T0218364

THE AGILE CONSULTANT

GUIDING CLIENTS TO ENTERPRISE AGILITY

Rick Freedman

Apress®

The Agile Consultant: Guiding Clients to Enterprise Agility

Rick Freedman
Lenexa, Kansas
USA

ISBN-13 (pbk): 978-1-4302-6052-3   ISBN-13 (electronic): 978-1-4302-6053-0

DOI 10.1007/978-1-4302-6053-0

Library of Congress Control Number: 2016951233

Managing Director: Welmoed Spahr
Acquisitions Editor: Robert Hutchinson
Development Editor: Matthew Moodie
Editorial Board: Steve Anglin, Pramila Balan, Laura Berendson, Aaron Black,
    Louise Corrigan, Jonathan Gennick, Robert Hutchinson, Celestin Suresh John,
    Nikhil Karkal, James Markham, Susan McDermott, Matthew Moodie, Natalie Pao,
    Gwenan Spearing
Coordinating Editor: Rita Fernando
Copy Editor: Lori Jacobs
Compositor: SPi Global
Indexer: SPi Global
Cover Designer: Isaac Ruiz Soler

Distributed to the book trade worldwide by Springer Science+Business Media New York, 233 Spring Street, 6th Floor, New York, NY 10013. Phone 1-800-SPRINGER, fax (201) 348-4505, e-mail orders-ny@springer-sbm.com, or visit www.springeronline.com. Apress Media, LLC is a California LLC and the sole member (owner) is Springer Science + Business Media Finance Inc (SSBM Finance Inc). SSBM Finance Inc is a Delaware corporation.

For information on translations, please e-mail rights@apress.com, or visit www.apress.com.

Apress and friends of ED books may be purchased in bulk for academic, corporate, or promotional use. eBook versions and licenses are also available for most titles. For more information, reference our Special Bulk Sales–eBook Licensing web page at www.apress.com/bulk-sales.

Any source code or other supplementary materials referenced by the author in this text is available to readers at www.apress.com. For detailed information about how to locate your book's source code, go to www.apress.com/source-code/.

Printed on acid-free paper

Apress Business: The Unbiased Source of Business Information

Apress business books provide essential information and practical advice, each written for practitioners by recognized experts. Busy managers and professionals in all areas of the business world—and at all levels of technical sophistication—look to our books for the actionable ideas and tools they need to solve problems, update and enhance their professional skills, make their work lives easier, and capitalize on opportunity.

Whatever the topic on the business spectrum—entrepreneurship, finance, sales, marketing, management, regulation, information technology, among others—Apress has been praised for providing the objective information and unbiased advice you need to excel in your daily work life. Our authors have no axes to grind; they understand they have one job only—to deliver up-to-date, accurate information simply, concisely, and with deep insight that addresses the real needs of our readers.

It is increasingly hard to find information—whether in the news media, on the Internet, and now all too often in books—that is even-handed and has your best interests at heart. We therefore hope that you enjoy this book, which has been carefully crafted to meet our standards of quality and unbiased coverage.

We are always interested in your feedback or ideas for new titles. Perhaps you'd even like to write a book yourself. Whatever the case, reach out to us at editorial@apress.com and an editor will respond swiftly. Incidentally, at the back of this book, you will find a list of useful related titles. Please visit us at www.apress.com to sign up for newsletters and discounts on future purchases.

The Apress Business Team

For Terri
Doubt that the stars are fire,
Doubt that the sun doth move,
Doubt truth to be a liar,
But never doubt I love . . .

Contents

About the Author

Rick Freedman, author of *The IT Consultant* (Pfeiffer, 2000), has experienced the agile transition from the inside. He has been working as an agile coach and trainer since the beginning of the agile movement. As Worldwide Project Management Director for Intel from 2001–2005, Rick evangelized, trained, and coached Intel project managers in the United States, UK, China, India, Germany, Sweden, and Australia. Since leaving Intel, Rick has trained and coached agile teams at clients such as Credit Suisse, Bank of New York, Turner Broadcasting, Motorola, U.S. Department of Homeland Security, U.S. Customs and Border Patrol, the IRS, Wells Fargo, TransCanada, and many others. He authored ESI's original Agile Project Management course and consulted with ESI as it expanded this offering into a suite of agile courses now delivered internationally. Rick's articles about agility for TechRepublic and DZone enable him to remain current with agile trends and engage with a worldwide audience of agilists.

Acknowledgments

Thanks to Jim Highsmith for introducing me to agility through our interview in 2000, to Tom Conrad for helping me understand how agility works at Pandora. Also to Ludwig and Rudolf Melik for their kind friendship. Thanks to agile geniuses Pete Behrens, Jean Tabaka, Ronica Roth, Mike Griffiths, Denise Vestin, Munir Bhimani, Scott Bird, Kay Harper, Jenny Tarwater: knowing you made me smarter. Matt Holt, my friend and my original believer: rock on, my brother. To the originators: Mike Cohn, Lyssa Adkins, Ken Schwaber, Jeff Sutherland, Dean Leffingwell, Jon Katzenbach and Doug Smith, Craig Larman, Rob Thomsett, etc.: You started a revolution that changed the world . . . no small feat.

Introduction

I began learning the basics of project management as a rookie in one of the biggest information technology (IT) shops in America, Citicorp's global data center. I was hired as a specialist in Citicorp's new PC and Network group. My first project went way long and over budget. I was invited to a chat with a systems manager, for what I expected to be a scolding. Instead, Jerry took me to a blackboard and explained the fundamentals of managing an IT project. Jerry drew four boxes on the blackboard, and put a "D" into each one. "What do you think the D's are for?" he asked. I just stared, stupefied. Jerry then explained a simple 4D methodology for delivering IT programs.

Discover, Design, Develop, Deploy

Being a typical New York guy, Jerry didn't explain this to me in terms of critical paths or network diagrams. "Discover what the client wants, and what you're walking into." Jerry advised. "Design a solution to fix the problem. Develop that thing that you designed, then Deploy it."

I, and thousands of other project managers, took Jerry's commonsense "4D" project philosophy and subsequently expanded it into phases, then tasks. We estimated those tasks, even though anyone who'd been in the IT field for more than a minute knew that estimates were invariably wrong. We created "phase gates" to ensure that no one illicitly progressed without permission. Those gates became codified, and eventually developed into the 17-binder proprietary project methodologies that were the rage in the 1990s.

I went to work for one of the Big 5 consulting firms, and was trained in its particular version of the multichecklist, highly enforced methodology. After a few months, I became such a zealot of the regimented, gated approach that I joined the Project Committee.

When I got some experience in the field I quickly understood why the "predict and plan" model was unworkable in a consulting context. Simply put, no client being billed by the hour will stand for dozens of hours of overhead, filling out forms, and passing through gates that don't add business value. The client, of course, believed that project management was just the consultant planning his own project, and so was reluctant to pay for it, while we were under orders to get at least 15% of the total gig in project management fees.

Most significantly, "predict and plan" didn't work. Upfront requirements were incomplete, as users couldn't articulate what they needed. Estimates were "magical," as if we could see over the horizon and know how the mix of technology, personality, and culture would play out. IT projects routinely failed. As I began to understand the fallacy of the "predict and plan" model, I noticed the shoots of a "light methodologies" movement budding, with thinkers like Rob Thomsett writing books like *Radical Project Management*.[1] I was determined to find a method that maintained the rigor of a phase-gated approach with the low-overhead of these new "radical" project ideas.

When the overhead of the big consulting giant became too much, I moved to a local system integrator. We dealt with smaller clients and less complex IT challenges, but nonetheless struggled with consistent delivery. We spent a long time experimenting with different versions of "project toolkits" and eventually reached a light, adaptable 4D-style model that was less likely to scare away clients. With the simple application of a lean project management discipline, we grew the consulting practice significantly, and delivered controlled, successful results.

I left this gig to write my first book, *The IT Consultant*,[2] and began to travel as an advisor to other IT shops. The more small IT shops I visited, the more obvious the patterns. Either they were strangling in bureaucratic predictive project regimes that destroyed their flexibility, or they were improvising their way through projects, usually by throwing technical bodies against them, and delivering chaotic, unmanaged engagements.

In advising these small IT shops or consulting firms, I discovered a secret: institute a few, simple project disciplines, apply some consulting skills, like collaboration and communication, and most IT shops will solve their own problems.

On a writing assignment during this time, I interviewed Jim Highsmith, soon-to-be signatory of the yet-to-be-written Agile Manifesto, and Highsmith introduced me to ideas that were about to revolutionize the world of software development. The concepts of high-performing teams that managed and motivated themselves, of enforced client participation, of lean thinking throughout the process, fell so neatly in line with the on-the-ground experience I was having in the [3]field, that I quickly became an agilist.

---

[1]Rob Thomsett, Radical Project Management (Prentice Hall, 2002), www.amazon.com/Rob-Thomsett/e/B001KD577M/ref=dp_byline_cont_book_1.

[2]Rick Freedman, *The IT Consultant: A Commonsense Framework for Managing the Client Relationship* (San Francisco: Jossey-Bass/Pfeiffer, 2000), www.amazon.com/Rick-Freedman/e/B000APKF5U/ref=dp_byline_cont_book_1.

[3]www.techrepublic.com/article/consultant-employs-quotlight-methodologiesquot-for-application-development/.

The "predict and plan," PERT (Program Evaluation and Review Technique)-method, Gantt-chart-style of project management taught us a lot, but it got strangled in its inconsistency. You can't possible predict how projects will go, no matter how many gates you set up or papers you sign. The technology changes constantly and unpredictably. We can't know what clients want, since they rarely know themselves. We can't accurately estimate huge programs, but we can time-box and cost-box projects and deliver valuable, useful increments quickly. We can't manage talented knowledge workers into compliance, but we can lead them to glory.

Agile is revolutionary for those who came up in a gated, waterfall world. It's going to become a lot more revolutionary in the next few years, as these agile ideas of collaboration, speed-to-value, adaptability, and iterative, incremental delivery evolve from a strictly IT discipline into agile marketing, and then to agile strategic planning in the executive suite.

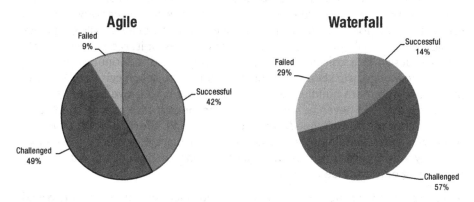

Figure I-1. Agile vs. waterfall success rates: The Standish Group CHAOS study, 2015

One thing is certain; the verdict on agile is in. Agile works, at least in some circumstances and for some organizations. The latest Standish Group CHAOS study,[4] a periodic review of project success, illustrated clearly that agile is more successful than waterfall.

Another thing is also true; the vast majority of self-proclaimed agile enterprises are far from being agile; most are not even doing agile. The distinction is meaningful; simply performing the ceremonies and techniques of agile won't help the marketing department prepare for agile's iterative cadence, nor will it convince leaders to accept the ambiguity and emergent nature of agile projects. Agile evolution is an agile, iterative process itself, and it usually takes a lot of iterations before the culture of agility begins to penetrate beyond the development team.

---

[4]www.infoq.com/articles/standish-chaos-2015.

Companies gravitate to agile approaches for a few simple reasons. First, as we saw, they work; the agile community is full of success stories from enterprises that have adopted agile techniques and gained significant advantage. The ranks of developers are exerting pressure from below. Many have experienced agile, and bridle at reverting to traditional techniques. The cadence of technology, the expectations of markets, the fickleness of customers—all increase the pace of change, putting more businesses at risk of disruption. It's no wonder executives are now looking at agility as the next holy grail of management theories. Agile consultants often see a significant drop in enthusiasm when leaders discover the depth of radical change agility requires.

My experience across the gamut, from strict Project Management Institute (PMI), CMM (Capability Maturity Model)-style predictive project management techniques to agile methods, leaves no doubt for me that agile is a revolutionary way to think about software development. Like many revolutionary ideas, now that it's the norm it seems obvious and inevitable. These practices and principles have the potential to profoundly enhance the competitiveness and productivity of global business; that's how important I believe agile's ultimate impact will be. Agile proves the business advantages of iterative, incremental, dynamic design in a collaborative, open atmosphere of continuous improvement. Knowledge workers, from the chief information officer (CIO) to the pair of programmers huddling over a terminal, want to move beyond fantasy strategies that will never be implemented, beyond fantasy specifications that the organization doesn't need, won't use, and can't afford, beyond arbitrary estimates and schedules that guarantee "death march" projects. The move to agility was a hard-fought battle against an entrenched incumbent, and it's triumphing only because it works.

Agile appeals to me because it's rational, and because I evolved to it based on my own experience. But its real attraction is on the human side; it creates a team-based, collaborative, consensus culture, and it promotes the values that I admire. Honesty, openness, intrinsic motivation, robust collaboration, reflection, and improvement; these values seem so obvious from a human perspective, and yet the enterprises we build are often the exact opposite. Siloed, politically charged, hierarchical, and demotivating cultures are still the norm in many enterprises. Agile values of teamwork, incremental refinement, and change readiness are inevitable in our tumultuous business environment. Once executives, their teams, and their customers absorb these ideas, agile will change everything.

---

[5]www.leadingagile.com/2011/01/untangling-adoption-and-transformation/.

Who Is This Book For?

Both Jim Highsmith and Mike Cottmeyer, influential agile thinkers, have recently weighed in on the distinction between "doing agile" and "being agile." As Mike Cottmeyer phrases it,

> *Agile adoption is about changing the agile doing side of the equation, while transformation is about changing the agile being side of the equation.*[5]

Highsmith writes passionately and persuasively about the need to take agility beyond methodology for agile to achieve its potential:

> *Many organizations seem to be stuck at Agile 101, the rule-based approach to Agile (do this, don't do that) that is a necessary first step towards becoming Agile, but it's only a first step. To take advantage of the fast-paced responsiveness of a continuous delivery environment, the entire organization—from delivery teams to executive management—needs to embrace the process changes required to respond rapidly, collaborate effectively between development and operations, and embrace an adaptive, exploratory mindset.*[6]

My ultimate goal as an agile consultant is to help clients evolve from doing agile, with select teams following the process-based methods and techniques of scrum, for example, to being agile, through deep cultural change to the structure, norms, purpose and style of the enterprise. As there is a contrast between adopting agile and transforming to an agile culture, I see a contrast between the agile coach and the agile consultant. This isn't a value judgment —there's plenty of need, at the current state of agile adoption, for both.

Coaches are often consultants as well, focusing on the entire enterprise and helping organizations discover the best approach to improving agility across their firm. In this early stage of agile adoption, however, many agile coaches will have limited interaction with the executive team, primarily spending time with the product development teams and product owners, helping them understand and adapt to agile practices.

The agile consultant plays that coaching role but, in the ideal scenario, is also working with senior managers to create an adoption framework for agile in the enterprise. The agile coach is often having a methods-and-practices conversation, while the agile consultant should be having a return-on-investment (ROI)-based, strategy-focused engagement across the entire enterprise,

---

[6]https://assets.thoughtworks.com/articles/adaptive-leadership-accelerating-enterprise-agility-jim-highsmith-thoughtworks.pdf.

evangelizing the benefits of agility and building support at the sponsor level. Agile consultants are also coaches, working on the nitty-gritty methodological details with teams and individual contributors if that's what the enterprise needs, or where it decides to begin. In my ideal scenario, the agile consultant is simultaneously building trust and expertise within the agile teams while advising leaders on the benefits and challenges of evolving to agility across the enterprise.

The methodology focus by many teams and firms in the beginning of their agile journey is understandable; in fact, it's inevitable. Despite all of the evidence of agile success, clients are skeptical until they see it for themselves. It's not reasonable to expect organizations to jump into a radical new set of behaviors and attitudes without some demonstration of its efficacy and fit. The agile adoption phase is a critical and necessary step on the path to enterprise agility. After all, even with all the hype around agility, in most situations the migration is still driven bottom-up, by teams of developers who have experienced or heard about the speed, transparency, collaboration, and self-management associated with agile methods. "Grassroots" agile sometimes works in the open, exhibiting quick wins to gain support, and sometimes it works in stealth, displaying the outward signs of predictive, traditional waterfall methods. The stealth teams incrementally build the confidence of the organization by reporting and delivering faster.

Existing practices are sticky, company history is sticky, culture is sticky, and hierarchy is sticky. Stickiest of all is personality. Agile evolution requires us to help the enterprise unstick itself from its traditions. It sometimes requires us to help teams and individuals unstick their most fundamental behaviors. The effort to change norms and habits requires much more than change at the tactical level. While the use of a small "tiger team" to introduce agile into the product development function is a good practice, any improvements solely within that team will be undone by the stickiness of "the way things work here." To make the leap from more efficient IT to a more agile enterprise, culture, history, and management style must be disrupted. I believe this requires, in addition to methodological expertise, mature consulting skills. Communication, facilitation, negotiation, organizational diagnosis, change management, strong business context skills—all are mandatory to effect evolution rather than mere adoption.

My hope is that, in reading this book, agile coaches, consultants, managers, and practitioners will gain some insight from my experiences and observations. For coaches and consultants, the obvious targets of this work, I'll point out tips, tricks, and pitfalls from my consulting experience, and describe tactics I've learned for working through challenges and barriers. For managers, I'll define the role of leadership in agile organizations and in enterprises as they become agile. I'll discuss in depth the evangelizing, consensus building, and reassurance that leaders are called upon to provide as organizations gain agility. For the stakeholder, such as the client or the product owner, I'll talk about the profound adjustments in the relationship between developer and client, and the heightened level of participation and collaboration that the agile enterprise expects. And for the practitioner, the developer sitting in a cubicle writing code or designing data structures, we'll review what it means to be *self-directed*, *self-managed*, and *self-motivated*, and the behaviors that these phrases imply.

The real skill of the agile consultant, or any consultant, is not in her ability to transmit the technical or domain knowledge in which she specializes; it is rather her sensitivity to the culture, history, and personality of the client, and her ability to guide this particular enterprise to the leanest, most efficient business model it can achieve. The tactical elements of agile practice are easy to teach and to learn, but, as with all profound ideas, enterprise agility is a journey. Agile consultants, whether acting as coaches or strategic advisors, are a necessary element of agile at this stage of its development. I believe we're on the cusp of a torrent of agile evolution, up to the boardroom, that will change organizational culture forever. Like Sherpas guiding climbers, it's our responsibility to thoughtfully and sensitively guide our clients to the top.

What Is Agile Consulting?

The Agile Consultant

Consulting matters. Our advice, good or bad, can affect the future of clients, their companies, their employees and customers. Some consultants, such as doctors and lawyers, can, by their advice, instigate reprieve or catastrophe. Mentors and managers are advisors, as are our peers and colleagues. Although we give and receive advice all day, the professional consultant has a unique responsibility. As a paid advisor, the consultant is ethically bound to focus on the client's best interest. The best consultants have the domain expertise and creativity to add value, the temperament to advise gracefully, the relationship skills to collaborate and guide, and the tenacity to adapt to the client and accept their boundaries. Clients of consultants expect more than counsel; they want us to implement the ideas we've proposed, and to be accountable for the business results we promised.

When I envision an agile consultant, I see a consultant with the experience, mature skills, and agile domain expertise to guide a client's evolution toward enterprise agility. He's seen agile adoptions from the inside, and experienced the tensions inherent in the migration process. He's run into some of the roadblocks of organizational culture and politics, and he's made the transition from predictive thinking and embraced the values of adaptation and self-direction. He's fallen into traps, from the team to the enterprise level, and has figured his way out of them. He's aware of the evolving theories of agile, from SAFe to tribes, and is thoughtful but enthusiastic about applying promising new practices with his clients.

© Rick Freedman 2016
R. Freedman, *The Agile Consultant*, DOI 10.1007/978-1-4302-6053-0_1

All of this agile experience and domain expertise, however, is essential but not sufficient. The participative, cross-functional, egalitarian instincts of agile require much more personal interaction than the old "expert from out of town" advisory style. At the team level, for example, modeling the right level of neutrality as a facilitator is critical to educating your team about collaborative behavior. At the management level, the ability to translate unfamiliar agile concepts into accessible, business-oriented language is more important than your mastery of story-point estimation. At the executive level, a strategic conversation about the competitive benefits of organizational agility will go farther than an explanation of the Agile Manifesto. The consultative skills that you can deploy in the face of conflict, resistance, failure, and reflection are more critical for success than is domain knowledge. Your ability to set the bar high, create a collaborative, performance-oriented team atmosphere with a sense of purpose and achievement, while keeping everyone's eyes on the business prize, will determine your success as an agile advisor.

Agile consultants are engaged in the intimate daily flow of human relationships, biases, feuds, and triumphs. We uncover broken team and enterprise dynamics that have been swept under the rug forever. We raise expectations of achievement, and of the joy of work, for individuals, teams, and companies. Agile consultants are introducing methods designed to disturb the status quo. We're not delivering a routine consulting project to "migrate the client to agile"; we're unleashing a revolution in the client's house. Then we must guide clients to accept, embrace, and finally capitalize on that revolution. As a kaizen[1] practice, agile evolution has no end but the unattainable, perfection. The expectations we set, the skills and experiences we bring, the humility with which we approach the client's culture and history, our empathy for those whose stability we've disrupted—these account for success. Agile domain expertise is expected. Mature consulting skills, the ability to guide an agile evolution that fits, and sticks, are rare and precious.

I'm also visualizing a consultant who applies an agile business model in her own consulting practice, building an iterative, experiential relationship with clients accustomed to "firm fixed price, scope, and schedule" contracts. As we'll see, the traditional consulting model is unsuited for agile evolution, and may be obsolete for any type of consulting engagement. The forces of digital disruption and lean thinking have swept over every sector, and the consulting business is not immune.

---

[1] Gradual, continuous improvement.

Agile Changes Consulting

Agile is both simple and complex. It's simple in that the basic practices of scrum or XP can be taught in a day. Simplicity is inherent in the agile principles. "Maximizing the amount of work not done" is one of the most elegant statements of lean philosophy I've encountered. It's complex, however, because it's designed to disrupt assumptions, processes, relationships, and hierarchies that are built to avoid disruption. Achieving the level of agility required to simplify our work is a complex endeavor.

Consulting is also both simple and complex. The five-step process used by consultants, whether doctor, lawyer, or architect, has been the same for centuries:

1. Understand the current state.

2. Define the desired state.

3. Analyze the gap.

4. Recommend a plan of action to address the gap.

5. Implement and monitor the plan.

This simple list of steps, however, contains multitudes. Understanding the current state can involve a quick walkthrough of a department, a month of interviews and surveys, or a year of due diligence. Defining the desired state is especially difficult when the aim is agility. The goal, as in all lean, kaizen exercises, is perfection through continuous reflection and improvement. It's a goal, like speed-of-light travel, that becomes increasingly elusive the closer we approach. Gap analysis is also a challenge in an agile transition, when many of the gaps don't become apparent until agile adoption begins and roadblocks start to emerge. Recommending a plan of action to proceed in an agile transition is also an emergent task. At each evolutionary stage in our agile expedition, the recommendations must change based on our experiences so far. We can perhaps overlay a map that points us to previously worn paths, but each voyage is distinct.

The traditional consulting engagement model, it seems, has been disrupted. The simple five-step approach outlined previously, used by Hippocrates with his first patient and by your doctor yesterday, is another victim of the "creative destruction" of the agile model. Once we abandon the predictive, big-upfront-plan approach to project management and software development, we see that it also has to go in the agile consulting world. As agile consultants, we are essentially contracting to undertake an experimental, experiential quest with our client to discover together how far toward agility their collective awareness, desire, and will can take them. We only learn their agile limit by trial and error. In agile evolution, when you push the boundary, the boundary pushes back.

The traditional consulting business model, at least at the top tier, isn't designed for speed-to-value. It's designed for lengthy, entrenched projects that intersperse a few veterans with legions of profitable rookies, and for which the firm then sells lucrative maintenance contracts, or extracts retainers, to sustain the changes they implemented. The fad-driven "program of the month" mentality, which now threatens agile, has demonstrated its bankruptcy, as the majority of Total Quality Management (TQM) and Business Process Reengineering (BPR) enterprises slide back into old cultural norms. The "scope extension" sales philosophy, in which every consultant is an inside spy, eavesdropping in the cafeteria seeking the next problem the firm can swoop in and solve, is deadly to trust in the consultative relationship.

If the sponsor is aware of both the potential for agile and the risks of his current circumstances, wants to change and understands the disruption involved, and has the will to adapt both himself and the culture around him, you've walked into the ideal scenario for a successful agile evolution. Good luck finding that guy. Even if you successfully discover this perfect, willing candidate, the evolution to enterprise agility is monumental. In the ideal scenario described earlier, with a willing client, the contracting phase alone can be daunting. Whether or not the CEO wants to "go agile," the procurement agent wants a signed scope of work. Training your sponsors to support and enforce corporate acceptance of an iterative, pay-as-you-go engagement with an ambiguous outcome is often an obstacle before you even engage. In our humanistic, participative agile world, every element of agile transition is negotiable by anyone in the conversation. The most mature consultant, with superior facilitation, communication, influencing, and coaching skills, will have his hands full, even with this ideal sponsor.

Now consider the other end of the client spectrum. Our executive sponsor has read a *Harvard Business Review* article on agility, heard her chief information officer (CIO) mention it a few times, and thinks of it as a software process improvement project. She's OK with trying it out in a "swat team" within the development group but still thinks the Project Management Office (PMO) should manage all projects, wants to see a project plan before she'll approve any expenditures, and still wants her quarterly strategic plan and budget from information technology (IT). The culture is an extension of her personality, which values stability and predictability over innovation and change. She's granted limited access to her best and brightest coders for this "pilot test" of agile adoption.

In each of these circumstances, the key success attribute of the agile consultant is adaptability. The boundaries will obviously differ vastly between the scenarios, and will require both the sensitivity to understand them and the tenacity to challenge them. The consultant, in either case, is called upon to learn a new culture, a new business scenario, and a new set of personalities. None of that should be new to any advisor. The understanding that each engagement is unique comes early to an alert consultant.

What's different is that we now have to revamp the traditional engagement model entirely. The big-scope consulting project, with a defined beginning and end, finely negotiated deliverables, and a tightly managed change control process, necessarily must give way to an iterative, collaborative, time-bound and change-ready engagement (perhaps serially extended) that delivers value throughout. The agile consultant is committing to a series of time-boxed value deliveries, rather than a 12-month study that produces a report. The value we deliver in early iterations may be only the first sparks of enlightenment, but when we can demonstrate progress, the spread of agile principles will become self-reinforcing.

The cornerstone of an effective consultative relationship in the agile world is honesty, openness, and trust. The agile consulting model is less predictive, less prescriptive, and more evolutionary. The current state, future state, gaps, and plans are acknowledged as unknowable until the engagement is underway. These things were always obscure; just because we called it predictive planning doesn't mean it actually predicted anything. Agile is reality-based, and we encounter and adapt to reality by living it. The incremental model of consulting, both for agile transition clients and for our traditional consulting clients, is the disruptive idea that must inevitably replace the traditional leveraged, predictive, eternal entrenchment model of the Big 5 (or 4, or 3, or however many are left).

The nature of the engagement does not have to change radically. It just becomes atomized. That big-bang, omnibus fixed-scope project now becomes a series of collaborative experiments, time-bound and targeted, in which you and the client will discover how agile ideas affect the enterprise. Many consultants are already familiar with the "discovery first" business model, in which the consultant charges a fee to perform some minimal due diligence, before committing to planning and delivery. Agile consultants are offering a series of discovery projects, typically expanding concentrically from the team to the team-of-teams, then incrementally through the enterprise. We're promising to apply our skills and experience to guide teams to agility; how their existing competencies, attitudes, and practices will adapt is unknown. Successful agile consultants start their engagements with the explicit mutual understanding that they are guides, not project managers, and their role is advising and mentoring, not enforcing process compliance. The agile consultant's key commercial challenge is ensuring that the client grasps the concept of variable scope. No coach or consultant can promise to "make you agile," especially in one iteration or "pilot." There are too many uncontrolled variables.

If we can't promise "agility in a box," what is our promise? We're committing to the client that we actually have the agile domain experience and expertise we claim. We're committing that we're coming to the engagement "pure," not trying to make ourselves indispensable and eternal but instead dedicated to using our domain knowledge and consultative skills to bring agility to their enterprise and make it self-sustainable. We're committing that we'll engage collaboratively, that we'll meet them where they are and help them adapt from there. We're committing that we'll view their agile evolution strategically, and ensure that our pursuit of agility is tightly coupled with the pursuit of their competitive goals. Most important, we're committing to embody the agile principles and to be a role model of the adaptable, humanistic, purposeful, and collaborative spirit that epitomizes the agile enterprise.

Agile Consulting Principles

When I wrote my first book[2] back in 1999, the predictive planning model for project management and consulting engagements was still the norm. At that time, I formulated a list of five fundamental ideas that, I felt, were the necessary underpinnings of any consultative relationship. Going back to them now, I'm proud to report that I believe they are still applicable in the agile world; in, fact, I'll make the argument that they are more pertinent than ever. Let me reveal those five fundamental ideas of consulting I put forth in 1999:

- Focus on the relationship.
- Clearly define your role.
- Visualize success.
- You advise, they decide.
- Be oriented toward results.

These principles clearly did not address technical issues back then, and they don't now. Instead they help define the consulting relationship you establish with your client, the clarity of expectations, the definition of "done," the collaborative nature of the relationship, the client's right to accept or reject your advice, and the orientation toward delivering value, not just white papers and migration plans.

I'll walk through these ideas and describe why I believe that, unknowingly, I was articulating some agile principles in my recommended approach to the client.

Focus on the Relationship

The relationship element is critical in any advisory relationship, since trust is the first prerequisite for advising and being advised. In my Big 5 days, the key relationship was often with a solitary executive, who commissioned a report

---

[2]Rick Freedman, *The IT Consultant: A Commonsense Framework for Managing the Client Relationship* (San Francisco; Jossey-Bass/Pfeiffer, 2000). Available at: www.amazon.com/ Rick-Freedman/e/B000APKF5U/ref=dp_byline_cont_book_1.

or program, with everyone else a spectator or, at best, a "stakeholder." The intimate nature of agile consulting, on the other hand, broadens our scope of relationships to every team and individual we touch in the process of agile evolution. This makes relationship cultivation central to agile consulting. We're not just interviewing and commenting on the behavior of teams, or making remote suggestions for improvement, like consultants of old. We're in the daily working life of our teams, making independent relationships with team members, managers, customers, and executives. More to the point, we're hands-on in helping change their behaviors, attitudes, and methods. The traits we typically display in a personal relationship, like empathy, patience, and respect, will be tested in an agile consulting relationship. Any consultant lacking the relationship focus and skills, the "emotional intelligence," to develop collaborative and productive connections will struggle as an agile advisor.

Clearly Define your Role

The advisory relationship is always ambiguous. That's why traditional consultants spend so much energy on writing pinpoint scope documents. The fear of implied expectations, role confusion, and scope creep made documenting the commitments of both client and consultant essential. Clients can imply all sorts of commitments and expectations. As I said in 1999, some clients believe that if you recommend a $99 accounting package, you're bound for life to rectify any bugs, act as the go-between with the software publisher, and build any reports they need. The chain of implied expectations applies equally to agile, where the end state is ambiguous and roles are emergent. *What do you mean, the team's not ready for continuous integration ... we've been at this agile thing for three months already!*

In the collaborative atmosphere of agile consulting, where the participation of the client and the upholding of commitments is vital, the importance of role clarity is magnified. Agile evolution isn't a project that a consultant can "go do"; it is by its nature a collaborative exercise that loses all meaning if the players don't understand and commit to their roles. In fact, a large part of the agile consultant's challenge is to help teams and individuals clarify and understand their new roles in a new world. This is not to say that we can determine these roles upfront. The true scrummaster in a rookie agile enterprise should arise spontaneously, not by a manager pointing to someone. At the least, as mentioned earlier, the consultant must ensure that the client understands we're not peddling "agile in a box" but rather a mutual expedition of discovery toward their maximum agility.

Visualize Success

As I've watched agile theory evolve since the Agile Manifesto, I've seen the debate around "the definition of done" increase exponentially. I've witnessed arcane arguments about "done" versus "done, done" versus "done, done,

done." If we accept the premise that agile product development, software or otherwise, is not a project, in that it has no end that can be defined at the beginning, then clear agreement about what we call complete is mandatory. The debate about the definition of done may have become extreme, but the importance of defining it, especially in a paid consultant arrangement, is fundamental.

The visualization of success is, to me, a humanization of the quest for a definition of done. Rather than a big, upfront specification that defines success criteria, we now need to help the client visualize a high-level roadmap that illustrates, in business language, how the disparate efforts or workstreams come together in a cohesive scenario that supports the business strategy. The "vision box" exercise that Jim Highsmith recommends[3] is great for the team that's trying to define priorities and overall feature mix, but my experience is that managers prefer a roadmap conversation that concentrates on strategic alignment, timing, and budgeting, one that helps them plan marketing, sales, and fulfillment campaigns.

Visualization of potential outcomes through roadmap planning is a powerful tool in the agile arsenal, but, in the consulting relationship, it's fraught with risk. The agile consultant's challenge is to present a possible future scenario, based on what's now known, and not have it turn into the dreaded "fixed firm scope" project executives naturally favor. Before the enterprise has embraced or internalized agile, the tendency toward predictability and artificial certainty will be powerfully ingrained. Agile consultants who help their sponsors understand the inevitable uncertainties and unknowns, and help them grasp the concept of emergent development, are more likely to succeed at visualization than those who confront a command-and-control culture with an ambiguous and variable roadmap.

Visualization is also about articulating the big idea that we're evolving toward. In agile evolutions, where the creation of momentum and enthusiasm is a success factor, the clarity and persuasiveness of the driving vision are key. Our message must speak to the fears and concerns of the teams, as well as the glorious future that awaits. The time to begin thinking about the enterprise communication and promotion strategy is at the beginning. The vision, roadmap, and our evangelizing should all send a consistent message: change is hard, what we're attempting is hard, we acknowledge that we're disrupting time-honored practices, but others have succeeded, and we can do this together and unleash creative power within the enterprise, to work with less friction and achieve more than we ever believed possible.

---

[3]Jim Highsmith, *Agile Project Management: Creating Innovative Products,* Second Edition (Addison-Wesley Professional; 2 edition (July 20, 2009)). Available at: www.amazon.com/Agile-Project-Management-Creating-Innovative/dp/0321658396/ref=sr_1_1?s=books&ie=UTF8&qid=1447619469&sr=1-1&keywords=agile+project+management+highsmith.

You Advise, they Decide

Consultants learn early in their careers that client ownership of the proposed solution determines project success or failure. Every veteran has experienced the "your idea" syndrome, when the inevitable delays and unknowns impact the project, and the client intones those famous words. If you, as a consultant, are in the position of having the customer tell you that this was "your recommendation" and you therefore are responsible for its success and risks, you're doing it wrong.

Even before the collaborative ethic that imbues agile was pervasive, client ownership of the solution and vision was critical. The advisor advises; the advised considers, then decides. The decision process can't be outsourced, and client attempts to turn consultants into "blame agents" must be resisted. We can explore options, describe the implications of choosing one direction or another, and anecdotally advise the client, *if it were me, I'd . . .*, but once that's done, the client, and the enterprise, must resolve to take a particular course and own that decision. As outside advisors, we bring many advantages; we can apply the experience of all the other clients we've worked with, cultures we've seen, and roadblocks and enablers we've encountered. From our vantage point, outside the prevailing culture and with "no dog in the fight," we can unstick problems, often with simple solutions that are apparent to the unbiased eye. However, even if the solution is obvious to us, we need to take the client and her teams there, facilitating them to make the right decisions themselves, and to own them.

For agile consultants, in an emergent and evolving organization that we're guiding through change and disruption, the client's ownership of the decision process must be explicit. Both agile transitions and the projects that agile teams undertake must have a product owner, the keeper of the strategic flame, of the priorities, and of the decisions and trade-offs that accompany any effort. We are unambiguously coaches and advisors, working with the environment and competencies we find. As we incrementally expand the breadth of agile within the organization, we should also be expanding the ownership and enthusiasm. The natural scrummaster becomes a natural coach, who mentors more scrummasters who coach in turn. As Sun Tsu said in *The Art of War*, "A leader is best when people barely know he exists. When his work is done, his aim fulfilled, they will say: we did it ourselves."

Be Oriented Toward Results

The connection between this principle and the value-driven nature of agile is obvious. The value ethic of agile requires us to stop measuring success based on documents produced, or steps followed, or tasks performed, or milestones reached. At each iteration, we commit to delivering a result that could potentially be released. It has working features that bring value. It can be both subjectively and objectively evaluated. While this may be a stretch when the project is an agile evolution, the ethic remains; agile consultants deliver value incrementally, and can demonstrate that value to their sponsors. Measuring progress in collaboration and purpose may be more difficult than in a software project, but as agilists ourselves, we maintain agile's value focus when we expand the cycle of enhanced creativity, collaboration, adaptation, and enthusiasm that successful agile evolutions experience.

Agile Change Models

Michael Sahota, in his widely read *Survival Guide*,[4] said

> *Let us consider the question of the skill level Agile change agents have in "helping organizations with Agile.. I make the assertion that the vast majority of Agile change agents are at the accidental [lowest skill] level. The key reasons are:*

1. Failure to understand Agile as a system of culture and values

2. Failure to understand the disruptive power of Agile in general and Scrum in particular

3. Not understanding the difference between adoption and transformation

4. Often no explicit adoption or transformation framework

5. Weak or mis-alignment with management goals and objectives

As we've discussed, agile is a set of values, not a set of practices. It's a culture, not a methodology. We've also emphasized the disruptive nature of agile, both practice and culture. Doing agile and being agile, as we've discussed, are two different things. And the clash of agile with current strategic planning methods, and indeed with big, upfront strategic plans themselves, should be obvious.

The lack of an adoption or transformation framework, however, is of real concern to the agile consultant. We may understand that we're embarking on an iterative, experimental voyage with the client, but we still can benefit from some structure around the engagement. No client will, and no consultant should, embark on an agile engagement without some guiding framework, in my experience.

---

[4]Michael Sahota, *An Agile Adoption and Transformation Survival Guide: Working with Organizational Culture* (InfoQ, 2012). Available at: https://www.infoq.com/minibooks/agile-adoption-transformation.

For instance, Mike Cohn, in his *Succeeding with Agile,*[5] recommends an adoption framework based on the acronym ADAPT:

- **Awareness** that the current process is not delivering acceptable results.

- **Desire** to adopt Scrum as a way to address current problems.

- **Ability** to succeed with Scrum.

- **Promotion** of Scrum through sharing experiences so that we remember and others can see our successes.

- **Transfer** of the implications of using Scrum throughout the company.

Cohn's framework, an adaptation of the ADKAR[6] model, has great applicability in defining the elements that must be in place for agile adoption in a scrum-based environment. For consultants, it presents a stepwise series of symptoms that we can look for, or encourage, within the client organization. Based on extensive ADKAR research, this sort of framework has rich academic credentials as a barometer of change readiness, and as a set of goals to achieve for change to self-sustain.

Twenty years ago, Harvard Professor John Kotter performed a study of change in the enterprise.[7] Kotter proposed an eight-step model that, based on his team's studies, was the most successfully path to sustained organizational change. His eight-step model 20 years ago was:

- Establishing a Sense of Urgency.

- Forming a powerful Guiding Coalition

- Creating a Vision

- Communicating the Vision

- Empowering Others to Act on the Vision

- Planning for and Creating Short-Term Wins

- Consolidating Improvements and Producing Still More Change

- Institutionalizing New Approaches

---

[5]Mike Cohn, *Succeeding with Agile: Software Development Using Scrum* (Boston: Addison-Wesley, 2010).
[6]Awareness, Desire, Knowledge, Ability, Reinforcement.
[7]John P. Kotter, *Leading Change* (Boston: Harvard Business Review Press, 1996).

It goes without saying that each of these steps had significant detail behind it, which I'll not try to expand upon here, as there are great references available online,[8] or in Kotter's book itself.

I'd prefer to concentrate on Kotter's recently revised eight-step model, from his new book *XLR8*,[9] which is much more aligned with an agile viewpoint. The original model, for example, took a phase-gated approach—you could only move on to the next step once the current step was complete. The new model, in contrast, is concurrent; multiple steps are incrementally advanced as organizational readiness increases. Twenty years ago, Kotter's model was focused on a core group of leaders selected from the hierarchy to drive change linearly; the new model focuses on a cross-functional network of enthusiastic volunteers, jumping on new opportunities and capitalizing on them quickly. For those agile consultants who begin their engagement at the strategic level, with a powerful sponsor who grasps the risks and benefits, and can mobilize the organization, Kotter's new "accelerators" of change can be a powerful renewal engine. It's demanding and radical, however, expecting much of the organization and its leadership. Agile consultants who, due to their assessment of the culture they've walked into, choose to take a more bottom-up, adoption-based approach won't have much immediate use for a complex organizational model like Kotter's. For those agile consultants who have the privilege of partnering with determined leaders pursuing a guiding vision of enterprise agility, however, Kotter's accelerators are potent.

Kotter's accelerators haven't changed that much from 20 years ago, but their intent is completely different, thanks to the inroads of agile thinking.

Create a Sense of Urgency

Kotter emphasizes the development of a big, guiding idea that generates momentum and enthusiasm, which he terms the *Big Opportunity*. In our case, of course, the big opportunity is agility in the enterprise. Our challenge as consultants is to help the organization frame a compelling "burning platform" that creates the urgency required to counter organizational inertia. We'll discuss in later chapters the disruptive challenges that are driving enterprises to seek agility.

Build a Guiding Coalition

In contrast to the hierarchical, executive-focused coalition that Kotter originally recommended, this new coalition is cross-discipline, cross-function, and cross-rank. All players are equal in this more participative, "swarm" consortium. This idea is congruent with one spread by Ken Schwaber[10] about the creation of an Enterprise Transition Team, itself a scrum team that manages the enterprise transition iteratively.

---

[8]www.rbsgroup.eu/assets/pdfs/2013_THE_8-STEP_PROCESS_FOR_LEADING_CHANGE.pdf.
[9]www.kotterinternational.com/book/accelerate/.
[10]Ken Schwaber, *The Enterprise and Scrum* (Redmond, WA: Microsoft Press, 2007).

Form a Strategic Vision and Initiatives

We commonly talk of the capital-v Vision statement in the agile community. Many of the original agile thinkers wrote extensively about different practices that teams could use to develop a guiding vision. While visualizing the glorious future state is essential, Kotter's insistence on initiatives to move it forward differentiates it. It's not just a vision we're creating here, it's a plan to achieve that vision through a specific portfolio of actions.

Enlist a Volunteer Army

In most development-centric organizations, finding a team of volunteers for agile adoption is not challenging. Those who have not transitioned usually want to, with a vengeance. Finding volunteers, however, among the concentric circles that surround the development team is the challenge. As agile practices in development teams create pressures in IT operations, which then roils outward toward marketing and fulfillment, our need to keep seeding the army of volunteers becomes more urgent, and more difficult. The ability of an agile consultant to work with the guiding coalition to keep the momentum going is a predictor of success.

Enable Action by Removing Barriers

Removing barriers, of course, is a lean and agile core principle. It's also a phrase that simplifies an extraordinarily complex idea. Every process, every human being, every historical artifact and cultural norm within any enterprise can be an obstacle to progress. As we've said before, when you push the envelope in agile evolution, the envelope pushes back. Existing processes and behaviors that have grown over years don't get obliterated in an instant. The removal of barriers is a key scrummaster competency. At that level, we're often discussing tactical barriers, like *I can't finish this until she does that*. At the enterprise level, removal of barriers is often a miracle of persuasion, desire, and will.

Generate Short-Term Wins

Again, this step is clearly in line with the agile principle of iterative value delivery. The celebration and visibility aspects are emphasized in Kotter's method. The visibility of short-term wins also appears, as Promotion, in Mike Cohn's ADAPT framework. The importance of visible progress in the creation of momentum is obvious. If the teams, and the entire enterprise, couldn't see incremental success and progress, why would they continue?

Sustain Acceleration

Sustainment of change is the hardest part, as the many failed adopters of TQM, BPR, and Enterprise Resource Planning (ERP) can testify. A resourceful leader can often generate enthusiasm and momentum toward a goal, and a horde of eager volunteers can adopt it with vigor. As change begins to penetrate the further layers of the institutional onion, embedded processes and cultural norms produce added friction. Whether you prefer the rubber band metaphor, in which culture is a rubber band that pulls rogue elements back into compliance, or the gravity theory, which proposes that organizational inertia is a natural force that can't be reversed, one thing is true: *Culture eats strategy for breakfast.* The agile consultant who can stretch his capabilities and guide clients to sustainable agility is truly having strategic impact.

Institute Change

The crowning step of the consultant's art is the ability to institutionalize change so that it, in turn, becomes the new "personality of the organization." Advising leaders on the mechanisms of communication, participative leadership, agile strategic planning, and operational dexterity is the summit of the agile consultant's achievement, and will take the summit of his efforts. The ability to guide a client through the disruptive process of agile evolution, and to see that enterprise embrace new values, live new ideals, and inculcate those ideals in its rookies and veterans, is an achievement worth celebrating.

Both Cohn's and Kotter's change frameworks have much to teach agile consultants, whether we're guiding the adoption of scrum practices within a team or driving an enterprise transition. Approaching a client engagement in a structured and orderly manner is a sign of professionalism. It reassures nervous clients that they're in competent hands. Agile consultants don't want to validate the negative view of agility, that it's just an excuse to make it up as we go along. We, instead, want to demonstrate that even though agile is iterative and experimental, we can approach its adoption and evolution in a disciplined way.

I'm humbled by the insight and real-world experience that both Cohn and Kotter have built into their change frameworks. Humbled, but not satisfied. I'm not satisfied because, as an agile consultant, they both have flaws for me. Cohn's ADAPT method, apart from its scrum specificity, seems to be addressed to inside change agents. It's not the consultant's Awareness that needs to be raised but the enterprise's and its leaders'. Similarly, the other elements of Cohn's approach are necessary conditions for agility, but not a prescription to take the client there. Kotter's model, while a bit more amenable to the outside advisor, makes the assumption that change starts at the top, and not until multiple steps into the model do we engage the actual teams in our volunteer army. In addition, neither of these models takes any account of the engagement model that consultants must apply from a commercial perspective. The first step for us isn't the awareness of the client or the creation of a sense of urgency, (although those things can be part of our sales strategy). First we must get engaged to do the work. We're essentially contractors, and our framework needs to acknowledge that fact. Our risks and concerns are different from those of the inside coach or agile leader. We have to ensure that the client understands and accepts our proposed approach, that we've defined what "done" means, and agree on the terms of our relationship. In short, agile consultants need a different change model, one that suits our special circumstances.

As we progress, I'll introduce my EVOLVE consulting framework, which, I believe, takes the core elements of the transition frameworks we've discussed and adapts them to the specific concerns of the agile consultant. Before we explore that framework, however, let's examine some of the challenges of dealing with existing culture in agile evolutions.

Summary

The agile consultant requires a unique combination of skills. Expertise in the agile domain, is, of course, critical, but the consultative skills of facilitation, negotiation, and persuasion are also key. Agile consultants, unlike many agile coaches, engage at the enterprise level, and so they need the capability to understand the business and strategic context in which agility is being implemented. Agile consultants must be able to navigate conflict, resistance, and individual agendas to be effective.

Agility has changed many industries, and the consulting business has changed as well. The big, upfront plans of traditional project management are becoming obsolete, which means that the big, upfront consulting contracts, with their fixed fees, fixed scope, and fixed schedule, must be replaced by a more agile engagement model.

There are many similarities between the principles of good consulting and those of agile consulting. These principles, however, must be adapted to the agile world and mind-set. We've reviewed some attributes of mature consultative behavior and noted how they must be adapted to the agile environment.

Finally, we examined organizational change models, like Mike Cohn's ADAPT framework and John Kotter's XLR8 model, and seen how they can aid in evolving an organization, and some areas where they are insufficient for an agile consultant engaging to remake the enterprise. We mentioned the EVOLVE agile consulting framework, and we'll dig into the components of that framework beginning in Chapter 3.

Agile Evolution: More Than Methodology

For the past ten years, VersionOne software, a provider of agile project tools, has performed a "State of Agile"[1] survey. In 2009, the survey listed "management opposed to change," "loss of management control," "team opposed to change," and "lack of discipline" as top challenges to agile adoption. In the ninth survey, five years later, top barriers to adoption are "lack of management support," "company philosophy at odds with agile," "external pressure to follow traditional waterfall processes," and "a broader organizational or communication issue." After five years of widespread adoption, it's still culture and management that obstruct agile evolution.

As illustrated by this graphic from the ninth State of Agile survey[2] (Figure 2-1), every issue cited here, with the possible exception of inexperience with agile, is a management or cultural issue. It's management that sets the tone of culture and drives organizational communication, that sponsors agile transition (or doesn't), that applies pressure to follow waterfall or systems development cycle (SDLC) processes, and that budgets for training (or doesn't).

---

[1]www.versionone.com/pdf/state-of-agile-development-survey-ninth.pdf.
[2]Ibid.

© Rick Freedman 2016
R. Freedman, *The Agile Consultant*, DOI 10.1007/978-1-4302-6053-0_2

Barriers to Further Agile Adoption

As in previous years, respondents continued to increasingly cite organizational culture and a general resistance to change as their biggest barriers to further agile adoption. Concerns about organizational culture increased from 44% in 2014 to 55% in 2015, and concerns about a general resistance to change increased from 34% in 2014 to 42% in 2015.

55%	Ability to change organizational culture
42%	General organizational resistance to change
40%	Pre-existing rigid/waterfall framework
39%	Not enough personnel with the necessary agile experience
38%	Management support
28%	Business/user/ customer availability
27%	Concerns about a loss of management control
25%	Management concerns about lack of upfront planning
18%	Confidence in ability to scale agile methodologies
18%	Concerns about the ability to scale agile
17%	No barriers
15%	Perceived time and cost to make the transition
14%	Development team support
13%	Regulatory compliance

SOURCE: VERSIONONE 10TH ANNUAL STATE OF AGILE™ REPORT
© 2016 VERSIONONE INC. ALL RIGHTS RESERVED.
*RESPONDENTS WERE ABLE TO MAKE MULTIPLE SELECTIONS.

Figure 2-1. Barriers to further agile adoption

Why Culture Matters

My favorite definition of culture is the simplest: "the way we do things here in order to succeed."[3] Other concise definitions are "the personality of the organization" or "the operating system of the enterprise."

Less concise, but more nuanced, is Edgar Schein's[4] definition:

> *A pattern of shared basic assumptions that the group learned as it solved its problems of external adaptation and internal integration, that has worked well enough to be considered valid and, therefore, to be taught to new members as the correct way you perceive, think, and feel in relation to those problems.*

Schein's definition, though academic, highlights a few important points for agile consultants. Cultures grow and adapt, based on external conditions. They may not adapt at the speed we, as change agents, would hope, but the General Motors (GM) of today is certainly different than the GM of 1960, or even 1990.

---

[3]William E. Schneider, *The Reengineering Alternative: A Plan for Making Your Current Culture Work* by William E. Schneider (Richard D. Irwin, 1994).
[4]Edgar Schien, *Organizational Culture and Leadership*, Fourth Edition (San Francisco: Jossey-Bass, 2010), www.tnellen.com/ted/tc/schein.html.

That culture only must have "worked **well enough** (my emphasis) to be considered valid" shows that organizations often make compromises and accept inefficiencies because they're "good enough." Finally, these cultural norms are swiftly taught to new members to influence the "correct" way they "perceive, think and feel." Schein's definition reminds us that while culture is tenacious, intentional, and influential, it's also adaptable and open to improvement.

I often hear other agile consultants complain that *the culture is broken* at a certain client's organization. Efforts to adopt agile will often falter or fail, and many consultants indict "dysfunctional" firms that are too bureaucratic, too political, or too change-resistant to successfully evolve. I'm not a proponent of the "broken culture" philosophy. My observation is that cultures evolve because the participants want things that way. They value the outcomes of the current culture, which are often measured personally: my title, my authority, my workload, my commitment level, my security and stability. An enterprise judged as dysfunctional at adopting agile is often highly accomplished at protecting rank, sheltering employees from disruption, offering a stable and secure environment, minimizing personal accountability or consequence, and blocking change. They may be dysfunctional from an agile perspective, but their evolution to their current cultural norms wasn't an accident; it was the result of conscious decisions by the entire community of what is valued, what is acceptable, and what is not. As consultants, our work is observational and diagnostic, not judgmental.

Another widely held belief is that "people naturally resist change." There's clearly truth to this, as all consultants have experienced, but it's ascribing resistance to the wrong motivation. People don't resist change when they get a raise, or win a prize, or find a great new job. They resist not change itself but the potential risk and loss it brings. From the executive suite to the newest rookie on staff, when rumblings of change begin to circulate, most people are immediately assessing the potential damage to their standing, reputation, power, workload, compensation, and accountability. The friction exists, in my view, not merely due to some irrational resistance to *any* change. People rationally calculate the risks of upheaval and loss created by change, compared with the stability and personal rewards of the status quo.

The Cultural Change Imperative

Whether starting at the top with an executive conversation about agile transformation in the enterprise, or beginning at the team level with a single scrum or agile team, the State of Agile studies make it clear that our greatest challenges as agile consultants are managerial and cultural. When we engage at the software team level, for example, we learn about the disconnections, miscommunications, stretched resources, and strained relationships that developers experience. At the executive level we learn about the challenges of misaligned priorities, legacy technologies and skills, failed projects, and unmet expectations. When 43% of survey respondents claim that cultural incompatibility with agile is the key barrier to adoption, and 38% cite lack of management support, it becomes obvious that, if the organization is seeking increased agility, a strategic, consultative approach is called for. Team-based coaching will always be essential to organizations starting their agile journey, but it is not sufficient if the aim is agility across the enterprise.

Executives understand that they are in jeopardy and must change. In the oft-quoted 2010 IBM study "Capitalizing on Complexity,"[5] a survey of over 1,500 chief executive officers (CEOs) in the United States, over 80% said they expected their organization to experience more volatility, more uncertainty, and more complexity in the next few years. Some 60% are experiencing high complexity now, and 79% expect to see more. Most alarming, in my view, is that while 79% expect higher complexity, only 48% feel prepared to deal with it.

Yet some organizations are thriving in these tumultuous times. IBM calls these the "Standouts." This small percentage of CEOs are thinking about their business differently. According to IBM's survey results, the Standouts have three key attributes that account for their leadership in turbulent conditions.

- Creative leadership
- Reinventing customer relationships
- Building operating dexterity

The connection of these traits to agile philosophy is clear. Creativity, not decisiveness or strong leadership, is now recognized by executives as the driver of competitive advantage. Drastically revamping the organization, enabling innovation, inviting customers and teams into the conversation—these all correlate directly to agile's emphasis on people-focused, collaborative, customer-centric practices.

Later in this chapter, we'll discuss in depth the reinvention of customer relationships, driven by Internet-enabled forms of customer intimacy. The customer may be an e-mail address, but the enterprise's knowledge of customer habits and preferences creates a new kind of familiarity. The feedback and data generated by a transaction are as valuable as the transaction itself, as the firm builds millions of interactive relationships with complete strangers. Netflix knows what I want from my transaction history and that of my demographic cohort, as does Amazon. Google knows what I want explicitly, as I tell them so when I search. The CEOs whom IBM selected as Standouts focused on using analytics, driven by these streams of data, to increase their customer obsession.

---

[5]www-01.ibm.com/common/ssi/cgi-bin/ssialias?subtype=XB&infotype=PM&appna
me=GBSE_GB_TI_USEN&htmlfid=GBE03297USEN&attachment=GBE03297USEN.PDF.

The data, unfortunately, has little value if the enterprise can't respond. Organizational dexterity is another way of saying enterprise agility. Dexterity, the ability to change in reaction to events and circumstances, is a strategic goal that far transcends the software development practice. For information technology (IT), it requires re-imagining data centers, cloud, hybrid infrastructures, and mobility, as well as new development methods. As agility spreads from software to IT infrastructure and then across the enterprise, thoughtful executives will be reimagining their entire value chain to incorporate agility everywhere. The agile consultant, by embodying the agile principles and helping translate them from product development to strategic thinking, has the opportunity to reshape enterprise culture and help teams and organizations prepare for tomorrow's tempestuous business climate.

Adapting Agility to Different Cultures

Focusing on IT for a moment, many agile consultants have experienced the complexity of reconciling the iterative, experimental nature of agile software development with the stability, security, and support concerns of IT infrastructure teams. We'll talk about DevOps and other approaches for IT to increase agility, but in the early days of an agile transition, IT development and operations teams have conflicting responsibilities. Agile software teams want flexibility; production IT requires stability. Agile teams want responsiveness and creativity; infrastructure teams seek efficiency and repeatability. Agile teams are cross-functional; infrastructure teams are typically specialized into functional server, data, and support silos. Each is prioritizing their own values and objectives responsibly, yet a clash is inevitable.

Consider these naturally opposing agendas and then amplify them across the entire organization to get a picture of the complexity of agile transformation. My emphasis on these political, cultural, and human complexities, rather than the techniques of scrum or XP, is based on one thing: experience. In every agile engagement I've undertaken, the basic methodology could be easily taught and practiced. The difficulty was in the discovery of the hidden web of personalities, alliances, duels, histories, and biases of the groups and individuals. Developing a strategy to evolve a resistant, fearful, change-worn firm into an agile enterprise requires deep understanding of both the overarching processes and practices that are out in the open, and the unspoken social structures that really influence behavior. It also requires empathy. Team members aren't resisting agile to be ornery, or to test you (most of the time). They are driven by the norms, fears, and insecurities of organizational life.

We've all heard of the "people, processes, systems" approach to thinking about organizations. While this is a useful high-level frame for thinking about the enterprise, it has a few flaws. Each of these areas can expand into a universe of subtopics. The "people" element, for example, encompasses most of the cultural, political, and personality issues we've discussed. Firms spend months on process mapping, often discovering that they don't really know how work flows, don't understand or follow their own guidelines, and the existing processes don't work. As IT becomes a strategic differentiator, the systems element of this model soars in complexity and importance. This is a functional view of the enterprise, but it doesn't reveal many of the things an agile consultant needs to know.

"People, processes, systems" has exploded into dozens of theories of organizational structure. Rummler and Brache, in their classic *Improving Performance*[6] refined this into "Organization, Process, and Job/ Performer," and applied a systems-thinking approach to the study of the organization. They offered a consultative, sober approach to reengineering, contrary to many of the radical, rip-it-out Business Process Reengineering (BPR) philosophies of that moment. *Improving Performance* was the mature refinement of an anarchic BPR movement that fed on its own radical ideas to become extreme and counterproductive.

In response to the criticisms of BPR, Schneider[7] proposed an organizational view much esteemed in the agile community. In his segregation of organizations into four key cultural types

- Control
- Collaboration
- Competence
- Cooperation

Schneider moved away from the systems view and toward a humanistic view. Cultures arise because the participants seek certain ideals and outcomes, and cultures evolve based on human traits, values, and decisions.

He compares the **Control** culture to a military organization. In a Control culture, "the individual motivation . . . lies in people's need for power. The leadership of a control organization values dominance most. Control cultures are prone towards territoriality. Control cultures manage performance by imparting rewards and sanctions. They also quickly suppress discontent or any signs of disruption. People are reluctant to give bosses bad news . . . leaders get told only what they want to hear. Subordinates feel compelled to comply and stick to business."[8]

In the **Collaboration** culture, values are aligned around people-driven, organic, informal participation, like a family or team, in which "little happens

---

[6]Geary A. Rummler & Alan P. Brache, *Improving Performance: How to Manage the White Space in the Organization Chart* (San Francisco: Jossey-Bass, 1995).
[7]William E. Schneider, *The Reengineering Alternative: A Plan for Making Your Current Culture Work* (Richard D. Irwin, 1994).
[8]Ibid. at 28–29.

that is solitary or solely independent. Harmony and cooperation are essential elements . . . the process is inherently win-win. This culture puts more trust in people than any of the others...the collaboration culture must be more adaptive, ready and able to make adjustments than the other three cultures. The organization moves ahead through the collective experience of people from inside and outside the organization."[9]

The **Competence** culture is based, in Schneider's view, on the academic model, in which the things that are valued are "imagined alternatives, creative options, and theoretical concepts. Its decision making process is analytical, scientific and prescriptive. Life in a competence culture is intense and high-strung. The work is rigorous and carries a sense of urgency. The norms are excellence, superiority and challenge." This culture "has competition at its center . . . this is a win-lose culture in which discord is present and less competent people fail. An organization whose goal is to create one-of-a-kind products . . . instinctively fills the organization with one-of-a-kind people."[10]

The **Cultivation** culture, modeled after a religious or social enterprise, "pays attention to potential, ideals and beliefs, aspirations and creative options." With a "focus on cultivating growth and development among their people. They strive to help people fulfill their potential . . . the culture is value-centered. Values and the value of people hold sway. Self-expression is highly encouraged."[11]

It's important to recognize that there's no judgment in the Schneider model. No culture is deemed better than the others. Each has different values and intentions, but all are useful, depending on the product, the team, and the customer. In fact, most organizations have some elements of each culture. A pharmaceutical firm, for example, could have a Competence culture in the research and development (R&D) laboratories, while exhibiting a Collaborative culture in the marketing team. Schneider is talking about the dominant culture, the culture that fits the criteria of "the personality of the organization."

The agile community has reacted to the rediscovery of Schneider's ideas with a robust debate over how agile consultants should apply this information. In a survey[12] performed by Michael Spayd of Collective Edge Coaching, agilists expressed a strong cultural preference for the Collaborative culture (47%) as an ideal for the agile team, with a Cultivation culture a strong second at 41%. With Competence at 9% and Control a tiny 3%, it's pretty clear that agilists value the interaction, team ownership, and self-organization that are epitomized by the Collaborative, Cultivating cultures, and appreciate the cultivation of skills and human potential these cultures champion. It's also obvious

---

[9]Ibid. at 44–59.
[10]Ibid. at 63–77.
[11]Ibid. at 81–98.
[12]http://collectiveedgecoaching.com/2010/07/agile_culture/.

that the hierarchical, authoritarian model of Control, or the hypercompetitive, win-lose ethic of the Competition culture, holds little attraction for agilists.

This, however, is an exploration of the ideal, a situation consultants rarely encounter. In the real world, as noted, agile consultants will encounter Control cultures that nonetheless want to benefit from some agile practices, and Competence cultures that believe agility can enhance their competitiveness and drive to results. As noted, in most instances consultants will encounter mixed cultural environments where different teams or "silos" have adopted different values. Can agile consultants simply write off any of these cultures as incompatible?

For the agile consultant, there is no judgment, only observation and diagnosis. Armed with this information about the types of cultures we are likely to encounter, our job is to determine the best route to the level of agility that each unique enterprise can achieve. The practices of scrum are a great fit when you walk into an existing Collaboration or Cultivation culture but will challenge the most experienced consultant in a Control environment.

In Control organizations, many agilists recommend beginning their agile journey with Kanban. Kanban, the systematic work-flow approach that enables teams to explicitly limit their work in progress to ensure low inventory and a just-in-time value chain, might be a better cultural jumping-off point. While embodying agile principles, Kanban's focus is not on the collaborative, iterative, team mentality, or self-directed teams—it's about the process-driven flow of work through a production process. It doesn't require organizations to rethink their Control-Based philosophies (at least at the beginning), or to grapple with foreign ideas like self-organization. As such, it seems a good fit for an opening foray into agile ideas for a Control culture.

The software craftsmanship movement, complete with its own manifesto,[13] is a reaction to the concern by coders that all the attention on agility and speed-to-value risks putting them in the position of writing bad code. Scrum, the dominant agile method, provides a process that promotes iterative, collaborative development, but it doesn't guide coders in the application of their craft. While quality and standards are explicit agile principles, their definition is up to the team and the product owner. The *Software Craftsmanship Manifesto* goes beyond the delivery of "working software" to the mandate for "well-crafted software" that "steadily adds value." This movement has strong affinity with a Competence culture, complete with the competitiveness that we often see in academic or scientific communities. Because agile values are more humanistic than a typical cutthroat competitive culture, I expect the software craftsmanship movement to be more collaborative than a strict Competence culture. When encountering a Competence culture, agile consultants can use the software craftsmanship model to promote a commitment to excellence that suits the prevailing values.

---

[13]http://manifesto.softwarecraftsmanship.org/

Whatever culture you encounter, there are simple techniques for easing the agile transition. In my career I've adapted to "the way things are done around here" by applying an *inside-outside* perspective. Inside the agile team structure, we're applying all the methods and practices, and measuring our progress, based on the agile approach we're following. Outside, to the existing structure, we're supplying some of the artifacts they expect to see, like project plans and status reports. Clearly a compromise with agile standards, these "adapters" enable us to begin the conversation about the difference between what they're used to seeing and what agile provides. The migration from a Gantt chart to a burn-down chart is not momentous, but a transition period with some coaching on the benefits of agile can make it smoother. Reminding the Project Management Office (PMO) of the stack of unread status reports that inevitably pile up on their desk, versus the daily interaction of the stand-up, can be an opportunity to embody the "individuals and interactions" value of the Manifesto.

Strategic Goals of Agility

PWC, the consulting entity of IBM, recently published "Agility Is Within Reach,"[14] in which it defines two goals that all enterprises seeking agility should focus on, *strategic responsiveness* and *organizational flexibility*. This focus on two key elements of agility summarizes nicely the goal we should be aiming for as agile consultants. The purpose of our engagement is not to immediately change their culture, or teach them agile concepts, or create a more humanistic environment. Those may be outcomes of the agile transformation, but the strategic goal of agility is competitive advantage and enhanced business results. Agile consultants, as opposed to scrummasters or team coaches, should focus on the strategic, measurable business results that agile offers the whole enterprise. The holistic, enterprise view of agile is ambitious, and may be too much for many firms, but the strategic outlook is what differentiates superior agile advisors.

The art of the consultant is to observe, diagnose, and then plan for the best outcome under prevailing circumstances. The likelihood of us changing a Control culture to a Collaborative one, at least in the short term, is slim. What we can do is diagnose the cultural proclivities of the enterprise and thoughtfully strategize on the best mix of agile philosophy, culture, and methods that will enable this particular enterprise, within this unique culture, to begin its individual agile journey. Not every enterprise has the will, or the desire, to evolve completely to enterprise agility. Most will make changes at the team level, and measure the impact of those changes, long

---

[14] www.strategy-business.com/article/00316?gko=9ee79.

before they commit to changing their core beliefs and practices across the organization. Part of the agile consultant's art is to help customers figure out where on the spectrum of agility, from scrum practice at the team level to enterprise-wide evolution, they'll get the most strategic advantage with the least pain and disruption. As agile proponents and believers, we may want every organization to transform completely to these ideals we treasure. When we take our personal objectives and emotions out of the equation, our responsibility is to take a sober inventory of the customer organization's current state, strategically, culturally, and operationally, and help the customer develop an agile roadmap that fits its will and desire to transform.

Is 20th-Century Corporate Culture Obsolete?

Alfred P. Sloan, president, chairman, and CEO of General Motors Corporation from the 1920s through the 1950s, is often regarded as the author of the hierarchical, departmentalized, top-down management style that typified American business during those years. This style was immensely successful at building the giant American corporations we all know. After World War II, despite an abrupt decline in government spending, the U.S. economy boomed. One of the greatest periods of economic expansion and consumer spending in history resulted, in part, from the efficiencies designed into Sloan's management style, where orders flowed from the top and compliance flowed from below, with no such thing as a "stakeholder," just a shareholder. The success of America's industrial war effort validated the autocratic, assembly-line, interchangeable worker mentality that characterized American manufacturing.

In the intervening years, however, Sloan's command-and-control business philosophy has been severely criticized. James O'Toole,[15] in analyzing Sloan's management philosophy, noted that

> . . . not once does Sloan make reference to any other values. Freedom, equality, humanism, stability, community, tradition, religion, patriotism, family, love, virtue, nature—all are ignored. His language is as calculating as that of the engineer-of-old working with calipers and slide rules: economizing, utility, facts, objectivity, systems, rationality, maximizing— that is the stuff of his vocabulary.[16]

---

[15]James O'Toole, *Leading Change: Overcoming the Ideology of Comfort and the Tyranny of Custom* (San Francisco: Jossey-Bass, 1995).
[16]Ibid. at 174.

Yet even Sloan, the champion of hierarchical management, knew that technology, markets, and consumer tastes would inevitably change. In his classic "My Years With General Motors,"[17] Sloan remarked that

> *The circumstances of the ever-changing market and ever-changing product are capable of breaking any business organization if that organization is unprepared for change—indeed, in my opinion, if it has not provided procedures for anticipating change. p. 508*

Decades later, Sloan has been proven right on that count. The disruption, by new Internet entrants, of everything from the corner book store to the taxicab industry, and from the garage sale to the real estate market, illustrates his point. The success of those companies like Google and Facebook that have abandoned the traditional, hierarchical model of management and embraced a collaborative, experimental culture confirms the obsolescence of the hierarchical Sloan model, at least for "new economy" firms.

The surprising thing is that these command-and-control managerial theories are still in wide application. They seem so obviously unsuited to the modern business climate that their survival is clearly cultural and historical rather than pragmatic. When I started at Citicorp, it was described to me by a colleague as "the world's largest paramilitary organization." Warren Buffet believes that we only know who's swimming naked when the tide goes out, and, during the financial crisis of the last decade, it was pretty clear that Citicorp and many other global financial institutions were skinny-dipping. Even in the staid financial industry, the top-down autocratic model I experienced at Citicorp couldn't manage the experimental, opportunistic tactics of floor traders.

Agile Disrupts Everything

We know what makes agile popular among developers. Working as a team, they focus together on an achievable and valuable goal, improving their skills and the customer's satisfaction with every iteration. Well-running agile teams work in an atmosphere of self-motivation, mutual respect, openness, and accomplishment. What's not to like for them? But what is it that's driving executives and managers to take agile seriously as a potential revolution in enterprise management?

In the executive suite, agility, like Total Quality Management (TQM) and BPR before it, is reaching its maximum hype cycle. From *Harvard Business Review* to *The Huffington Post*, the idea of scaling agile within IT, and then across the entire enterprise, is widely discussed and debated. Now that

---

[17]Alfred P. Sloan, *My Years With General Motors* (New York: Doubleday, 1963), p. 504, https://hbr.org/2014/03/my-years-with-general-motors-fifty-years-on.

agile has proven itself in software, everyone else, from product development to marketing and operations, wants in. Executives want to see if they can get away from their fantasy[18] strategic plans,' with dozens, sometimes hundreds, of projects that will never get funded or executed, and replace them with iterative, incremental planning techniques that actually arrive at consensus and deliver value.

Let's examine the economic forces that are driving business thinkers to consider agile as their next candidate for modernizing a faltering business model. There are, in my view, four strategic themes that are setting off light bulbs for academics and executives worldwide.

The biggest fear, of course, is digital disruption. In the early days of the Internet we used to say that nobody wanted to get "Amazoned"; now that services are also being disrupted, nobody wants to get "Uber-ed." In either case, every business owner knows that there's a young entrepreneur lurking somewhere, dissecting their business model and trying to figure out how to automate it, put it in the cloud, and take their market. The software market has evolved from omnibus, all-in-one business products to an atomized world of apps, where every niche or microprocess has the attention of startups and investors. In this granular market, every existing business and process is a target.

The concern about digital disruption is so widespread that respected management authors like Clay Christenson[19] and Larry Downes[20] have proposed making the evaluation and assessment of potential disruptors a strategic focus of every business. As Downes says in his *Harvard Business Review* article "Big-Bang Disruption":

> *You can't see big-bang disruption coming. You can't stop it. And it will be keeping executives in every industry in a cold sweat for a long time to come ...*

According to Christensen, even the business of consulting is vulnerable.

> *The same forces that disrupted so many businesses, from steel to publishing, are starting to reshape the world of consulting...undermining the position of longtime leaders and often causing the "flip" to a new basis of competition. The implications for firms and their clients are significant.[21]*

---

[18]https://hbr.org/webinar/2015/05/bring-agile-planning-to-the-whole-organization; www.huffingtonpost.com/great-work-cultures/scaling-agile-to-create-a_b_7537818.html.
[19]www.immagic.com/eLibrary/ARCHIVES/GENERAL/JOURNALS/H950130C.pdf.
[20]https://hbr.org/2013/03/big-bang-disruption/ar/1.
[21]https://hbr.org/2013/10/consulting-on-the-cusp-of-disruption.

I was engaged by a smartphone manufacturing company to deliver training on Agile Project Management, and, as I got to know the students, one told a definitive story of disruption. Her team was building prototypes of new phones, and, in the middle of their project, Apple's first iPhone was released. Prototypes just a few weeks from production were scrapped, and the design team did the proverbial "back to the drawing board" exercise. The innovative technologies built into the iPhone were far beyond anything they'd been prototyping, and they realized that day that their market had changed irrevocably. Which explains why they suddenly were anxious to begin a conversation about agile.

This is an example of digital disruption, but it also speaks to the **exponential growth in the rate of change in technology**. Product cycles compress tighter and tighter, queues form for the next version of a gadget immediately after its last release, and feature wars accelerate. Ray Kurzweil, well-known author and winner of the 1999 National Medal of Technology and Innovation, says of accelerating technical change:

> *An analysis of the history of technology shows that technological change is exponential, contrary to the common-sense "intuitive linear" view. So we won't experience 100 years of progress in the 21st century—it will be more like 20,000 years of progress (at today's rate). Within a few decades, machine intelligence will surpass human intelligence, leading to technological change so rapid and profound it represents a rupture in the fabric of human history. The implications include the merger of biological and nonbiological intelligence, immortal software-based humans, and ultra-high levels of intelligence that expand outward in the universe at the speed of light.*[22]

While most businesses aren't yet concerned about "software-based humans," they do understand that technological change threatens their business models, their current products, and even their R&D function. How can you research and plan a product when, like the smartphone I described above, your prototypes may already be obsolete?

Another key factor that explains the hype surrounding agile is **price and product transparency**, or the death of unequal information. Before the Internet, the auto dealer had much more information about the price, lease structure, profit margin, and options than the customer. The insurance salesman knew much more about the likelihood of your accidental death. The for-profit school had private information about its success rate, as did the hospital. That unequal information gave the seller a decisive advantage. Those days of information inequality are gone, thanks to the Internet.

---

[22]www.kurzweilai.net/the-law-of-accelerating-returns.

As in the stock markets, price discovery and product information are now transparent to the customer. Every car buyer goes to TrueCar or its competitors to learn about the car he is considering, read reviews, and check invoice and local pricing. The graduation and job-entry rates of for-profit schools are now widely available, as is the hospital's mortality rate. I can go to eBay and, in an instant, learn the going price for a guitar, a table, or a pair of vintage earrings. Amazon reviewers will tell me which books to stay away from. So much data is being generated that many "big data" firms are springing up just to help businesses sort, categorize, and capitalize on these momentous data flows.

This transparency, of course, is the perfect catalyst for agility. Companies that can use this flow of data to understand the needs and desires of their marketplace, and make small, incremental changes to products in order to be responsive, have a deep competitive advantage. In fact, responsiveness to customer needs has overtaken sheer efficiency as a market differentiator. The Samsungs and Apples of the world, whose entire value chain can be redirected for every new product, use their agility to keep other players off balance. Amazon can, and does, incrementally change both the business model and the customer experience. These aren't the low-cost producers, a sign of efficiency. They are the responsive producers, using data flow analytics and customer intimacy to quickly give the market what it wants. While Steve Jobs may have been right in his particular niche when he said that "people don't know what they want until you show it to them," for those businesspeople who are not Steve Jobs, data-driven responsiveness, not intuition, makes the competitive difference.

As Michael Treacy and Fred Wiersema, authors of a mid-1990s best-selling book,[23] explained, there are three key strategies for any business: operational excellence, product leadership, and customer intimacy. Operational excellence, of course, refers to the efficiency that Alfred Sloan valued, while product leadership refers to the Apples, Teslas, and Gilead Sciences of the world, who can command premium prices for their innovative and superior offerings. These strategies have remained pretty much the same, though achieved through technological capabilities that were unavailable until now.

Customer intimacy, however, has changed completely. When Treacy and Wiersema published, they described customer intimacy as "the extraordinary level of service, guidance, expertise, and hand-holding" that companies provided. Their idea of customer intimacy was based on building multiple individual relationships with customers through great customer service, outstanding support, and the human touch that cements relationships.

---

[23]Michael Treacy and Fred Wiersema, *The Discipline of Market Leaders: Choose Your Customers, Narrow Your Focus, Dominate Your Market* (Perseus Books, 1995).

In the time of big data, however, customer intimacy is based on the streams of data that both individuals and groups throw off, transaction by transaction. Amazon has no personal relationship with me, but it has intimate knowledge about my reading and shopping habits, my demographics, and my likelihood to respond to a product or promotion. Facebook doesn't know me, but it sure knows *about* me; who my friends are, what posts I favor, my politics, religion, and marital status. From Facebook and Amazon to Google and Twitter, personal information is currency, driving ad revenue and product sales. So is the collective information, captured from millions of transactions and analyzed by sophisticated algorithms, which enables Netflix to make recommendations to individual subscribers.

When Land's End, for instance, was a catalog company, its ability to collect data was limited to individual transactions from anonymous customers. All Land's End usually saw was an order form and a check. Now, on the Web, It can trace every click, every purchase, and all the demographics of every customer, even those who are just browsing. The web world of customer intimacy may be intrusive and invasive in some people's eyes, but, in most cases, customers are volunteering this data gladly to gain the benefits of the technology.

In the 1950s, during GM's heyday, the industrial mantras of efficiencies of scale, interchangeable parts and workers, and long production runs on standardized models created the industrial giants. Many of these corporate behemoths, including GM itself, have faltered in the new economy. The threats of digital disruption, exponential technology advances, price and product transparency, and collective customer intimacy have changed the game completely. For many executives and management theorists, agile across the enterprise seems like it might be the solution to these threats.

Summary

Agility is about much more than methodology; in fact, a methodological approach to agile adoption is a key indicator of failure. Agile disrupts business models, culture, hierarchies, and operations. Studies have shown convincingly that, in order to evolve to agility, organizations need to address change from the team level up to the executive suite. Legacy cultural and managerial ideas and styles are cited as the key barriers to agility, and consultants need to assess the culture, history, business model, and managerial style in order to adapt their approach to the reality at hand.

The standard top-down, hierarchical corporate culture is showing its age, as modern workers reject the command style of management and expect input and creative freedom. We've surveyed many cultural styles, and discussed how an agile advisor can apply the right style to the existing culture.

Change is not an option. We've illustrated that the basics of every business model, from customer intimacy to product cycle time, have been changed by new customer expectations and disruptive technologies. Businesses that fail to keep up with these changes are in mortal danger. From price transparency to exponential increases in technical innovation, the forces of disruption require enterprises to rethink the traditional way of doing business and adopt new, more responsive and agile models. William E. Schneider, *The Reengineering Alternative: A Plan for Making Your Current Culture Work* by William E. Schneider (Richard D. Irwin, 1994)

The EVOLVE Framework for Agile Evolution

In Chapter 1 we looked at existing transformation frameworks, like ADKAR (Awareness, Desire, Knowledge, Ability, Reinforcement), ADAPT (Awareness, Desire, Ability, Promotion, Transfer), and Kotter's "accelerators." Each of these frameworks has a lot to recommend it. So why do I feel the need to develop a completely new framework, rather than just advising you to learn and use one of these existing change models?

As mentioned, there are gaps in these frameworks for an agile consultant. Cohn's ADAPT framework gives a consultant a basic overview of the necessary conditions for an agile evolution. Cohn expands it beautifully in his book *Succeeding with Agile*, the essential work on the techniques of agile adoption. The elements of the ADAPT framework are not, however, addressed to the needs of a consultant, who must structure a commercial agreement that suits the client and sets up for a successful engagement. To evolve the enterprise, consultants must be sure they've set reasonable expectations in the client's mind. We must know what the client is envisioning. We've got to explore the current state, and do a bit of due diligence, before we even engage. Is this a

© Rick Freedman 2016
R. Freedman, *The Agile Consultant*, DOI 10.1007/978-1-4302-6053-0_3

client you want to partner with on this complex and delicate transition, in a culture with which you can successfully engage? Can you do it yourself or do you need partners? What result are you responsible for, and to what is the client committing? What constitutes success?

This framework is certainly no original creation. I've shamelessly stolen those ideas that fit the consulting context from Cohn, Kotter, and others. We'll discuss situations where, armed with Cohn's book, I learned in practice what works and how to frame it. From consulting on large-scale acquisitions and organizational designs during my Big 5 days, and on agile projects now, I've encountered the persistence of history, legacy, and personality that makes change so challenging. I've incorporated elements from everything I've learned about organizational dynamics and change leadership, and brazenly arranged the concepts to fit my preordained EVOLVE acronym. My original contribution, if there is one, is to use these borrowed ideas fairly and wisely, from an agile mind-set, to incorporate my pragmatic experience, and to try to shift the conversation from team-focused practice adoption to enterprise-focused agile evolution.

We apply a framework because the complexity and sensitivity of agile evolution necessitates consulting discipline. Enterprise clients must know that we can engage strategically as well as tactically. They want to see an approach that indicates that the consultant has pondered their unique qualities, and thought through a tailored roadmap to their agility. Even if the move to agility is vigorously encouraged by senior management, sponsors of agile evolution projects want to know they're partnering with a consulting professional who can negotiate, plan, and carry out a successful engagement. A framework is a marketing tool as well as a consulting tool. It illustrates that you're credible, you're experienced, and you know what works.

I want to make one important disclaimer: this is not by any means a "big, upfront plan" for "going agile." As I hope I've clarified, engaging on this road with a client is an odyssey that will evolve and mutate as we're experiencing it. There isn't, and can't be, a static plan for a dynamic engagement. This framework doesn't predict anything, and it doesn't promise any outcome but kaizen, the eternal search for perfection.

We'll walk through the key ideas within each step of the EVOLVE framework (see Figure 3-1), and then I'll expand on each concept in its own chapter. Of course, in the spirit of agile, I invite you to inspect and adapt. EVOLVE is just a convenient way for me to structure my ideas and experiences, and perhaps a way to encourage a bit of consulting discipline in the emerging field of enterprise agility.

Figure 3-1. The EVOLVE framework

What drives a sponsor, whether executive or information technology (IT) manager, to engage an agile change agent? The IT manager is experiencing pressure to deliver more innovation, more throughput, and more functionality, for more platforms. His teams are clamoring to try, or to expand, agile. The executive is in fear of, or already experiencing, digital disruption from innovative competitors. The business press is extolling the wonders of agility. In Kotter's *XLR8*[1] and Denning's *Radical Management*,[2] the agile ethic is applied to the enterprise. Their arguments, and the experiences they chronicle, are persuasive. In short, the belief is spreading that agility just might be a way to retain or advance their competitive advantage, customer responsiveness, and innovation. Whether focused on market position and financial metrics only, or sincerely striving toward a more humane, frictionless, adaptive workplace, executives understand that the impetus behind enterprise agility is growing and will soon be overwhelming.

When a client decides to engage an outside advisor, she's already made a few admissions that may not be flattering. She's accepted that she doesn't have the inside resources to solve her problem, or that her leadership team can't come to consensus on an approach. She may feel uneducated about agility and seeks an expert who can help her visualize an outcome. She may have concluded that her teams just can't manage the change without a professional change agent, or she may just want the opinion of an objective outsider. Whatever the case, or combination thereof, an agile consultant must consider the situation and adapt the approach accordingly. An autocratic, hierarchical executive in a Control culture will have sharply differing concerns and expectations than the leader who has created a Collaborative culture, encouraging participation and valuing each individual. Those differing concerns and expectations will lead to a completely unique engagement and outcome for each.

Explore and Engage

This **Explore and Engage** step in the EVOLVE framework prompts us to consider the personality of the sponsor and the organization. It reminds us that not all clients are good clients, and not all cultures are places we'd choose to work. It reminds us also of three fundamental rules of consulting:

- Every client and engagement is unique.
- Explore before you engage.
- Engage judiciously.

---

[1] John P. Kotter, *XLR8 (Accelerate!)* (Boston: Harvard Business Review Press, 2014).
[2] Stephen Denning, *The Leader's Guide to Radical Management: Reinventing the Workplace for the 21st Century* (San Francisco: Jossey-Bass, 2010).

Even when, early in the sales cycle, the client invites us in for an initial chat, we're exploring all the elements: business context, enterprise and individual personality, culture, and atmosphere. As we're advising the client on how to proceed, we're incrementally observing every clue that might inform us of the best way to plan and execute this particular engagement. If the physician's Hippocratic Oath is "First, do no harm," then the consultant's oath should be "Don't prescribe before diagnosing." Before we start to propose and negotiate an agile roadmap, we need to understand what we're stepping into, and where the boundaries, taboos, and pitfalls might lay. As I've said, in an experimental, experiential engagement, we'd better consider the landscape we're treading, and negotiate and engage with understanding and with clear expectations all around.

Visualize Success

Long before the debates on the definition of "done," the skilled consultant learned that client expectations can be ambiguous, and that helping the client create a vision of a successful outcome is an essential practice. Experienced consultants know that organizational gravity is powerful, and that people have an emotional investment in their rank, their role, and their work. They're invested in their culture, as they're part of the community that built and sustains it. People and teams define themselves by their place in the enterprise, the enterprise provides them stability and solvency and reflects the common values and history that took them here. In short, enterprises have a powerful, organic inertia.

When we **Visualize Success** with the client, we're preparing for agility in a number of ways. We're clarifying what success looks like, and ensuring that consultant and client are anticipating the same process and outcome. We're also helping the client develop a communication scheme that can be used to create momentum around agile evolution. Momentum is the opposite of inertia, and its only cure. The wise agile consultant will validate the client's vision of agility, what it means, and its perceived benefits. For enterprise-level evolution, the prudent consultant begins to test the edges as early as possible, to determine how far on this journey he expects to go. He educates clients about the possible challenges and learnings they'll encounter along the way. He helps the client craft a vision of agility that resonates with the enterprise strategy and culture.

Part of the consultant's art is the ability to help the client communicate, educate, and reassure the enterprise community. I intend for Visualization to be an agile exercise, cascading through the organization, with sponsors initially participating to set the vision, and then opening participation to widening circles. I've called this Visualization step out separately because I believe it to be a critical predictor of success. If we can come to a common understanding of agility's potential strategic impact, its iterative, exploratory nature, and the roles, commitments, and success criteria for all players, we've prepared for the agile transition. We've helped the client envision our agility roadmap, we've reassured the client that we can do this, and we've started the process of articulating an agile vision across the enterprise.

Observe and Plan

In our initial exploration, we've started to get a glimpse under the covers of our sponsor's enterprise, but it's only a glimpse. In order to plan the effort required to migrate an entire organization toward agility, it's prudent for agile consultants to know as much as they can about the client's business, culture, and challenges. We often start our engagements at the "grassroots" level, allowing us the chance to see these factors from the team's perspective. These initial encounters are very revealing; in an iteration or two, we can start to expose the challenges inside the team, and the external obstacles of weak process, hierarchical management, and unhealthy culture.

Agile consultants have a complicated mix of responsibilities: training, coaching, mentoring, persuading, and executing. They have a complex mix of teams that they're doing it with; from gung-ho coders to reluctant server teams within IT, radiating out to resistant accountants and busy executives. There may be teams of scrummasters already in-house who've developed practices that need refinement (to be polite). There may be a Project Management Office (PMO) that's emotionally married to a complex systems development life cycle (SDLC) that it has developed over the years.

If we look back at Kotter's accelerators, we see that once we've created a sense of urgency behind a "Big Opportunity," which we should have started in our Visualization exercise, Kotter recommends we create a guiding coalition, and enlist a volunteer army. The observation and planning I recommend includes guiding the organization to empower a Product Owner as its key representative during the agile evolution. It includes determining what the role of any guiding coalition is: does it have veto power and decision rights, or is it a "cheering committee" of enthusiastic sponsors, or both? We'll be orchestrating teams that are set up in a traditional project management PMO "resource pool," or as a function-centered technology team, as they dissolve and reform to become agile teams. If we're bringing in partners, or engaging with incumbents, we'll need to figure out a mode of working that suits all parties.

The keys to observation and planning, in my experience, are transparency and discipline. Transparency is, of course, a central agile value, but I see it as a central consulting value as well. One of the reasons we were invited into the client's house is because we're objective. We're not driving toward an agenda, as internal advisors might. As agile change agents, we're enthusiastic and committed to agile ideas, but our role is not to implant our own vision. It's, instead, to objectively advise and guide clients through the delivery of their vision, within their competence and will. That leads us to be transparent; to be honest, open, and truthful about triumphs, obstacles, successes, and failures. Transparency builds the trust that underlies any agile transition. When trust develops, the boundaries among teams start to evaporate and new forms can emerge.

Discipline is also key. As democratic and egalitarian as agile is, groups need leadership. If you're lucky as an agile consultant, 95% of the leadership toward enterprise agility is coming from committed managers and volunteers. If you're like the rest of us, you have to prod, goad, and then end up leading the communication program, the training program, and the hands-on coaching of teams across the enterprise. I'm disappointed to report that I've worked with agile change agents who fluttered from one training course to another planning poker session, with no overarching plan or program. This misinterprets agility; we're not making it up as we go along. In my vision of agile consulting, we're trying some stuff that we've seen work, such as good scrum practices, and adapting our techniques and expectations every day, as the enterprise stutters toward agility. The orchestration of forces to deliver agility requires trust, adaptability, and discipline.

Lead Teams to Agility

In 1993, Jon Katzenbach and Douglas Smith wrote the classic book on team-work in business.[3] Based on years of experience as a McKinsey consultant, Katzenbach, with his partner Smith, presented a set of six "team basics":

- Small number
- Complementary skills
- Common purpose
- Common set of specific performance goals
- Commonly agreed upon working approach
- Mutual accountability

Katzenbach and Smith called teams that exhibited these characteristics "real teams." Over 20 years later, I call them agile teams. The characteristics clearly coincide.

The small number theory has become the "two pizzas" idea popularized by Mike Cohn, or the "7 + / - 2" theory all agilists know, but the underlying concept remains. The communication and consensus overhead of large teams

---

[3]Jon R. Katzenbach and Douglas E. Smith, *The Wisdom of Teams* (Boston: Harvard Business School Press, 1993).

inhibits innovation and throughput. Complementary skills are aligned with cross-disciplinary teams and integration of Dev and Ops. Common purpose is now a vision statement, performance goals are now roadmaps, iterations, and valuable features. Scrum (or whatever practice you've chosen) is the common working approach. Mutual accountability is manifested in the big visible charts by which we measure ourselves and the kaizen manner in which we approach reflection and adaptation.

The performance indicators revealed in this classic text demonstrate that the team concepts within agile didn't come out of nowhere, and that empirical observation proves these fundamentals are valid. At the team level, there are some well-known success factors that have been shown to improve results. The success of the agile movement has finally made these ideas, which seem the opposite of real life in the typical big company, accepted as "best practice."

The results of teaming successfully and adaptively, from Katzenbach's time to ours, are so strongly validated and so compelling that enterprises can't resist. They also can't do it alone, at least not yet. As agility migrates across levels, helping managers and executives understand, accept, and support these team concepts is an agile consultant's big challenge. The team approach isn't trivial in a single team of like-minded and like-dispositioned coders, but as we ascend the organizational ladder, motives become less transparent, and interests come to the fore. Guiding Dev and Ops to a continuous delivery cycle is tough enough. Getting sales and marketing to collaborate, or siloed division heads to team up cross-functionally, is a whole 'nother thing. From agile organizational design, to team, tribe, and squad theories of teaming, the agile consultant will need to adaptively apply multiple, various team forma-tions as she engages across the enterprise. Agile consultants at the enterprise level are engaged in multiple interdependent layers of disruption and change. The composition, objectives, styles, and expectations of development teams, operations teams, marketing teams, finance teams, risk-management teams, and executive teams will differ sharply, and the iterative process of advising, inspecting, and adapting these teams is demanding. We'll outline the experi-ence and knowledge required to successfully advise teams at every level.

Visible Results Now

It's an axiom of change management that visible results encourage enthusiasm, engagement, and optimism. From Cohn's ADAPT model to Kotter's accel-erators, the promotion of successes, large and small, is a key element of the transition process. Even without a sophisticated change model, most people know intuitively that "low-hanging fruit" is a metaphor for selecting some immediately achievable goals and demonstrating that we can actually produce results with a different approach. Any experienced consultant has bumped against the outer limits of culture, protocol, personality, and structure. As I gained experience as a consultant, I learned from painful experience that the generation of momentum is the primary sustaining element of change. Gravity, inertia, culture, or bureaucracy, whatever you call it, all advisors experience it, and all change agents must navigate it in pursuit of their goal. Their complexity expands exponentially with the size of the enterprise.

Luckily for agile consultants, our iterative, incremental approach to agile evolution is a great fit with the promotional concept. Based on our roots in IT, we typically start with development teams. When that atomic unit is working effectively, and producing observable results, we use all the venues at hand, from web sites to "lunch & learns" to posters and celebrations, to make those successes visible enterprise-wide. We augment that with leadership, putting those improvements in strategic context and underlining their business significance. We generate momentum by producing "potentially shippable code" (whatever the product) and collaborating with the entire enterprise to optimize the value of that product. I visualize a set of concentric circles, starting at the team level and radiating progressively outward, in which, at least within some individuals, we can plant a spark that encourages them to seek out agility and join the volunteers. This is the vision that inspires me to keep using the phrase *agile evolution* rather than the popular *transition* or *transformation*. By succeeding at the team level, and evangelizing our success, we incrementally and organically evolve to our maximum agility. The momentum created by visible success is one of the emotional levers that energizes change.

I have a pet peeve in consulting; I hate "drive-by engagements." A drive-by engagement occurs when a salesperson makes unreasonable promises, drops the project in a consultant's lap, and drives away to the next victim. Drive-by engagements are often perpetrated by consultants themselves. I often see this in the "consultants" that are actually dedicated product implementers for a software provider. They come into the enterprise, configure a working instance of the software, train an administrator and a couple of users, and are gone. In consultant-led change programs, beginning the change effort is often relatively easy. The organization has already acknowledged a problem that it can't fix itself, just by hiring you. Especially with agile, there's usually a bottom-up groundswell of desire to participate. There are always volunteers so motivated by their contempt for the current circumstance that they'll join the revolution. In agile, I've usually experienced more enthusiasm than resistance at the grassroots level. It's in evolution and sustainment that the real heavy lifting emerges for the agile consultant.

I've mentioned earlier the tendency of "program of the month" efforts to succeed for a minute, based on leadership's enthusiasm and staff's compliance, and then to get dragged back by the infinite gravity of culture. But what actually occurs when programs fail? As a former (or reformed) Big 5 consultant, I've observed problems across the change spectrum from the initial idea, to the strategic meaning, through planning, implementation, and sustenance.

Programs get initiated by a software salesman or a golf-course conversation. No connection is made to the strategic outcome. Plans are unrealistic, with big, upfront predictions and arbitrary schedules. Communication is weak. Implementation is sloppy and "drive-by." These are all clear failure patterns.

But the most significant failure pattern in change initiatives, in my experience, is the failure to sustain. That's why I hate drive-by consulting so much; it leaves clients unable to unlock the value they thought they were buying. By not implementing a sustainment program, they've doomed their product to grudging acceptance at best, or shelfware at worst. It's our responsibility to ensure that the client understands the pull of inertia, and considers the long-term implications of sustaining disruptive change.

When the first agile team is successful, visible, and practicing kaizen, we've planted the first tiny seed. That seed sprouts when agility spreads to other teams. As agility propagates across the enterprise, experienced agile consultants can help the client foresee the elements of gravity that might pull the new practices into the black hole. By collaborating with the client to understand the unique circumstances within their enterprise, we can craft strategies that enable the organization to become self-sustaining and continuously improving. By inspiring agile ideals for quality, standards, craftsmanship, and value, we can aspire to guiding whole enterprises not just to gain agility but to keep it.

Summary

While there are many organizational change frameworks, none of them fits precisely the unique needs of a consultant guiding an enterprise to agility. We've looked at Kotter's accelerators and Cohn's ADAPT frameworks, and then walked through the EVOLVE framework that I'm proposing specifically for agile advisors. The evolution to agility is too complex and fraught to simply feel our way through; we need to apply a structured framework, based on mature consulting practices mingled with the principles of agile. We've taken a brief tour of the elements of the EVOLVE framework, as a roadmap of the topics we'll address in subsequent chapters. The emphasis is on an adaptable, lean, and agile approach to agile consulting engagements, and on the idea that each engagement will be different and each enterprise requires a unique approach.

The EVOLVE Agile Consulting Framework

Explore and Engage

Is there an agile personality type? Is agile evolution destined to succeed or fail based on the personalities of the executive team and the culture of the organization? Are Industrial Age companies, like Ford or Proctor & Gamble, with their history of hierarchical management styles, doomed to fail at agile? Agile consultants must consider these and many other questions before they embark on the mutual effort to enhance agility and responsiveness.

Explore the Environment

Before we tackle these questions, let's discuss why they matter. If there is a recognizable type of personality that is more or less likely to engage successfully in agile evolution, as agile advisors we should be prepared to identify those types, and adapt our training and consulting to the personalities we're confronted with. If an executive asks us in to discuss agile adoption, it would be helpful to be able to put his, and his team's, personalities on some type of spectrum that might give us guidance for the voyage ahead. If some particular types of cultures are inherently prone to fail at agility, should we steer clear of them, or take on the challenge to help them adapt? I raise these points because many agile advisors, acting at the "accidental" level of engagement that Michael Sahota describes, walk into every engagement with the same tools, methods, and practices, as if there's a single roadmap to agility and these cultural and personality issues are immaterial.

© Rick Freedman 2016
R. Freedman, *The Agile Consultant*, DOI 10.1007/978-1-4302-6053-0_4

The question of agile personality types has actually been widely studied. From the academic studies[1] done at Goethe University in Germany, to the anecdotal analysis performed by Mario Moreira[2] for *The Agile Journal*, the idea that there are specific personality types that are suited for agile has been analyzed both formally and informally. Even Mike Cohn has gotten into the conversation, with a post[3] on different types of resistors that agile change agents might find in organizations.

As illustrated in Figure 4-1, Cohn's analysis isn't specifically about distinct personalities but more about the attitudes that some resistant individuals might bring to the agile evolution process. He divides the resistance camp into four quadrants:

- Skeptics
- Followers
- Saboteurs
- Diehards

He contends that team members adopt these positions based on two criteria, their desire to either sustain the status quo or oppose agile methods and their passivity or activeness. Skeptics both dislike agile and are passive participants, while Diehards are invested in current processes and are actively resisting change. Here's Cohn's diagram, from the cited post, illustrating his theory:

---

[1] aisel.aisnet.org/cgi/viewcontent.cgi?article=1015&context=ecis2015_cr.
[2] cmforagile.blogspot.com/2011/04/knowing-your-agile-personalities.html.
[3] www.mountaingoatsoftware.com/blog/four-types-of-resistors-when-adopting-agile.

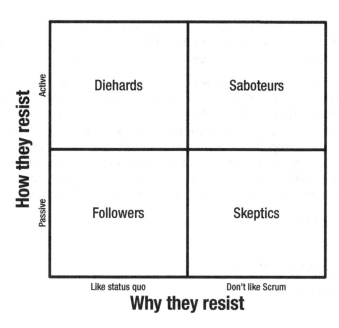

Figure 4-1. Mike Cohn's resistor spectrum

Cohn's experience-based analysis is important, but it only addresses resistors. Moreira digs a bit deeper. Though not a rigorous study, it raises some interesting ideas about the sorts of team members we might encounter. He categorizes these personalities as follows:

- Innovator
- Champion
- Workhorse
- Bandwagon
- Cowboy
- Deceiver
- Denier

From the Denier, who actively disputes agile theories but typically has little experience with agile concepts, to the Innovator, who provides agile leadership from within and has deep experience in agile culture, this continuum is quite useful for understanding and handling the objections, resistance, and impediments that an agile change agent will encounter, especially as agile spreads beyond information technology (IT). The Denier plays an important role in agile evolution, enabling agile consultants to confront head-on the myths and misconceptions that many first-time agile participants may be carrying. The Cowboy confirms the worst mythology about agile, using it as an excuse to jettison all discipline and make it up as he goes along. The titles Moreira has assigned are self-evident to any experienced change agent, agile or not.

On the academic side. the research[4] performed by the team at Goethe University in Frankfurt takes a more formal approach to the question, using familiar personality models like Meyers-Briggs[5] and the Five Factor Model (FFM)[6] to understand how different personality factors might influence the acceptance and competence of individuals in an agile team. Through a series of interviews with agile team members, they evaluated individuals against the FFM personality traits and analyzed these traits against their attitudes and effectiveness in agile settings. The five traits in the FFM model are:

- Extraversion
- Agreeableness
- Conscientiousness
- Neuroticism
- Openness

They found that Agreeableness is a key factor for developer success with agile, while Conscientiousness is a key trait for scrummasters. The research goes into considerable depth about the individual traits that apply under these five broad categories, which I won't reproduce here.

The point is that the personality traits of individuals, from the executive sponsor to the individual developer, have a significant influence on the ability to adopt agile techniques. While I scoff at the study's recommendation that every agile team should undergo testing to uncover these attributes, I believe that the agile consultant who understands these personality elements, and is on the lookout for them when she engages, is less likely to apply a one-size-fits-all approach, and will instead design and implement a strategy that fits the team.

The clues are all around us when we start to engage. Is the sponsor genial and welcoming or austere and formal? Does the sponsor take his time to describe the scenario, or is he rushed and harried, answering the phone continuously while we chat? Is she enthusiastic, or does she seem to be responding to an edict from above or pressure from below? Is the client in immediate crisis and clutching at straws, or applying a reasoned, strategic approach to enterprise agility? Experienced consultants will spend as much energy evaluating

---

[4]Ruth Baumgart, Markus Hummel, and Roland Holten, "Personality Traits of Scrum Roles in Agile Software Development Teams—A Qualitative Analysis," ECIS 2015 Completed Research Papers, Paper 16 (2015).
[5]www.myersbriggs.org/my-mbti-personality-type/mbti-basics/.
[6]www.personalityresearch.org/bigfive/costa.html.

the personalities as they do understanding the client's scenario. When I engage with a new client, I'm observing the demeanor, the physical setting, and the client's attitude as methodically as I am the potential engagement.

Remember also that clients, especially at the sponsor level, are considering agile for strategic reasons, and that it's our job as advisors to consider the strategic as well as the tactical objectives. As I've noted before, I still encounter many coaches who can recite the Manifesto and principles verbatim but never have a strategic, value chain, or process conversation with their sponsor (except as it exclusively relates to software development). At the enterprise level, this can't succeed. If we don't understand how clients make money, how they compete, how they deal with customer feedback, or what processes they follow to achieve their outcomes, how can we know if we're addressing the right improvement opportunities?

When it comes to assessing the personality traits of a potential client, I believe that consultants must evaluate the potential for success, and make engagement decisions based not on their need to pay the bills but on the probability that the engagement can succeed. If the potential client enterprise doesn't understand what it is asking, can't articulate a strategy or a set of success criteria, or simply is someone you don't think you can advise successfully, it's your professional responsibility to decline the engagement. Just as an ethical judge will recuse himself from a case he can't judge impartially, ethical consultants will consider the likelihood of a successful outcome and recuse themselves from doomed engagements.

Mapping the Value Chain

During this exploration process, it's not just the client personalities we need to discover; we also need to dig into processes and value chains. When I engage in a change project, agile or otherwise, I often engage an experienced process mapping partner to help walk through both the value chain and the individual processes that produce the outcomes desired. My particular partner of choice is ProcessTriage,[7] a local (Kansas City) firm that specializes in both value chain and process mapping and improvement. The specific firm you choose is not the point: evaluating the value chain, and the processes that go into creating value, is a fundamental element of guiding the client to agility. We'll explore the concept of value chain here, but it's not my intention to give a full tutorial; there are many other sources for that, from Michael Porter's book,[8] where the idea originated, to multiple web pages[9] that provide insight into the usage of value chain, or value stream, analysis.

---

[7]https://processtriage.com/.
[8]Michael Porter, *Competitive Advantage* (New York: Free Press, 1998).
[9]www.netmba.com/strategy/value-chain/ is one example; there are many others.

Let's first look back to Porter's original idea, from his 1985 book. We'll start with a couple of definitions, and a graphic (Figure 4-2) depicting Porter's conception of a value chain, and then we'll dig into the details:

Value chain represents the internal activities a firm engages in when transforming inputs into outputs.

Value chain analysis (VCA) is a process where a firm identifies its primary and support activities that add value to its final product, and then analyzes these activities to reduce costs or increase differentiation.

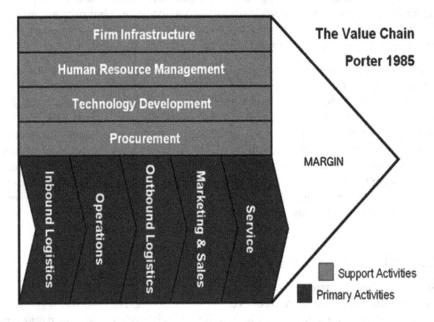

Figure 4-2. The value chain

The idea is a simple one, although performing the analysis is not. Enterprises have inputs and outputs, and they create competitive advantage and profits based on the value they can add to their inputs. According to Porter, firms can create competitive advantage two ways: through lower cost or through differentiating features. As illustrated in Figure 4-2 in the "Primary Activities" section, the firm receives inputs (e.g., raw materials in an automotive business, or intellectual property on a content-based web site), transforms these inputs by performing some operation on them, creates a mechanism for distributing the end product, identifies customers and their needs to create demand for the product, and provides services to customers as they use the product to gain value.

Enterprises also have a set of "Support Activities" as shown in the figure, such as IT, HR, procurement, and infrastructure, which includes elements like the physical plant or office, the organizational structure, and the firm's culture. The tip of the arrow, in Figure 4-2, represents the margin that firms can achieve when their sales are greater than their costs. When a firm can perform these activities efficiently and effectively it can achieve superior margins and competitive advantage.

For businesses that primarily rely on cost advantage, like Wal-Mart, their analysis of the value chain will focus on removing costs from any, or all, of the value chain activities. They seek to identify economies of scale, high utilization, and efficient linkages within the chain. Those that focus primarily on differentiating features, like Google, concentrate on innovation, uniqueness, and continual responsiveness. This is not to say that firms concentrate solely on one or the other. Manufacturing firms like Ford Motor Company attempt to excel in both categories, and web-based businesses like LinkedIn, while focusing on a unique niche and innovative features, must also maintain low costs to achieve margin.

I don't mean to imply that, in the exploration phase, I'm going to drag a process expert into the initial sales meeting and start drawing diagrams; that piece comes later. I'm emphasizing here the agile consultant's responsibility to start thinking strategically about the client's value chain from the outset. This is, again, where the consultant's powers of observation are critical. As we begin to understand the client's business, culture, and structure, we should start creating a mental model of the business, with Porter's value chain ideas as a foundation, so we can start to identify improvement opportunities. When we think about an enterprise holistically, it becomes obvious that, while improvement in the software development process, for example, may optimize a tiny element of the entire value chain, the progressive optimization of surrounding elements, and their support structures, is where the real impact lies. Agile advisors must make the distinction between "suboptimization," or the optimization of one local element, and holistic optimization, in which we're looking at the linkages, interactions, and effects of change across the entire chain, and targeting our efforts at the right improvement opportunities for this unique client. As I noted, this is a brief fly-by of VCA, and there are many great references to help you dig deeper.

Explore the Incentives

In many firms, the climate is competitive, hostile, and judgmental. Team members are evaluated quarterly and, in many companies, are "stack-racked" against their peers, creating a combative, rather than a cooperative and collaborative, atmosphere. Some firms even have a forced "up or out" mentality, in which the bottom 10% of ranked employees is put on a performance plan, and "managed out" if they don't improve their rankings. While some more enlightened firms will incorporate a "360 measurement" approach, in which teammates and other managers also get a chance to weigh in on the employee's skills and accomplishments, those firms are in the minority.

Since these rankings determine pay, promotion, and prestige, they are important in terms of their effect on careers, attitudes, and atmosphere. The theory, based on Peter Drucker's Management by Objectives (MBO) philosophy outlined in his 1954 book,[10] claimed that MBO was the cure for military-style command-and-control management, by setting agreed objectives for each manager, team, and individual, thereby freeing managers to focus on strategic issues rather than task management. Drucker's original idea was that the MBO process would be a constructive dialog between managers and their team members, in which they would collaboratively determine realistic goals for the next period, whether quarterly, semiannually, or annually, and together build a sense of ownership, commitment, and improvement areas.

It hasn't quite worked out that way. MBO works under the theory that objectives stay constant over the evaluation period, when in reality, especially in the agile, responsive enterprise, work is dynamic and objectives change frequently. There's little space for creative activities that don't fit into static objectives. Managers are typically the judges and juries in these organizations, and the externals, such as weak peer skills, broken processes, poor organizational communication, lack of vision, and lack of leadership are disregarded, as employees are instructed that it's their responsibility to live with the culture that exists. The overall problem with MBO-based management is that it stifles creativity, creates a hostile and competitive environment, saddles team members with tactical goals that don't have meaning to them, applies a reward-and-punishment system that is known to demotivate knowledge workers, and creates a "not in my objectives" atmosphere that values compliance over creativity. Although MBO was designed as an interactive exercise in which team members develop their own objectives and then iterate through them with their manager's guidance, in most firms it has devolved into a mechanistic system in which those conversations never happen, team members are encouraged to take on objectives that they don't believe and have no interest in, and managers are put in the uncomfortable position of force-fitting some team members into low ranks in order meet an arbitrary quota.

What gets measured gets managed is a common quote in executive ranks. That may be true, but, in agile terms, what *doesn't* get measured and rewarded, like intrinsic motivation, creativity, team collaboration, and a focus on customer value, creates disincentives for the behaviors that the

---

[10]Peter F. Drucker, *The Practice of Management* (New York: Harper Collins, 1954) (reissued April 20, 2010).

agile enterprise needs the most. We'll discuss in later chapters the techniques that agile consultants can use to guide the changes organizations must make, from these type of measurements to metrics that encourage agility, responsiveness, and creativity. I give this overview here to again emphasize the observational powers of agile consultants. Guiding the enterprise to evolve its thinking, from these traditional, individual-focused, static measurements to the dynamic, team-based metrics that encourage collaboration and creative thinking, is an example of the heavy lifting that enterprise-level consultants must take on. Observing and thoughtfully considering them is the first step of the eventual education and persuasion that we'll need later in the evolution process.

Engaging with Trust

Nothing happens without trust. From the auto mechanic to the doctor or accountant, if the expert can't develop a sense of trust and confidence with the client, then relationship issues are likely to be a drag on current and future engagements, even if the service is exemplary. For the consultant coming in to help evolve the agile maturity of an enterprise, trust is even more critical. The client organization is taking a risk by inviting us into its house, introducing us to its colleagues, and exposing the organization's challenges and flaws. If the consultant turns out to be incompetent or untrustworthy, all the agile knowledge in the world won't save the engagement. Immature consultants, I've observed, sometimes make the assumption that being selected for an engagement means the client trusts them already. Big mistake. Trust is never granted, it's always earned.

The development of trust is an uphill climb. With consultants, as with auto mechanics, the "trust curve" follows a typical path from transactional interactions to favored vendor status and then toward trusted advisor standing. I laugh when I see LinkedIn profiles in which the individual describes herself as a "trusted advisor." Trusted by whom, and based on what? Like Abe Lincoln's fifth leg,[11] calling yourself a trusted advisor doesn't make you one. The progression to trust requires consultants to display honesty, forthrightness, and clarity from the beginning. Our consultative skills and our personal demeanor are under constant evaluation with every team member we meet. Those are the qualities clients gauge long before they have an opportunity to assess our agile domain knowledge. From the initial meeting to the conclusion of the engagement, there's only one way to earn trust, and that is to deserve it. Clients don't hire consultants to tell them what they want to

---

[11]Abraham Lincoln is purported to have posed the riddle, "If you call a tail a leg, how many legs does a dog have?," to which the answer was usually "five." Lincoln's response? "No, four ... calling a tail a leg doesn't make it one."

hear; they're surrounded by that type of advisor all day, each typically pushing a personal agenda. They hire us to tell them those things that only an objective outsider can utter. Of course, they expect domain expertise, but it's our ability to stand outside the culture, and to observe and report on the unproductive behaviors we see without the ego, emotion, and agenda of insiders, that clients value most.

When I think about consulting behaviors that work against trust, I think of the "eternal engagement" business model, in which consulting firms try to make themselves indispensable and embed themselves for life. I'm talking about the "inside spy" model I've mentioned previously, in which, in the name of scope expansion, consultants turn into eavesdroppers, searching for opportunities to expand their footprint. I'm talking about the notorious bait and switch model of the Big 5 firms, bringing in veterans for the sales process and then loading the engagement with green rookies. I'm talking about consultants who inflate their own knowledge and experience to get the gig, with the idea that they can learn as they go, on the client's dime. I'm also talking about those consultants who still propose a big, upfront plan model, perpetuating the illusion that they can know, in advance, how a project will proceed and what obstacles they'll encounter on the way. All of these behaviors doom the relationship to an adversarial, unproductive encounter, with unfulfilled expectations all around.

The customer-value focus that we preach within the agile principles also applies to the agile consultant. If we're more concerned about our longevity in the engagement than on the client's interests, we are behaving unprofessionally, and sabotaging or own credibility and trustworthiness. The instant our credibility, competence, or trustworthiness is questioned by the client or the client's team, the engagement is on thin ice. Through my long experience as a consultant, I've learned one simple motto: tell the truth. If you don't have a specific skill that the client expects, admit it. If you have concerns about the potential for success, state them. If the engagement is a stretch that you think you can conquer, say so. If you fear, from your exploration, that there are significant challenges that the enterprise will need to overcome, explain them, and describe your ideas for conquering them. Prospective clients appreciate honesty and self-knowledge above braggadocio and wishful thinking.

One error I often see consultants make is to assume that the client knows how to engage with an outside advisor. Even for large, established firms that frequently use outside advisors, I make it a point to clearly state the process I foresee, and both the client's and the advisor's role. How will we kick off the engagement? What homework might you have to do, and what background information do you expect the client to provide? At what cadence do you expect to engage? Who will be the Product Owner of this engagement from the client side, and what will the client's role and commitment look like? What are you committing to do, and to what is the client committing? What are the expected deliverables? What is the expected outcome?

What does success look like? To avoid misunderstandings and recrimina-tions later, clarity of expectation and commitment is vital. In an ambiguous and incremental project like agile evolution, in which we can't possible know the client's desire, capacity, or commitment to change until we experience it, missed expectations are a constant danger, so answering these questions becomes imperative.

It's imperative also that we are upfront about the risks and challenges of an agile transformation. Clients who have never undertaken a disruptive change program like agile evolution may believe that it's merely a matter of training and coaching a couple of scrum teams. If that's the ultimate goal, that's fine, but if the client believes that doing so equals enterprise agility, you're setting the engagement up for disappointment. On the other hand, clients that have already experienced an attempted agile migration that's fallen on its face or "snapped back" to the prevailing culture will bring skepticism and doubt into the engagement. A candid conversation about obstacles we've experienced before, or failed adoptions that we've participated in turning around, can go a long way to counteract any negative perceptions. In short, a large part of build-ing trust is based on building confidence in your abilities, and in your sincere belief in the ultimate success of the engagement.

When I interview any project manager, scrummaster, or consultant for a potential engagement, I ask him to describe his skill set, and then to prioritize those skills. The magic phrase I'm seeking is *managing expectations*. When the candidate can only articulate a set of technical skills or domain expertise and never mentions consulting skills or the ability to manage client expectations, my finger starts reaching for the eject button. The clarity of expectations, and the ability to help the client visualize a successful engagement and understand the boundaries of that engagement, separates the Subject Matter Experts from the consultants. Clients frequently have built fantasy castles, both in their own minds and across the enterprise, about the cost, schedule, and difficulty of achieving their agile goals. Consultants, especially in the agile realm, who have difficulty correcting false assumptions or reporting on adverse circumstances that might affect the project have a tough road ahead of them. Obstacles will inevitably arise, and bad news will inevitably need to be conveyed. Agile evolu-tion, like agility itself, is reality-based, and reality is messy, unpredictable, and not subject to brute force or wishful thinking.

Framing the Engagement

When we have evaluated the personalities of the players and the potential for a successful engagement, thought about the enterprise value chain, taken a peek at the current performance-measurement and incentive practices, begun to build trust and confidence with the client, and articulated roles, commitments, and expectations, it's time to start developing an agreement that documents those findings. As I've noted, the traditional big predictive plan approach is obsolete in project management, and is therefore inappropriate in agile engagements. In fact, agility emerges from the recognition that we can't accurately predict and plan. Acknowledging this, let's also acknowledge that the predictive, all-in plan is exactly what many sponsors are expecting. Educating the sponsor and guiding her away from that expectation falls to the consultant. For many clients, the acceptance that traditional project management techniques have failed is a component of their decision to embrace agility. Others are experimenting with agility, but still clinging to the traditional management techniques that reassure them with the illusion of control.

The first step to reaching agreement is to test your understanding of the client's current state of agility, the client's perceptions and expectations. *So what I think you're saying is* ... and *help me understand how* ... are two of the most potent phrases in the consultant's toolkit. Our goal is to come to agreement on what we're there to do, what constitutes both a reasonable approach and a successful outcome for the sponsor, and who is committing to do what to further that goal.

Just as I scorn the big, upfront plan, I also reject the big, upfront consulting contract. "Customer collaboration over contract negotiation" is an important precept of agile theory, and I have much respect for the values that produced that principle. Equally important to me is the iterative nature of agile evolution. Unlike a data center project or the building of a bridge, we can't know, or even approximate, the end at the beginning. When we enter an engagement with a new client, we have no visibility into the teams' competence, will, or desire to adopt agile practices, and little insight into the culture and obstacles we'll discover along the route. Our engagement documents must reflect that reality.

The agreement I visualize with the client looks much more like a letter of engagement than it does a formal contract. I'm agreeing that I'll apply my agile domain knowledge, and my consultative skills, to help the client discover its own agile destiny, and my agreements reflect that fact. I'll state explicitly: *I'm engaging to assist and guide the client enterprise to their agile objectives, based on my experience and domain knowledge.* I'll acknowledge the client's goals, but I'm not promising anything except to apply my best efforts to help the client reach its maximum agility within its boundaries. If the client responds that this is too "squishy" and ambiguous, I'll remind him that that's exactly what agile evolution entails. Just as in an agile development effort, I'm prepared to agree to a predefined time box and "cashbox," and to commit to guiding the client to its organic limit of agility within those constraints, but there's no circumstance in which I'll commit to a fixed scope with a promised level of agility guaranteed at the end.

That's often the rub. Clients that are experienced with "big bang" consulting contracts are often stuck in the perception that only a fixed-scope, fixed-fee, fixed-budget contract protects them from unfulfilled expectations. Traditional consultants are equally convinced that only a fixed-scope project protects them from dreaded scope creep. We'll talk in depth in later chapters about the business model of an agile consultant, but my key point here is that many clients, especially those that have not internalized the agile mind-set, will struggle with the iterative approach to agile evolution. Nimble consultants will invest significant energy in building trust at the start, educating sponsors about the known successes of the iterative, incremental approach, and partner with the client to develop an engagement agreement that reassures the client without putting the consultant in an untenable position.

If we're committing to a time box and cashbox, it's urgent that the client enterprise is prepared to document its own obligations, and I'm not talking about fees. Participation, commitment, interaction, and a robust feedback loop are central elements of any agile project, and they are equally critical in an advisory relationship. Every experienced consultant, agile or not, has dealt with the client that makes all kinds of grandiose commitments to participate during the contract negotiations, only to disappear in a puff of smoke when it comes time to actually collaborate. There's nothing we can do to drive agility without the client's participation, enthusiasm, and desire. Even the simplest letter of agreement must spell out the consultant's expectations for customer access, clear project ownership on the client side, and the roles and commitments of all key client players. Clients are frequently accustomed to the "throw it over the wall" style of consulting engagement, in which their involvement occurs at the beginning, to toss the specs across the desk, and at the end, to evaluate the consultant's results. The burden is on the consultant to ensure that client participants understand and commit to their roles, and honor these commitments.

Summary

"A bad beginning makes a bad ending," said Euripides back in 400 B.C., and that wisdom has not changed. The Explore and Engage phase of an agile engagement sets the stage for success or failure. Agile consultants who dive in to an agile evolution project, especially at the enterprise level, without respecting Euripides's logic, defeat their own purpose. The consultant who disregards the unique circumstances of every enterprise, and brings out the same tools no matter the on-the-ground conditions, may have some success at the scrum-team level, but evolving out across the enterprise requires mature observation and consultative skills, and the ability to inspect the situation and adapt to the culture, competencies, style, and boundaries that reality imposes. If you're operating, as an agile consultant, at the accidental level of skill, don't be surprised when you crash.

On the positive side, agile consultants who engage thoughtfully, observantly, and intentionally, and meet the enterprise where it is, in order to guide it to where it wants to be, have an excellent chance of starting off on the front foot and achieving breakthrough results for the enterprise and teams they have the privilege to advise.

Visualize Success

In an ideal world, all clients would be able to clearly articulate their business objective, their success criteria, and the capabilities they expect to gain from any project. In reality, most can't. Studies of software development[1] show again and again that clients can't articulate their needs, can't communicate with specialists, and can't define what success means. Consultants are usually called upon not just to deliver the client's vision but to help define it. Skilled consultants can guide clients from a vague project concept to a clear, concise, and persuasive vision.

In the ideal *agile* world, client participants have thought through their guiding vision of agility, phrased it in pithy and compelling language, and evangelized its benefits. In reality, most haven't. They may see a version of an agile future, but every participant sees it through a different lens. Clients may desire the benefits of agility without recognizing its inherent disruptiveness. Even if they have crafted a common vision, it's often poorly composed and unpersuasive. And then, when they have a compelling message that they've agreed upon, they've probably not planned a campaign to communicate and evangelize it.

---

[1]See the Appendix for insights from those studies.

© Rick Freedman 2016
R. Freedman, *The Agile Consultant*, DOI 10.1007/978-1-4302-6053-0_5

Why Visualize?

Our goal in Visualization is to build a consensus, at the highest level with which we're engaged, on a vision of the future state, the capabilities that will be gained, and the challenges that will be addressed. If we're engaged at the team level, we need a team-level vision built on participation and consensus. The same is true if we are engaged at the enterprise level. In either case, we're encouraging ownership, buy-in, and enthusiasm. We're trying to craft a concise, logical, positive, and persuasive message, aligned with the sponsor's agile strategy and the participants' agile expectations.

John Kotter calls this vision "The Big Opportunity," and I prefer this to the common "burning platform" phrasing. Language matters, and I prefer a positive vision, not one that implies roasting to death. The threat of impending doom may be motivating, but it's certainly not inspiring. It may be true that existential disruptions are on the horizon, and that current methods are broken; that's an important part of the message. The enterprise agility vision, however, should emphasize the future capabilities and benefits awaiting the enterprise when it embraces agility, instead of focusing on fleeing the coming inferno. Part of our visualization work is to keep the enterprise focused on what it's driving to, not what it's running from. Many teams and enterprises are panicked enough about merely adopting basic agile practices. Ringing the fire alarm in the middle of that transition isn't helpful.

During our exploration and engagement time, we've had some substantive conversations with sponsors about vision, expectations, and the problems they're trying to solve. In the initial engagement cycle, however, we've only gone so far. Most clients aren't prepared to reveal the depth of their dysfunction or poor performance, in fear of scaring you away. Most consultants can't afford to spend many hours in initial discovery, especially in the sales cycle, before the meter is running; we need to bill hours. We've seen the outline, but we haven't seen the Big Opportunity. And usually, neither has the client.

Acknowledging this reality, agile consultants must be prepared to guide the sponsor, and the enterprise, through some bare minimum elements of a Visualization exercise, including agreement on:

- A guiding agile vision or "Big Opportunity,"
- A definition of success,
- A compelling message, and
- A plan to communicate it.

I emphasize the word *guide* here; no consultant can build the vision for a sponsor. The client must own it, and, so should the teams. I differ here with Kotter; he still recommends that a leadership committee creates this vision. The committee may set the strategy, and have greater visibility into the enterprise portfolio, but I'm a proponent of a broad community participating in visualizing. That, in my view, is both consistent with the values of agility and likely to deliver a more persuasive message. This is a tightrope, as "vision by committee" can often mean long and impenetrable language, as the vision statement tries to address everyone's input and interests. Agile consultants need to thread the needle between a "tablets from the mountaintop" vision, handed down from executives on high, and an endless cycle of word-by-word debate.

The Enterprise Agile Opportunity

As agile consultants, we are initially engaging with a sponsor, or a committee, and not the entire enterprise. Sometimes that's someone in the executive suite, sometimes a functional manager focused on a particular silo. I'm not a fan of top-down vision building, but there are advantages to starting the conversation at the top. Agile consultants that have the endorsement, and the attention, of influential leaders should take advantage of their strategic and portfolio visibility, to get a business-minded view of the opportunities agility presents. We're starting from the core of information we gathered during our exploration activities, but, now that we're engaged, sponsors will begin to be more candid about the challenges they face and the flaws in the system.

When we engage at the executive level, one of most important imperatives is to help leaders evolve from their strategic language to plain talk. "Increasing market penetration by 11% in Asia" is an example of a strategic objective, but few coders or testers are going to be inspired by it. That's why I stay focused on capabilities. In a vision of agility, I want the organization to articulate the capabilities it hopes to achieve, not the strategic objectives it wants to apply them to. As an agile consultant, I can guide the enterprise toward faster delivery cycles, a more intimate relationship with the business, and a more collaborative environment. I can't help the enterprise achieve market penetration in Asia, except indirectly.

Another reason to focus on enhanced capabilities is that they're less like to be controversial. "Increasing market penetration" can sound like a challenge to those responsible for achieving that goal, rather than a vision of future opportunities. It can cascade negatively across the organization, as every individual ponders the repercussions on his personal role, responsibility, and workload. "Achieve faster delivery cycles" can also be threatening, but, since it applies across the organization, it's less likely to set off a reaction of dueling silos.

Most important, the agility guiding vision must be inclusive. The worst possible vision statement looks something like this:

> *From the Executive Suite, we command that you achieve these goals. You didn't participate in setting them, you don't understand how they align, and we're not going to tell you how to achieve them, but we **will** hold you accountable at review time if you fail. Now go forth and do!*

How do we help organizations migrate from a top-down, hierarchy based mandate to an inclusive, inspirational vision? First, we must acknowledge that, especially in enterprise-wide transitions, it's difficult work. With all the strategic and technological variables, all the personal and cultural sensitivities, and all the individual agendas that arise, getting to a consensus, putting it into persuasive language, and communicating it effectively can be a marathon. We're trying to craft a concise, logical, positive, and persuasive message that is aligned with the enterprise strategy. At enterprise scale, this is obviously an iterative, incremental exercise, as the chance we will craft a message with all these attributes the first time through is nil. If we do it right, we're using the agile practices we apply in product development to craft the vision. We start with a business need (in this case agility), articulate it as best we can, run that message through a feedback loop, and refine it until we have a potentially shippable product. In this case, of course, the product we ship is an **Enterprise Agile Opportunity** that is clearly communicated and compelling.

Om the other hand, I've gone through successful visualization exercises with a single agile advocate over lunch. If the sponsor is a knowledgeable inside agile coach or advocate, it's pretty easy to agree that "we want three teams, capable of applying the basic scrum practices consistently over three months of iterations, achieving stable velocity and quality." It's certainly not an enterprise vision, but it's enough to work with if that's the situation. The point is that, as with all agile projects, we can take a "barely sufficient" viewpoint on visualization; if there's no wider team to inspire, and a core team that gets it and is eager to proceed, a short agreement on intent is all we need to get started. Let's maximize the work not done; I'll lay out a lot of practices here, but in many grassroots adoptions, a simple, tactical statement can define the effort.

The visualization process requires leadership. As Jim Highsmith notes,[2] "This is one area where effective leaders lead—they help cut through the ambiguity and confusion of creating an effective vision." Whether we're dealing with a single product owner trying to build a single scrum team or a leadership committee that is striving for full enterprise agility, we must have someone who owns the vision and brings the clarity required to avoid spiraling into an endless semantic debate. Leadership is also required to ensure that the teams participating in visualization do so in a productive manner, with an enterprise, strategic viewpoint, and avoid any parochial, siloed instincts that may have developed in their culture. We'll look at an overview of the process I recommend, and then decompose it for a bit more detail.

---

[2]Jim Highsmith, *Agile Project Management: Creating Innovative Products,* Second Edition (New York: Pearson Educational, 2010), pp. 91.

Experience in building project visions, from the Project Charters of the waterfall days to the Enterprise Agility Vision statements I've developed with clients, has led me to a process that is both rapid and inclusive. To perform inclusive visualization, agile consultants should:

- Identify the Agile Opportunity product owner or committee.

- Craft a set of capability goals.

- Integrate feedback.

- Craft a Consensus Vision.

- Execute Their Communication Plan.

Identify the Agile Opportunity Product Owner or Committee

While agility is an egalitarian movement, there are moments in a company's agile evolution that require leadership. Whether the aim is agility across the organization or agile adoption at the team level, leader sponsorship and enthusiasm build the momentum that kick-starts agility. When the conversation starts at the executive level, I'm a proponent of the Enterprise Transition Committee approach recommended by both Ken Schwaber[3] and Mike Cohn.[4] An executive committee of agile proponents willing to craft a vision and evangelize it is obviously an enormous boost. Just by helping our executive sponsor build a small, cross-functional transition team, the savvy consultant can learn a lot about who's trusted, who advocates agile, and who the messengers of change would be. As in any agile project, we want a clearly designated product owner as the representative of the business through whom business decisions flow. The transition team owns the project, and must come to decisions and take actions depending on the product owner's feedback. The agile consultant will often be called into transition committee sessions, both to facilitate and as a domain expert, but the designated product owner is accountable for driving business decisions and priorities.

In engagements starting at the grassroots level, the product owner is usually a functional manager, of, say, software development or project management. Whether executive-led or team-focused, the product owner is the resource with whom we visualize the outcome, and is the owner of the Agile Opportunity message. Agile advisors can begin the conversation by walking the product owner through a roadmap discussion that helps them articulate their high-level

---

[3]Ken Schwaber, *The Enterprise and Scrum* (Redmond, WA: Microsoft Press, 2007).
[4]Mike Cohn, *Succeeding with Agile: Software Development Using Scrum* (Boston: Addison-Wesley, 2010).

expectations. The outcome of that conversation should be a graphic roadmap that then enables them to further articulate their more precise vision. The objective of the consultant's initial conversations with the designated product owner is to agree on our capability objectives, our roadmap, and our roles.

When I begin any consulting engagement, I scrutinize and probe the enterprise's structure, formal and informal, to see who should be included in the vision conversation. There are always technical specialists, business managers, and other domain experts who have a stake in the outcome of agile evolution. "Who else should I be talking to?" is one of the most useful questions for any consultant, and I ask it early and often. We must be judicious in how far we inquire, and how wide a circle we include, but representatives of key constituencies will add both insight and momentum to the agile vision.

For the consultant, the value of correctly identifying product owners on the sponsor side is incalculable. In traditional consulting, we often had to ask the question, "Who is the client?." We were engaged with executives, managers, contributors, and users, each of whom had different interests, expectations, and decision rights. This is the problem that the "product owner" concept tries to solve. By designating an individual, accountable representative of the business, we've now guided the organization to grant ownership to the product owner, who then is accountable for convening and caucusing the leadership team, for coming to group vision for agilityand for communicating the vision to the enterprise. At enterprise or team level, it's in the consultant's interest to have a single product owner who has the explicit decision rights for the Agile Opportunity, and selecting the right representatives is decisive.

Craft a Set of Capability Goals

Why is the enterprise considering agility? Does it believe adopting agile will help it increase market penetration in Asia next year? Probably not. The enterprise is instead seeking enterprise or team-wide capability enhancements that will enable it to achieve its strategies. Agile, whether at the team or enterprise level, is about reducing waste, increasing responsiveness, and removing friction from the value stream. We strive to enhance the organization's capability to execute efficiently.

Capability planning[5] is a facilitative method that helps the organization identify gaps in its performance. This process generates capability goals, quantified objectives that describe business execution capabilities. The capabilities they describe are cross-functional and hierarchical lines. Rather than strategic goals, like "Sales will increase our reach in the generics market by 22%," the enterprise capability goals we seek look more like "The Enterprise will be

---

[5]See The Open Group Architecture Framework's (TOGAF's) in-depth description here: http://pubs.opengroup.org/architecture/togaf9-doc/arch/chap32.html.

capable of identifying new target markets, and establishing measurable progress within six months." Other examples of capability goals are:

> The Enterprise will provide a friendly, positive response to any inquiry or complaint within 24 hours.

> IT Development will deliver a set of running, tested features for client review at the end of every iteration.

> Marketing will be capable of designing an initial campaign within 8 days of shippable product delivery.

Capability planning is the essential building block of agile visualization. We must know, at whatever engagement level, the business capabilities our sponsors expect to enhance. The previous examples illustrate that, whether it's the entire enterprise or one eight-member development team, there is a clear, concise, and measurable capability that the team can identify.

In the process I apply, I begin capability planning with a process-mapping session, so we have a visible model on which we can plot barriers and broken connections. Team or enterprise, every entity has an input-process-output cycle that can be mapped and analyzed. Simple process mapping is a great way to coach teams in thinking about process efficiency, and to help them visualize obstructions. This practice can be simple or complex, of course, depending on the scale of your transition and the enterprise business model. I've been in mapping sessions that lasted a half hour, and sessions that took four days. I want just enough visibility so they can walk me through the flow of their value stream and point out obvious pain points. As we discussed earlier regarding value streams, it's hard to target high-impact improvements if we don't understand how the enterprise works.

From executive teams to small contributor teams, my practice is to develop capability goals by convening a brief mapping session, getting the basic flow on a whiteboard, and then asking participants to point out blockers and enablers. With executives, the flow will typically be a high-level fly-by of their value stream. For developer teams, it might be "from software request to application acceptance." With the basic map in front of us, we can start to probe. Where do we get stuck, and where might added capability solve a problem? I'll then ask participants to propose solutions to the obstructions they've identified. If the problem is "Too many defects get through unit testing and blow up integration efforts," the solution might be to "Enforce completed-test standards on all code passed to integration." The move from solution to capability is natural. The capability goal in this case might be to "integrate successfully with no passed defects 85% of the time."

Size capability planning to the scale of your agile engagement. Capability planning in a small team can be an informal exercise; team members know where they're stuck. You can generate a set of capability goals in a beginning rookie scrum team in an hour or two. Just ask them what's broken, and steer the conversation to a positive scenario rather than the current negative situation.

Help the team articulate the solutions they envision for the broken places, and their capability goals will write themselves.

This list of capability objectives becomes our Agile Opportunity backlog, replacing vague goals like "be more agile in responding to customers" with explicit improvement expectations. Capability planning should be run like any agile planning session, building consensus on a backlog, prioritizing backlog items, and soliciting commitments from team members. The agile consultant facilitates the team through capability planning, helps them frame the language for positive impact, and assists in consolidation and prioritization. When capability planning is complete, the agility product owner or committee will have accepted a prioritized backlog of measurable enhancements, upon which the Agile Opportunity can be based.

Capability planning has a lot of advantages for the agile consultant. It develops consensus around the agile capabilities the sponsor expects. It subdues the inter-silo debate, and focuses instead on cross-functional process innovation. It enables the consultant to probe disconnects and dysfunctions, since each capability goal recognized is also a gap identified. It takes the focus off suboptimized, siloed improvement efforts and envisions enterprise capabilities that enhance results. Most important, it provides the raw material to be filtered down into a persuasive Agile Opportunity.

Integrate Feedback

Every lean and agile process has a feedback loop. Without feedback there is no kaizen. The creation of an Agile Opportunity vision must be inclusive if we want to avoid the dreaded executive proclamation. Leaders can shape the strategic direction of agile evolution, and be enthusiastic evangelists for the coming changes. What leaders *can't* do is create ownership and commitment. That requires participation and a responsive feedback loop.

The feedback mechanism for an Agile Opportunity vision is obvious, because it is a straight application of agile practices. We iterate through drafts of the Agile Opportunity, solicit feedback from our target audience, and synthesize that feedback, all within a defined time box. The first iteration of draft and feedback is often the raw capability goals we built in our mapping session. At the enterprise scale, the transition committee has probably ironed out a lot of the disputes and created a set of capability goals that are not controversial. At the team level, team members often have already agreed that they want to adopt these practices and enhance their capabilities. Still, the feedback process is designed to surface disagreement and innovation. Capability goals should cycle a few times, especially in politically charged environments.

The target audience for our Agile Opportunity communications must be, well, targeted. I wouldn't advocate an enterprise-wide communique at this point, before we've crafted a complete vision. An individual team can have an all-hands conversation and agree on the capabilities it is striving to achieve. At an enterprise level, a small, thoughtfully selected, and representative sample of informed, influential, and interested stakeholders is a wise strategy. We want to include enough diversity of opinion for a meaningful dialog, while avoiding a firestorm of confusion, resistance, and rumor in this initial stage of our agile journey. As we've emphasized, visualization of an agile outcome requires leadership, and, while the feedback loop is essential, it must also be prudent. Leadership still has a role to play in agility, and aligning the effort to strategic priorities is still leadership's prerogative.

The time-boxed nature of the visualization effort is important, as a participative feedback cycle can be eternal, and agile enterprises can't afford endless loops. Iterating through drafts, with a targeted feedback opportunity embedded in the cycle, can take us from capability goals to a broad, consolidated, and compelling Agile Opportunity statement rather quickly. The development of a set of capability goals, even in complex enterprises, can be done in a day. The dissemination of them, by e-mail or survey, with request for comment, can have a two-day time box. Another few days to integrate commentary and start to wordsmith and condense it into an Agile Opportunity, and another round or two of draft and feedback, and you're on the way to an integrated synthesis of the enterprise's agile expectations and hopes.

Of course, inspect and adapt this process; some Enterprise Transition Committees can rocket through iterations and reach an Agile Opportunity statement quickly, and others are slow and deliberate. Some team-level sponsors are agile advocates with a deep understanding of where they're headed, and some have been assigned agile transition from on high, and need education and guidance. If the agility product owner, with the agile consultant's guidance, articulates a set of concise cross-function capability objectives and puts them out for comment, we learn what is important to the enterprise community, what motivates them and what concerns them. Just as in a software development project, we allow the community to course-correct as we determine what agility means to the enterprise. What's important to the agile consultant is that the Agile Opportunity vision we iterate toward is ultimately an elegant and urgent statement, and is owned by all the right participants.

Craft a Consensus Vision

Building consensus is a core consulting skill, and it requires delicacy, diplomacy, and resolve in equal measure. In the pursuit of an agile vision, we'll frequently have to condense and modify language, prioritize objectives, and, in the process, strip out some group's favorite phrases and descope someone's urgent need. At the Visualization stage, the agile consultant hasn't been around long enough to build much trust, and frequently applies collaborative, participative practices with which teams are unaccustomed. To evolve from capability goals to an Agile Opportunity statement will require us to refine a backlog of possible future outcomes into a crisp and compelling statement. Again, the consensus we seek at this point is not across the enterprise; it's among the agility product owners and the selected domain representatives.

The dangers of "vision by committee" are obvious. Every team has its own language, its own pet phrases, and its own strategic priorities. Our first job as consultants is to keep the team's eyes on the prize. Skilled consultants can facilitate a conversation that focuses on enterprise value rather than narrow interests. We can help the team move from the specific to the general. A capability goal that we mentioned earlier, to "integrate successfully with no passed defects 85% of the time," may have great urgency for the application development team and be perfectly suitable if that's the target. For impact across the wider enterprise, this might be better articulated as "Deliver running, tested applications, fit for use, within an agreed time box."

Let's recap. We've worked with the product owner of the agility initiative, whether executive committee member or team leader. We've done some preliminary process mapping or walked through the value stream, identified barriers, and derived a set of capabilities the business would like to improve. We've communicated these expected capabilities to a select group of domain representatives, and integrated their comments and ideas into revised versions of those objectives. We've gone through that cycle some number of times, and our product owners are ready to start crafting an Agile Opportunity statement. This statement will be the vision upon which we will build consensus and enthusiasm. It will be addressed to the enterprise at whatever level we are engaged, from the team to the entire organization.

The crafting of an Agile Opportunity may require us to broaden the circle of participation. Human resource experts, technical specialists, and additional domain representatives can often offer insights and help avoid landmines. Marketing specialists or technical writers can bring critical writing and persuasion skills. We still want to apply our "barely sufficient" discipline to team participation, but we need to be deliberate when developing a communique that broadcasts change and disruption.

The ideal team for crafting an Opportunity vision includes an executive sponsor or product owner, representatives of the critical teams within our engagement scope, and the writing and marketing talent to compose a compelling vision. The consultant plays a facilitation role, and often needs to reel the conversation back to the work at hand. My practice is to convene a single facilitated work session, with the right participants and a strict time box, in which the team commits to producing a final draft of an Agile Opportunity vision. Final, because we don't have the luxury of eternal iteration, and draft, because we acknowledge that there will be feedback when we communicate, and attempt to evangelize, the vision.

To illustrate my view of compelling Agile Opportunity statements, here are three examples, from informal to enterprise scale:

> The RED user experience design team will pilot the application of agile methods. We'll learn and apply scrum techniques in their pilot project, build a prioritized backlog, and iteratively present a valuable package of design functionality for customer review at each iteration. We'll achieve scrum proficiency, including a steady and consistent velocity and the ability to manage a backlog, within the next three months. We'll use the learnings from our pilot to migrate scrum to five additional teams this year.

> The GOLD software development team delivers quality software to our customers rapidly and responsively. We help customers articulate their needs and expectations, collaborate with them to ensure they can guide our development, and respond to their changing business needs. We present complete transparency of our progress through big visible indicators, and we work in cross-functional teams that focus on business value instead of activities. Our products add value across the enterprise, resulting in improved agility and responsiveness for our company. We apply continuous improvement to ensure we refine our practices with every iteration, and collaborate openly within our team and with our customers. We will achieve these capabilities by applying scrum practices with discipline and craftsmanship.

> The Blue Corporation has a long history of meeting customer needs in personal care products. We recognize that our customer's needs evolve constantly, and that competitors are developing and marketing innovative products faster than us, and threatening our market share. We intend to protect and grow our market share by becoming a more agile and responsive organization. We'll build a strong connection and feedback loop with our customers through social media. We'll apply that feedback to developing innovative products within months instead of years. By applying agile methods, we will drive innovative new products through our R&D function at twice the current speed. We will create an agile software development community that can deliver quality applications on a regular cadence, with predictable and consistent speed. Our marketing team will be capable of developing a new campaign within two weeks, and our logistics chain will be prepared to put our products on shelves within a week of launch.

By transitioning the enterprise to agile mind-set and methods, we'll be capable of changing products quickly to meet evolving expectations, of marketing and delivering those products faster and better than our competitors, and developing the supporting software rapidly and accurately. We'll build a collaborative, low-friction culture that empowers teams to make decisions and take ownership of their outcomes. By building agility and adaptability into our enterprise, we'll have fun and dominate our market.

These are modified examples of agile visions I've worked with in the past. They reflect my style of writing and persuasion. I'm sure yours is better, because you are collaborating with your client and adapting to the client's unique situation. As an agile advisor, you've led the client to reveal its hopes and flaws, develop its own solutions, and convert the client participant into concrete capability goals that will inform its agile vision. By facilitating the team or the enterprise through the creation of a compelling opportunity vision, it has told you what success looks like. You've prepared the team or enterprise for the heavy lifting of building enthusiasm and commitment.

Execute Your Communication Plan

Ineffective communication is the root of most business evils. In the worst cases, the strategic plan is impenetrable, objectives are unconnected, expectations are obscure, and direction is muddled. The culture is accustomed to long periods of silence, indecision, or controversy from leadership. The communications that randomly cascade from executives to managers, and from managers to staff, all seem like disconnected mandates rather than a coherent strategy. The response is more likely to be "here we go again" than it is to be enthusiasm, much less commitment.

An agile evolution program must begin with a clear and persuasive communication campaign. Organizational inertia is weighty, and won't be moved by the issuance of an e-mail. If our Agile Opportunity is truly a Big Opportunity, it must stand out from the reams of corporate proclamations, and inspire teams to action. We'll get a range of responses, from cynicism of "another fine program" to enthusiasm from agile advocates. The feedback is the point; it makes visible the fears, concerns, and hopes of the community, whether team or enterprise. In true agile form, it exposes the weak spots, so we know what to prioritize. The community transitioning to agility will tell you how to succeed through your interactive campaign of communication and persuasion.

Long before our Agile Opportunity vision is composed, we should be advising our clients to consider their communication and momentum program. Through what venues will we be communicating with our enterprise? Should we go beyond e-mails and surveys and create a Facebook page, a series of training videos, an executive presentation, or a "big room" work session? Are we asking for understanding, compliance, or feedback (or a bit of each)? Persuasive communication of an Agile Opportunity is our chance to demonstrate executive support, evangelize the benefits, acknowledge the challenges, and build some momentum.

As we've seen in the State of Agile Surveys, organizational inertia is the major factor in agile adoption obstacles. The management team isn't ready for "servant-leadership," the culture is change-weary and skeptical about another new program, and the "way we do things here" has encouraged and rewarded bad habits. Moving just one team to a new conception of work is a challenge. Moving the enterprise to a new mind-set is Herculean.

I use the word *evangelizing*, but bluntly, this is a marketing effort. As in all such, we must think about our target market, our appeal to their interests, and the behavior we hope to influence. While I believe the Agile Opportunity vision addresses the entire enterprise audience, framing it will differ in IT, where the pilot will take place, and in accounting, which won't be immediately affected. IT wants to hear, probably from a technical manager, that it will be supported through adoption, that there's benefit to the department, and that there's nothing to fear. Accounting, like all other functional departments and all individuals, wants to know how this affects its members.

At the enterprise level, my recommendation would be to select a small team, with representation from human resources (HR) and marketing, to build the campaign. The individual team can have this conversation over lunch, but once we grow beyond, we need to be sophisticated in our approach. HR will guide us to appropriate language, and marketing expertise can add flash that makes this more than just another e-mail or program. We've already derived an Agile Opportunity message, but to complete it, we need to answer the questions I posed earlier. A broad set of communication channels, from the executive presentation to the social media campaign, and from video tutorials to scheduled training sessions, will reach different audiences with different interests and learning styles. Executive support, through team visits and all-hands presentations, can be a burst of jet fuel to momentum, especially if the message is positive, honest, and passionate.

The Big Opportunity is an opportunity lost if its communication is not compelling. Consultants have a large role to play in the framing of the message, due to our agile domain expertise. Sensitivity to agile theory, practice, and language will be critical. Starting to acclimate the enterprise to a new language and a new mind-set begins here. Consistency is also important, as inconsistent delivery of the agile vision will lead to rumor, speculation and negative interpretations. Inconsistent messaging often occurs when the message is cascaded verbally from top down, as in "tell your teams that we're going agile and it'll be great!." We must also campaign honestly. While I talk about this as a marketing campaign, there's a difference between manipulating and influencing. Agile is transparent, and our communication should be as well. Good agile vision messages emphasize the positives but acknowledge the challenges. We know this will be hard; we should tell them so. We also know that it works, and that teams and enterprises that adopt it are happier and more productive. If the agile consultant ensures that a compelling Agile Opportunity has been envisioned, articulated, and communicated, he's done a service to the client. He's also done himself a favor, having ferreted out the initial set of challenges, resisters, and advocates.

Some agile evolutions are team-focused, some are enterprise-wide. In either case, there is a natural progression from vision to roadmap to backlog. When the project is an agile evolution, the items that land in the backlog are improvement features, elements of the value chain that we intend to enhance with agile practices. The enterprise can't get to an improvement backlog without a vision, whether accepted over lunch or cascaded through a marketing campaign. In Chapter 6 we'll discuss the development of a roadmap, based on the vision we've just articulated and circulated. Without an overarching, vision, the roadmap is just a set of tasks. The Agile Opportunity vision opens the door for us to observe more directly, and to create a roadmap that reflects the client enterprise's consensus on the capabilities they expect.

Summary

Every agile project begins with a vision that defines the guiding goals and objectives of the effort. The same must be true for an agile evolution project; the consultant and the sponsor must agree on the business reason for the effort, the results we're expecting, and the path we choose to take. That path may be long and winding, and it may lead us to unexpected destinations, but the vision should be constant and consensual. Agile consultants help their clients understand the strategic meaning of the evolution, and help them craft and execute a communication plan to build understanding and commitment across the enterprise. Organizational inertia is strong. Only a persuasive vision and communication program can turn inertia into momentum. Agile consultants omit this key activity at their peril, and at the peril of the client's agile expectations.

Observe and Plan

Every agilist knows that, when developing products using agile practices, planning, design, development, and testing are no longer sequential, as in traditional waterfall methods, but are occurring in parallel and being refined incrementally. The same is true for the visualization, observation, and planning work we've been discussing in these chapters. Although necessarily presented sequentially, in real client engagements we typically don't have the luxury of completing a fully vetted agile vision or roadmap before we begin to engage in the development of agile teams. Although some agile transitions are driven by a clear strategic consensus at the executive level, in the majority of cases agile engagements start at the grassroots level. Agile consultants are more likely to be tasked with getting teams transitioned to agile and coaching them to consistent delivery and velocity than to develop strategic agility and responsiveness across the organization. Sponsors usually expect agile consultants, and especially agile coaches, to jump right in and start training, persuading, and guiding teams to adopt agile practices. Although I've broken out exploration, visualization, and planning into separate chapters for clarity, the reality is usually much different. Don't misinterpret the serial order presented in this book as a sequence of start-to-finish events. Agile consultants engage with agility, which means that we're refining our exploration, visualization, and planning incrementally as we go.

© Rick Freedman 2016
R. Freedman, *The Agile Consultant*, DOI 10.1007/978-1-4302-6053-0_6

Figure 6-1 illustrates the idea of incremental refinement, from vision to roadmap to backlog. Whether the desired outcome is a software application or the introduction of agility to an organization, a guiding vision leads to the development of a product roadmap, which in turn is decomposed into the stories or features that make up the product backlog. As we progress through the iterative development of the product, we discover and experience circumstances that require us to loop back and revise the roadmap and vision. Ideally, the vision remains relatively constant, the roadmap is more fluid, while we expect the features and their priorities to change and evolve as we progress. All will evolve based on the reality we encounter, but when the vision changes radically it's usually prudent to revisit the entire effort and make sure we still understand what we're aiming for. Again, all is not as tidy as it is depicted; roadmaps breed epics (or the other way round), which are decomposed into features, and every element can change and evolve rapidly and continuously.

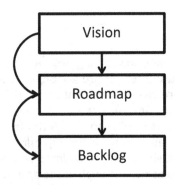

Figure 6-1. Agile roadmap sequence

Since agile consultants often begin at the team adoption level rather than the enterprise level, we have the opportunity to observe intimately both the enablers and the inhibitors of agility. The narratives we get from executive sponsors rarely disclose the tactical barriers we discover once engaged. After a few weeks of coaching teams to adopt basic agile practices, we often encounter disjointed or absent tool sets, counter-agile management behavior, and ingrained waterfall thinking that constrains the enterprise's ability to progress. Within the teams themselves, the willingness and capability to adopt agile practices will vary widely. That's why, although executive consensus is a significant enabler of agility by clearly demonstrating the support of management and the strategic results expected, it's no substitute for team-level observation.

Agile Exposes Obstacles

Agile methods are simple to learn but difficult to instill and sustain. Not only do the practices of daily stand-ups, iteration reviews, and retrospectives uncover dysfunctional practices within the team, they also expose weaknesses at every connection point. If the development team is working toward an iteration goal, but information technology (IT) operations is uncooperative or offering limited "sandbox" and deployment services, we'll uncover that as soon as we try to develop, test, or promote a package. If the Project Management Office (PMO) is talking agile but still expects a task-oriented, Gantt-style project plan, we'll have to deal with that obstacle soonest. If management is calling itself agile but refusing to let the team "waste time" on retrospectives, we risk losing the kaizen benefits of the agile feedback loop. If the project manager is now called a product owner but has none of the customer intimacy or business knowledge required to play that role, then we are engaging in agile theatrics, with little chance for positive change. If our client enterprise is trying to force-fit agile development into a waterfall toolset, we'll need to engage with the entire software selection, implementation, and support chain to encourage adoption of appropriate technology. All of these impediments are outside the team, but even the most eager and capable team can't benefit from agility until we address these external obstacles.

For the agile consultant, observation is active, not passive. Even as we're in the thick of daily coaching and consulting, we must be cataloging the obstructions thrown up by the enterprise environment. Daily stand-ups will quickly reveal impediments to the current iteration, but, more important for agile consultants, they'll also tell us where we need to concentrate our advisory efforts. Scrummasters look for, and strive to solve, immediate impediments to the commitments of the current iteration. The wise agile consultant is building an improvement backlog that extends far beyond the team, and incorporates the cultural, historical, and technical issues that impede evolution. Addressing these externalities, rather than simply focusing on today's deliverables, differentiates the agile consultant from the adoption-focused coach.

We've reviewed many organizational change frameworks, from Kotter's accelerators to Cohn's ADAPT (Awareness, Desire, Ability, Promotion, Transfer) structure. I'm a fan of the ADKAR approach, from which Cohn built his ADAPT techniques. ADKAR, which is an acronym for Awareness, Desire, Knowledge, Ability, and Reinforcement, is a helpful way of thinking about agile evolution, at both the team and the enterprise level. It's incumbent on the consultant, once she's begun to observe obstacles like the ones outlined previously, to consider solving them by applying an ADKAR mind-set. For each interface, from management to IT operations, the consultant should walk through the ADKAR framework mentally and ask herself where the problem lies.

ADKAR serves as a simple root cause analysis technique which allows the consultant to consider the people, processes, and systems in question and develop a solution approach that is connected to the real issue. If, for instance, the PMO is not aware that agility requires it to abandon the traditional Gantt chart, the consultant's challenge is to raise awareness. This may be accomplished through conversation, education, or examples of previous projects that were planned to the most granular task level, yet still failed. If the PMO team is aware of the global migration to agile, and understands that agile is succeeding elsewhere, but lacks the desire to change, consultants must move from education to persuasion, by focusing on our compelling Agile Opportunity, by celebrating every win at the team level, and by motivating the PMO team with a team vision that addresses its fears and concerns, both organizational and personal. Lack of knowledge is clearly a significant handicap, as it breeds rumor, mythology, and uncertainty. Consultants must engage in continuous education, from the executive to the individual level, both in formal training settings and in every one-to-one conversation. I find that I can do more to educate reluctant executives or managers with a "chalk talk" on a whiteboard than in a crowded classroom. Face to face in front of a whiteboard, I can explain how agility affects their specific role, and help them understand the general advantages of agility to the enterprise.

Mature consultants address the ability challenge, not only through coaching and mentoring on agile practices but by observing how each individual affected is rising to the challenge of transition. Many developers, for example, have technical ability to spare, but have personal concerns with practices like pair programming or daily stand-ups. Managers may have outstanding leadership skills but are reluctant to surrender their control over teams or their need for predictive plans and estimates. When we address ability challenges, we need to look beyond the questions of technical or management capabilities and examine, with patience and compassion, the personal ability to share responsibility and to abandon false beliefs in prescience and predictability. Too many coaches operate solely at the practice-adoption level, and lack the consultative skills to guide individuals and teams through the thickets of pride, ego, power, and insecurity. While a clear and compelling Agile Opportunity statement is helpful, it takes delicacy, empathy, and individualized attention to guide each human being through the adjustments required for agility to take root. Coaches and consultants who preach the fiction that "just doing the practices will propagate change" are discounting the decades of research that illustrate the deep complexity of transitioning both organizations and individuals. Even teams that are following every letter and concept of agile practice will quickly find that team-based agility is not enough, if the enterprise that surrounds them lacks the attributes of ADKAR.

We'll talk about the Reinforcement element of ADKAR in later chapters when we address the challenges of sustaining agility. Suffice it to say here that many successful adoptions have "snapped back" to cultural norms swiftly once the consultant is gone, and that the sustainability of agile evolution is dependent on the actions we take at the outset of our engagement to ensure that acceptance, desire, and ability are real and internally motivated, and not just a temporary response to external pressures and mandates.

Planning the Roadmap to Agility

The roadmap to agility is one of the consultant's most important tools. Not only does it position us to set expectations and begin to outline time boxes, it also sets big, visible goals for our teams. When the outcome expected is team adoption, the roadmap reminds the team of its commitments, time boxes, and the enterprise's expectations. At the team level, a typical roadmap, as illustrated in Figure 6-2, will present an iterative approach to adoption, proposing, for instance, that we'll guide three teams to consistent quality, delivery, and agility within the first six months, and that we'll propagate those learnings to four other teams over the following six months. This simple roadmap is honest but incomplete. A more definitive roadmap will include some of the connection points mentioned above, and remind the sponsor that guiding teams to successful adoption includes moving the enterprise, at least at the critical junctions, to understand, accept, and encourage agile methods. The epics that might issue forth from such a roadmap will, of course, include training, coaching, and measuring the team's progress, but also might include epics such as "As an agile developer, I need an isolated development environment so I can develop and test my product without risk of interrupting production systems." Roadmaps that don't include any mention of enterprise obstacles create a false narrative, set the wrong expectations, and ignore the focus areas that will have the most impact on agile success. Of course, we can't know every obstacle upfront, and so roadmaps and epics will necessarily evolve as we observe and experience. That's a core concept of agility. We can, however, anticipate some of the more obvious impediments, such as reluctant PMOs and siloed functional teams, and ensure that we're thoughtfully observing all the intersections so we can foresee some of the traffic jams we're likely to encounter. Clients hire agile consultants because they assume we can, through our experience, anticipate and address some of the ubiquitous challenges they're likely to face. Failing to advise clients about the challenges and disruptions ahead is, put simply, malpractice, as it would be if a doctor tells his patient that a heart transplant will be painless and risk-free.

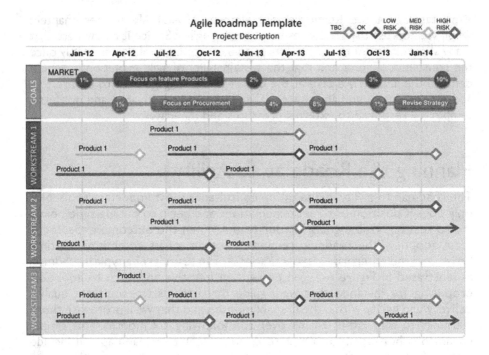

Figure 6-2. Project roadmap

At the enterprise level, developing a roadmap to agility is exponentially more challenging. The impediments at the management level are ingrained, historical, and cultural. The agile consultant engaged at this level must have the depth of business experience to grasp the client's business model, its strategic advantages, its processes and personalities. She must be able to follow the value stream, understand the legacy cultural remnants and artifacts that impede agility, and observe organizational disconnects, with neutrality and sensitivity. She must have the diplomatic skills required to tell senior executives that "they're doing it wrong" without upsetting egos or losing support. Most important, she must be able to highlight dysfunctions and inhibitors at the management level in a persuasive manner, motivating leaders to listen and heed rather than to escort her out of the building.

Constructing an enterprise agility roadmap is an extension of the Agile Opportunity visualization exercise we examined earlier. The examples of enterprise visions that we reviewed in Chapter 5 are aspirational, inspirational, and, frankly, ambiguous. They describe the attributes of an agile future, and some of the capabilities the enterprise hopes to gain but don't present any details on how we'll get there. The enterprise-level consultant who has assembled a guiding coalition, helped the enterprise develop an agile vision, and helped communicate a consistent and persuasive message now has the responsibility to take that vision a step further and encourage the leadership team to build a roadmap of the features, time boxes, and investments associated with its agile journey.

Opportunity visions and roadmaps have very different purposes, and skilled consultants should help leaders turn their vision statements into epics that describe the outcomes and expenditures they envision. A vision statement may inform the enterprise that "BIG Corporation will be agile and responsive to user needs, based on feedback obtained from our markets and social media relationships," but it gives no hint of how we'll accomplish that. Agility epics, on the other hand, can state that "As a marketing manager, I want to see a summary of all social media interactions every morning so I can plan for market and customer responsiveness." Part of the complexity of enterprise-level migrations is that each department, silo, and function will have its own agile epics to tell and may need significant help to tell them.

Traditional PMOs may know that agility is in their future, and may accept that their predictive methods aren't working. That doesn't mean that they'll be able to articulate the changes required to get there without the consultant's guidance. It may be obvious to us, as experienced agilists, that the PMO may have an epic like "As a PMO leader, I need access to burndown charts and scrum boards so I can understand the team's progress against commitments," but agile rookies won't come up with epics like this themselves. Functional departments, such as accounting or logistics, may be surprised to learn that changes to the software development function will affect them, and surely won't know how to create epics illustrating that. The role of the consultant in guiding, mentoring, and coaching leaders in the development of an agile roadmap is essential, and we haven't even mentioned the likely disputes or contradictions, in which one function's aspirations directly collide with another's.

Many consultants fall into the trap of concluding that the challenges, and the solutions, for every client will look like those of their previous clients. I've seen consultants "go on automatic," or jump to solutions before they've thoroughly observed and analyzed the particular scenario in front of them. We can't arbitrarily assume that the challenges we find in one organization will turn up in another. That's why I named this chapter "Observe and Plan." In agility transitions, as in all agile projects, planning is based on our experiences and learnings as we do the work. Consultants face a paradox; our clients expect us to bring the knowledge and experience we've gained in other engagements, yet to also honor their unique situation. They want us to have the foresight to help them avoid pitfalls, yet are rightfully touchy about "canned solutions." Because we're billable by the hour, clients often expect us to reach solutions quickly, but, especially in agile evolution projects, we can't solve challenges we haven't identified. Observation, and the ability to put those observations into context, is the agile advisor's indispensable skill.

In the debate about "big bang" versus incremental agile evolution, I'm clearly in the incrementalist camp. Agile evolution is too complex, even at the team level, to expect the enterprise to migrate from a predictive mind-set, adopt a set of new practices, work through the initial bumps, and identify roadblocks and impediments in one fell swoop. Mike Cohn does a great job of outlining the pros and cons of each approach,[1] so I won't recount them here. Many teams and organizations have already tried agile and failed, or have been through serial "change of the month" efforts, so, on top of the challenges I've laid out here, we often face a skeptical and weary atmosphere. Most clients want to see improvement on a very short time scale, and so part of our work is to instill patience in our sponsors and inform them of the realities of wading through the swamps of misperceptions and broken practices, which hamper the road to agility. Agile evolution is an iterative and incremental process, and is best run as an agile project itself, using the vision, roadmap, and backlog approach outlined above.

It's no accident, in my view, that the lean practices that underlie agility were initially perfected in Japan. I see the agile journey as a Zen exercise, requiring us to shed the fictions of control and predictability and embrace daily adaptation to reality. This quality also applies to scrummasters and agile consultants; if we approach the agile evolution with a ticking clock in our heads, with frustration and irritation when the teams stumble over obstacles, or with a preconceived notion about the enterprise's ultimate level of agility, we send the wrong messages to our teams, and we drive ourselves nuts. The proper attitude to agile guidance is patience, adaptability, receptiveness to reality, and empathy for our fellow voyagers. By observing the real conditions in the enterprise, adapting to them through our teaching and coaching, and mentoring our teams with composure and compassion, we model the qualities that will help teams evolve to a better version of themselves.

Summary

Observation and analysis are the core consulting skills. Mature consultants understand that every enterprise, culture, and personality is unique, and that an ounce of observation is worth a pound of premature diagnosis. Experienced consultants are always in observation mode, listening more than they speak and allowing the organization to devise its own solutions and get out of its own traps. Assuming that all engagements will be the same, and will be subject to the same sets of practices and methods, is a rookie mistake that does disservice to the client and the consultant.

---

[1]Mike Cohn, *Succeeding with Agile: Software Development Using Scrum* (Boston: Addison-Wesley, 2010).

Every enterprise's unique characteristics and challenges must be analyzed with care, and the plans that come from this diligent observation must fit the circumstances. In short, inspect and adapt. Guiding teams and organizations to agility is a Zen exercise, in which restraint, compassion, and patience pay off ultimately, even when the customer wants to "get agile now!" The development of a broad overall roadmap to agility sets the proper expectations with the sponsor and, although it must change as we learn and adapt, serves as a guide to the agile journey and enables us to ensure that we've created a timeline that's realistic and achievable based on the real conditions in the enterprise.

Lead Teams to Agility

"The team is always smarter than even the smartest individual." We've heard this proverb so frequently that it's become a cliché. But is it true? And, if so, why is that the case? Einstein had no team around him when he developed the general theory of relativity, nor did Newton when he discovered his fundamental laws of physics. From Galileo to Picasso, lone geniuses have advanced our knowledge and civilization through individual efforts. On the other hand, from The Manhattan Project[1] to the Beatles, and from Jobs and Wozniak to Watson and Crick,[2] the power of teamwork is undeniable. Even Newton, the typical example of the lone genius, stated that he "stood on the shoulders of giants" to make his calculations.

The Fundamentals of Teamwork

We've seen earlier the concepts of teamwork developed by Katzenbach and Smith.[3] To refresh, their study concluded that teams perform best under the following conditions:

- Small number
- Complementary skills

---

[1] The U.S. wartime effort to develop the atomic bomb.
[2] The final discoverers of DNA.
[3] Jon R. Katzenbach and Douglas E. Smith, *The Wisdom of Teams* (Boston: Harvard Business School Press, 1993).

© Rick Freedman 2016
R. Freedman, *The Agile Consultant*, DOI 10.1007/978-1-4302-6053-0_7

- Common, meaningful purpose
- Common set of specific performance goals
- Commonly agreed working approach
- Mutual accountability

These concepts, articulated by Katzenbach and Smith and confirmed by numerous studies since, back up the conclusion that teams with these attributes are more effective than lone geniuses in achieving their objectives.[4] Let's examine how these characteristics apply in an agile context, and how they inform the behavior of agile consultants as they lead teams, and their managers, to embrace agility.

Small Number

Agile or not, small teams have certain attributes that make them more conducive to high performance. Anyone who has tried to schedule a meeting with a large group of busy individuals knows that the simplest logistics become increasingly complex the bigger the group. While I'm a fan of big room planning, with representation from across the enterprise, these large gatherings often require weeks of groundwork just to get the group into the same room. In a high-pressure, high-expectation environment, we don't have weeks to wait for the team to make a decision or allocate immediate tasks. Small teams can meet frequently and (relatively) easily, and can convene emergency sessions to address the unexpected situations that arise every day in an innovative product development environment.

Communication also becomes more challenging with larger teams. Two people have a direct link, three require multiple links, and six need a complex network of interactions just to ensure that everyone gets the message. Even in teams that small, the message often gets garbled, as each individual re-interprets and retransmits the narrative. A small team can gather in a room, and everyone can hear the issue and collaborate on the solution, while large, distributed teams require more channels of communication, often including e-mails, phone calls, web chats, and other communication avenues that are not suited for immediate action. These alternate channels reduce the team's ability to interact, as anyone who has attended a web call can attest. The Agile Principles tell us that:

> The most efficient and effective method of conveying information to and within a development team is face-to-face conversation.

While today's global, distributed teams can make face-to-face communication challenging, the ideal still stands. With the product owner in the room representing the client, and with a small, empowered, cross-skilled team, we

[4]Michael Klug and James P. Bagrow, *Understanding the Group Dynamics and Success of Teams* (Vermont: Department of Mathematics & Statistics, University of Vermont, 2016).

can usually solve problems rapidly and come to consensus efficiently, without weeks of back-and-forth debate across multiple, impersonal mediums.

In a large group, it's common that many of the attendees, even if they come from the same enterprise, don't know each other, and are unfamiliar with the roles, responsibilities, and personalities of the people in the room. Many such sessions require a round-robin, in which we go around the room and describe our roles, often with the most cursory overview. In small teams, we incrementally gain intimate knowledge of our teammates' skills, capabilities, and personal attributes. We progressively build trust, and migrate to openness and honesty as we work through challenges and triumphs together. We learn the habits and proclivities, the unique skills and deficiencies, and the human characteristics that define our teammates. After a while, especially in persistent teams, we can predict the responses to a particular situation around the room and adjust our communication to the various sensitivities of our comrades. By building this trust and openness, we can collaborate effectively to address challenges and obstacles without having to pussyfoot around each other or soften our messages to avoid offense. Avoiding offense, of course, is critical for trust, but in teams that know each other and have been through the fire together, we instinctively learn how to frame issues to encourage teamwork rather than set off emotions.

Once we've developed this level of trust and honesty, it becomes easier to determine if we have the right skills in the room, or if we need to reach out to other experts or specialists to help us deliver our commitments. We can openly state that Michele is not the database expert we need for a particular challenge without insulting her. We can come to the conclusion that our training commitments need augmentation from the Training Department without humiliating our teammate who "sort of" has training experience. More important, the individuals themselves can volunteer that their skills or experience are not at the level required, thus sparing us the tiptoeing that this conversation would require in a large team of virtual strangers.

In an agile context, in which we have a defined time box in which we commit to specific deliverables, honesty, openness, and trust are indispensable. We simply don't have the luxury of dancing around delicate feelings when we're striving to develop innovative, emergent products. We never purposefully offend, but neither can we avoid issues that are impeding our progress. Small teams, with cohesiveness, collaboration, and trust, can call them as they see them, and uncover the flaws in our thinking and our process. Without that open exchange we'll never approach kaizen, let alone the perfection for which we ultimately strive.

Complementary Skills

In the typical enterprise, skills are clustered in functional silos. The developers sit, and work, together. The operations team has its own responsibilities, and reports to an operations manager. The same holds true for database experts, network teams, and quality assurance teams. Each functional, or component, team has its own chain of command, and its own goals and metrics. When a project is identified, temporary teams are pulled together across functions. They meet and collaborate on the project at hand, and then dissolve back into their respective silos until the next cross-functional project arises. This structure goes back to the industrial age, when individuals had very specific, repetitive tasks to perform, and, as long as each individual performed his task as expected, the final product rolled out the door. In fact, this separation of duties, along with interchangeable parts, is heralded as part of the industrial revolution that changed the world.

In the industrial enterprise, and in the administrative functions that grew to support it, this specialization made perfect sense. Specialist teams can be shared among multiple product lines, thus sparing the enterprise from hiring specialists for each product, increasing the expense and creating utilization problems. Specialists who work together can help each other, learn from and teach each other, and keep evolving efficiency within their speciality. As they enhance their capabilities, they can set standards of performance that lead to higher quality, easier handoffs, and more uniform practices and processes. All of these capabilities are focused on cost reduction. By carving out specialty, or functional, teams, we can keep the expertise in a controlled, closely managed team of shared resources that can be deployed as needed but kept together for ease of management, training, and cost control. We pay for this in the form of multiple handoffs, which decrease efficiency and increase the chances of miscommunication and error.

In the post-industrial age, cost control is still important but is trumped by innovation and customer responsiveness. Of course, costs need to be managed, but, as the management axiom goes, you can't cost-cut your way to product leadership. From Apple to Tesla, customers will pay a premium price for distinctive and unique products. The current marketplace values products, even if they are centered on hardware, that have a broad ecosystem of services and applications associated with them. Building the best smartphone hardware is great, but it is useless without great services and apps on offer, and this trend will only accelerate as the Internet of Things takes off. When even the automobile becomes a platform for software, it's clear that the pure hardware play is fading, to be replaced by physical products that are merely the platform for an array of additional, software-powered capabilities.

As hardware products become platforms, and as innovation and responsiveness become the differentiator, the industrial model of organization starts to show its age. The hierarchical, siloed structure is becoming obsolete as fast as the last generation of smartphones, and a more flexible, cross-functional, and self-managed workforce becomes the pathway to competitive advantage. Cross-functional teams, rather than silos of specialists, have been demonstrated to enhance the creativity and customer focus required in today's marketplace. Lean manufacturing practices have proven that those closest to the actual work have the most insight into efficiency and innovation. As firms experiment with this new cross-functional structure, certain attributes become clear, as do certain challenges.

Cross-functional, or complementary-skilled crews, enable the enterprise to build high-performance teams that contain all the capabilities necessary to take product ideas or new features from inception to completion. A team that includes analysts, developers, testers, technical writers, and customer representatives can take a product from ideation through quality assurance, and deliver a running, tested feature set to the ultimate customer without having to beg for outside resources, wait for other specialties to become available, or accumulate stores of work-in-progress while waiting for testers or documentation writers to be borrowed from functional silos. This is the ideal, of course, as most agile teams don't have every specialty required, and still have to wait or borrow, but teams that can take ownership of the product development cycle and avoid the serial, assembly-line practices of the industrial age have been shown to be more creative and invested than those in disconnected silos.

When we discuss complementary skills, many people think only of the technical or specialty diversity described earlier, but it's also important to consider interpersonal and collaborative skills as well. Some team members are great problem-solvers and decision makers, while others are stumped and frustrated by the smallest obstacle. Some are talkative and participatory, while others are timid and reserved. Some are argumentative and blunt, while others are collaborative and discrete. The best teams have diversity of personality as well as technical specialty, as each of these personality types adds something useful to team dynamics. The opportunity to watch the diverse skills and attributes in action, to learn from those who see the problem at hand in a different light, is itself a key strength of agile teams, both in the technical and in the interpersonal realms. The agile consultant who advises the enterprise in the composition of agile teams does well to ensure that technical and interpersonal diversity is encouraged, and that the ultimate objective for each team member is to develop a broader range of skills through exposure to her peers, and through the daily interaction of solving problems together.

Of course, most teams will need to reach out to other functional specialists to deliver a complete solution. Not many teams will have the luxury of a full-time technical architect, writer, or training specialist. Agile teams need to develop practices around coordinating with other specialists, who are often still working in functional silos, in order to fill team gaps and satisfy the customer's expectations. These interfaces can be fraught, as managers in silos attempt to ration their expertise or protect their positions. Agile leaders, such as scrummasters or product owners, often have to run interference in these situations, so team members can focus on their commitments without getting drawn into political disputes. Agile consultants should encourage teams to develop the required skills within the team when possible, and to reach out for expertise only when required. Teams that have grown up in functionally siloed organizations often stop forward progress as soon as they encounter an obstacle, before trying to design a creative solution within the team, a practice that only raises resistance and skepticism from functional managers.

Agile teams are often surprised at their ability to figure their own way out of the box, and guiding them to success in this is a major triumph for the agile consultant. Agile consultants should aim to develop "generalizing specialists," team members who have distinct areas of competence but also, through inter-action with their fellows and insight into other specialties on the team, build increasingly deeper understanding of the capabilities required to become self-organizing and self-managing.

Common, Meaningful Purpose

We've devoted much space to discussing the importance of a guiding vision for the migration to agility, but each agile project we undertake must also have a clear and compelling vision of its own. Teams need a meaningful purpose big-ger than themselves, bigger than the daily grind of paying the bills, to inspire them to persevere and collaborate. They need to feel that purpose in their hearts as well as their heads in order to achieve high performance. The Agile Opportunity vision we've discussed is an overarching, organizational vision, but teams need their own vision as well, one that suits their personalities both individually and as a group. As I illustrated above, roadmaps and back-logs derive from a consequential vision, particularly one that is developed and refined by the team itself. Visions that are handed down from on high, with no input or participation from the team, are interpreted as marching orders rather than inspiration. If the organization's objective is to "develop a new platform for processing insurance claims," the team can then derive a vision that articulates its aspirations for its role in achieving that mission. A cross-functional agile team may aspire to deliver the most running, tested features in the least number of sprints possible, thus pushing itself to high performance while supporting the enterprise goal.

Words are slippery, with the possibility of each team member interpreting any vision statement differently and approaching the achievement of any objec-tive in a different way. It's important that the entire team creates and inter-prets the project or product vision the same way. It's also important that the vision is concrete and measurable, with a binary outcome of achieved, or not. Vague visions, like "be the best team" or "create superior products," don't lend themselves to objective measurement or a clear outcome at the finish line. An agile consultant can help by coaching the team to develop a product vision that defines a SMART[5] goal that also contains both a hint of inspiration and a bit of a stretch. Ideally, I hope to see an agile team develop a product vision that its members can articulate and defend with passion, that they can refer to as a guiding principle, and that can drive them to greater achievement in their personal and professional goals.

---

[5]Specific, Measurable, Achievable, Realistic, Time boxed.

Common Set of Specific Performance Goals

In agile, the backlog is our version of the project plan, but, rather than reciting a list of tasks and activities, it defines a set of features that add value for the client and can be articulated and committed to by the team. This product backlog is our set of specific goals, and the roadmap and release plan is our visible articulation of what we've committed to deliver, and on what schedule. This granular set of goals is not only SMART but is also customer-focused and value-based. The goals are defined in such a way that they enable the team to demonstrate progress incrementally to both the customer and the broader organization, so the team can celebrate "small wins" and demonstrate that agility works.

To create a true product backlog, some team attributes are required. The team members must agree on the features or stories that comprise the product, and they must phrase them in a way that expresses the specific customer they're delivering value for, or the role or persona they address. The team must also agree, with the help of its product owner or business representative, on the relative priority of the backlog items, and on the level of effort required to achieve them. The practices of writing user stories, assigning them relative priority, and estimating the effort required, are clearly described by Cohn, Schwaber, and other authors I've cited, and I won't repeat them here. These basic mechanics of agile practice should be well understood by any agile coach or consultant, so reiterating them here is not our goal. We are, rather, focused on their importance from a team perspective. Skilled agile consultants know that the process of defining stories or features, coming to consensus on the roles, actions, and results that they represent, and deciding how to groom them to acceptable length and clarity is where the team dynamic is built and solidified. When a team looks at a large product vision, and collaboratively decomposes that into epics, stories, and priorities, it builds its understanding of each other's skills, personal attributes, and points of view that then enables its members to work in increasing harmony toward a common objective. As often stated, the plan is nothing; planning is everything. While I think this is an overstatement in the agile context, where the backlog is a critical artifact of our work that guides everything we achieve, I do believe that the act of planning is the element that solidifies the team and creates the knowledge, intimacy, and sense of shared purpose that creates a high-performance environment.

Those consultants who have coached a planning poker exercise have seen first hand what I mean. The story point estimating process is significant in itself, as it sets the expectations for effort required and gives us a quantifiable metric by which we can measure progress. Equally important is the team interaction. When one team member estimates a story as 5 points, and another estimates it as 40, it opens a dialog that enhances team understanding of the story, surfaces issues and technical challenges that may not be explicit, and teaches the team how to reach a consensus without argument or drama. The agile consultant should be a role model for neutrality, and for managing the emotions and egos of the team. The consultant who can guide the team to a productive discussion that uncovers the risks while acknowledging the expertise of the players leaves behind a team that can work through its disagreements in a productive manner. Once the team has reached consensus on the backlog, including features, roles, estimates, and priorities, it has achieved the clear set of specific performance goals that were identified as a critical success factor by Katzenbach and Smith back in 1993.

Commonly Agreed Working Approach

For teams adopting scrum, or extreme programing (XP), or test-driven development (TDD), the commonly agreed working approach should be obvious; we follow the rules of the agile discipline we've chosen. This, as any experienced agilist can attest, is a fantasy. I've never encountered a team, or an enterprise, that doesn't have unique circumstances, unique personalities, and unique constraints. I've also never encountered two teams, or two enterprises, that apply their selected agile discipline in exactly the same way. A team building smartphones may require longer iteration lengths to develop a valuable product, as I encountered in my consulting relationship with a major manufacturer. A team first learning agile methods may need to be eased into the process, by, for example, using t-shirt sizing before it evolves to story-point estimating. Enterprises with strong traditions of predictive, sequential project planning and estimation techniques will not automatically adopt relative estimating or backlog-based planning simply because we advocate it. While scrum, or the other approaches I've mentioned, have clear sets of rules and practices, the likelihood of those being adopted wholesale without training and evolution is nil. One of the critical areas of value that skilled agile consultants can add is their ability to observe and grasp the unique characteristics of the players and the environment, and figure out how to help teams adopt a version of their agile discipline that reflects the reality on the ground. I've followed up on too many failed agile transitions in which the sponsor told me that the previous coach was too rigid. "All he cared about was a set of rules; he had no sensitivity to our unique circumstances." To me, that description typifies a rookie just out of scrum training. Consulting is an exercise in observation, sensitivity, and adaptability.

This is not to say that the rules are to be wantonly abandoned or applied in an ad hoc manner. Agile advisors should have a clear vision of where they expect to land, and should have a roadmap for getting the organization there. The practices must be respected; they've been refined, over the many years since Kent Beck first applied XP at Chrysler, because they work, and because they inculcate a healthy, high-performance culture. This being true, agile consultants need to determine the best way to get teams to accept these practices and internalize them. A book of rules, slavishly followed, is not an effective map for completing this journey. Teams must have input into the manner and speed with which these practices are shaped and adopted. They must own the process, it must reflect their opinions, personalities, and skills, and cannot be imposed.

This is an area in which I'm at odds with many agile experts, who advocate following the rules exactly before trying to introduce changes. My experience is that this rules-based approach often confounds the uninitiated, and discounts the enterprise history, culture, and business model. As I've noted, I'm an incrementalist, for many reasons. My overriding concern is that teams understand and own their version of agility, not that they get to agile adoption on the shortest possible timeline. By training on the meaning of the practices, their historical basis, and the successes they've achieved in other settings, the agile consultant can help teams develop the *desire* to adapt, rather than follow a "thou shalt be agile" dictum. I've consulted with teams that benefited from incrementally adopting the practices, migrating from task-based backlog items to user-centered stories, or initially thinking in hours and activities rather than relative points and value. While we respect the practices, we can allow teams to absorb at their own pace the meaning, rather than merely the methods, of agility. Most critically, they invest in the creation of their own version of agile, and own it. Incidentally, I've found that this approach actually shortcuts the dissemination of agility in the enterprise, as you avoid having teams and individuals blindly following practices that they don't understand or invest in. Instead of questioning every technique and resisting the imposition of unfamiliar methods, they see for themselves how the practices they've devised help them achieve.

Shu Ha Ri,[6] a martial arts philosophy that can be roughly translated as Imitate, Assimilate, and Innovate,[7] is often cited as a central technique for training agilists. Shu Ha Ri was designed, however, for a physical discipline like karate, in which the development of "muscle memory" by imitation is a precursor to success. It is much beloved by many agile coaches, as it allows them to focus on rote repetition of a set of rules. Unfortunately, my experience is that teams coached in this manner never reach the assimilation or innovation stage, because they never understood or absorbed the underlying principles in the first place. Agility is a philosophy, not a physical practice; it requires understanding and acceptance, not muscle memory. As should be clear by now, I scoff at rote repetition; if that's all that is required, new agile teams don't need a consultant; they can learn the practices from a book. The consultant adds value through specificity; the ability to observe and absorb the unique circumstances at hand and guide the team to adoption of the practices in a manner and at a pace that fits their environment.

---

[6]/www.solutionsiq.com/shuhari-agile-adoption-pattern/.
[7]www.jazzadvice.com/clark-terrys-3-steps-to-learning-improvisation/.

Make no mistake; the ultimate goal is a disciplined adoption of standard agile practices, with only the modifications that absolutely fit the enterprise's, and the team's, distinct requirements. I'm not advocating assembling a random collection of agile techniques, cobbling them together, and calling it good. "Fractional agile" is no agile at all. The agile practices that the team adopts cannot violate the spirit of lean, agile mind-set. It still must honor the basic tenets of the Agile Manifesto and the Agile Principles, as well as the kaizen nature of all lean enterprises. But Katzenbach and Smith use the language of "commonly agreed approach" for a reason. Agreement on a method that capitalizes on the team's unique skills, requires measurable contribution by all participants, enables reality-based problem solving, and is unanimously accepted; these are the attributes that encourage team formation and results.

Mutual Accountability

When enterprises become agile, they abandon one thing that is precious in many cultures: the ability to hide. Many, perhaps most, organizations have a troubled relationship with truth. They tell themselves everything is fine when any outside observer can see massive dysfunction. They manipulate the numbers to misrepresent to the Wall Street analyst community, and to befuddle their own employees. They "work around" unproductive employees and broken processes to spare themselves the pain of decision, confrontation, and change. As we've seen, the speculators who caused the financial crisis through wild and self-dealing recklessness walk free. Management deals harshly with those who blow the whistle on unethical or dysfunctional behavior. In short, many enterprises lack accountability, transparency, and consequence.

In truly agile teams or enterprises, there's nowhere to hide. Big, visible indicators show every interested party the precise state of affairs at any moment. Visible scrum or kanban boards enable both the team and the enterprise to see the progress, or lack thereof, that the team is making on a daily basis. Velocity metrics and burndown charts clearly illustrate the capacity for creating value that the team has achieved over time. Iteration-based demos and retrospectives enable the team to show the value they've added on a regular cadence, and to quickly correct suboptimal practices. Every practice or ceremony of agility is specifically designed to make progress visible, and to bring commitment and accountability to all team members, from the developer to the executive. Agility is a disruptive practice precisely because it eliminates hiding places and removes the ability to sweep broken processes under the rug.

Mutual accountability relies on more than simple visibility. It requires that the team embrace both individual and team ownership of the final outcome. Every team member must accept that they succeed or fail together as a unit, and that each individual has a specific role to play in order to deliver. The entire team must commit and own every element, from vision to roadmap to backlog, and every work product that makes up the whole. Rookie agile teams often struggle with the concept of collective and individual ownership. Agile consultants must define what commitment means, and help teams grasp the idea that they can't passively accept roadblocks and challenges but instead must take action to achieve their goals, with the help of an active scrummaster. Teams accustomed to waterfall processes often simply send an e-mail and wait, versus picking up the phone or walking across the hall. Members who are used to being judged as individual contributors have difficulty adjusting their mind-set to the "whole team ownership" concept.

Unfortunately, we've all encountered those colleagues who have made a living by either hoarding their specialties or specializing in work avoidance. Agility will make these folks extremely uncomfortable, whether teammates or managers. That discomfort often spreads to their teammates as well; the "go along to get along" mentality is bred into many conflict-averse organizations. Agile teams tell the truth; that's one of their defining features. If we don't hold the non-producers, blockers, and hoarders accountable, kaizen is impossible. Helping teams change their accommodative behavior and start to expect higher performance from every member is one of the agile consultant's most delicate jobs. Agile consultants need to role model honesty without encouraging confrontational behavior. As skilled facilitators, mature consultants understand how to avoid turning accountability into argument. By guiding teams to take the emotion out of the conversation, and to focus on work products rather than personalities, we can add value to the retrospective process without becoming a blame agent when teammates feel threatened or exposed. The delivery of running, tested features is binary; it's either completed and demo-ready or it's not. Coaches and consultants can often have problems with their own emotions as well. It's easy to get frustrated with the team member who consistently misses targets or hands off a poor-quality product. Mutual accountability includes us as well. We need to remember that mutual accountability lies within the team, not at the scrummaster or consultant level. We're there to guide, not enforce, and we guide through influence alone.

I've been an advocate of team rather than individual commitment long before agility, for a simple reason. I've observed, in my corporate career, that individual contributors quickly become immune to the scoldings or poor performance ratings of managers. If I'm not bad enough to fire, and I'm not particularly ambitious, what do I care if I have to endure a periodic chastening from some remote manager? On the other hand, if the team looks around the room and focuses on me and my inability to deliver, that cuts to the bone. The likelihood of influencing behavior rises exponentially when the team chastises me, even gently and indirectly, than if some manager whose opinion I scorn gives me a lecture. Teams that can get beyond the discomfort of holding their teammates (and friends) accountable, without triggering argument and emotion, master the art of kaizen and quality delivery quickly.

Self-Management and Self-Organization

Team self-organization is a central tenet of agility, but what exactly does that mean? In most large enterprises, the idea of allowing teams to self-select, self-organize, and self-manage is a non-starter. Teams are usually selected by a functional manager, assigned to projects based on availability and skills, and expected to work in the manner endorsed by existing processes and hierarchical norms. The theory of self-organization is, in my experience, the idea most maligned and ridiculed by traditional managers when the concept of agility is introduced. "I can't get these teams to perform when I'm micromanaging every step they take. How can I trust them to manage themselves?." It takes a patient explanation of the meaning of self-organization by the agile consultant to help both managers and teams understand what it means for teams to own and manage their own commitments and performance.

One fallacy that many managers believe is that self-organized teams can be indiscriminately assembled from whatever staff members happen to be handy. As I learned early in my career, availability is not a skill set. I often say, when I train teams in agility, that "you wouldn't get on the New York City subway, randomly point at nine guys, and tell them they're the New York Yankees." You can, of course; just don't expect them to win the pennant. The Agile Principles encourage us to "Build projects around motivated individuals." As the enterprise migrates toward agility, management's role shifts from telling teams what to do and how to do it, to selecting the right mix of talents and temperaments to work together successfully, motivating them with a meaningful goal, and then running interference for them so they can avoid obstacles.

This evolution is often more threatening to managers than it is to teams themselves. Managers might see their authority and prestige evaporating in a haze of "empowerment." The teams themselves, especially if they are composed of self-motivated achievers, crave the opportunity to decide for themselves how they'll divide and conquer the work ahead. For the agile consultant, educating and guiding both managers and teams toward self-organization requires the right mix of education, reassurance, and guidance. Skilled agile consultants help managers understand the concept of "servant-leadership," a term that many command-and-control style leaders find demeaning and unrealistic. Hierarchical managers think of their teams as "my people." That's OK, but they need to migrate from "my people" as a term of ownership to "my people" as a term of ministry. When a pastor or rabbi thinks of his people, he thinks not of a pool of resources to command but of a congregation that he leads to grace, and guides to actualization. That's the role of leadership in the agile enterprise; leading the team members to uncover their best selves, and guiding them to achieve the highest level of actualization possible.

Teams that are at the beginning of the journey to agility are often reluctant to make their own decisions or to own their commitments. Years of having to go up and down the chain to make any decision, and of enduring long periods of latency before they get access to needed resources or discover the results of executive decisions, often suffer from a state of "learned helplessness." Like mice in a scientific experiment that learn that, no matter how they behave, they still get the same punishment, they just stop trying and become passive. These teams reach out for management guidance every step of the way, afraid to set themselves up to be overruled or chastised. Helping these teams turn the corner to self-management requires the agile consultant to engage at both the management and the team level.

Managers who wish to "go agile" without relinquishing the role of task management must be led to acceptance of team empowerment. This is one reason why celebration and promotion of small victories is so important to agile evolution. With each deliverable completed, each customer satisfied, and each team that displays the advantages of agility, managers learn to let go of control, a bit at a time. Once managers experience the ability to let go of micromanagement, they are usually delighted to find that they can start to focus on the strategic issues that they were hired to manage. Enlightened managers relish the idea of leading motivated, high-performance teams that make their own decisions, and find that the chance to lead and guide is more fulfilling than the responsibility to rank and chastise.

Of course, not every manager is enlightened in this way. We started this section by noting that agility allows no hiding place. That is true also of managers, many of whom are not adding value, or are sometimes even impeding value, in their quest to make themselves relevant and indispensable. The path to servant-leadership for these managers is more fraught, both for them and for the agile consultant. I've emphasized repeatedly that the agile consultant is neutral; we're not here to grade anyone, manage anyone, or enforce any change in behavior. Our role is to observe, inspect, and adapt, or help our sponsor adapt. When we observe that specific managers are clinging to hierarchical, decree-based management styles, we can relate that to our sponsors and suggest mechanisms for helping overcome that resistant behavior, but, as hired coaches, we must tread lightly on rating both managers and their teams. Just as the mantra for a scrummaster is "take it to the team," the agile consultant's mantra, when encountering resistance at the management level, is to "take it to the management team." Again, we focus on the behavior and its impact, not on personalities and names. As a blunt and forthright New Yorker, I've had a career-long struggle to keep myself from just saying "Mr. Jones is a knucklehead who is blowing up this project." Over my career, I've finally learned to apply some Zen to these sorts of problems, after the painful lesson that the blunt approach creates more animosity and resistance than a neutral, data-based, name-free observation. It's not our role to "name and shame," and, with an agile, kaizen mind-set, we shouldn't want to.

Summary

Agile methods are designed to develop the self-organization of teams. They enable teams to determine their own vision, roadmap, and backlog, to decide on the team's commitments and their own. Agile practices provide the markers that inform teams and leaders on the progress, the capacity, and the contributions of the team and its members. They reveal the dysfunctions and broken processes that can guide the scrummaster and the team to optimization. Agile ideas of teamwork are based on sound and confirmed analysis and experience, and have been proven to benefit organizations and teams whether agile or not. Agility, applied correctly and fearlessly, both creates and relies upon the ability of teams to organize, motivate, and manage themselves.

Visible Results

Visible results, in a traditional enterprise setting, often refer to the promotion and marketing of successful efforts, in an attempt to persuade the organization that new methods are working. When I was a traditional project manager (PM), I frequently convinced clients to put up posters, place scrolling slide shows in prominent places, and stand up in front of audiences in various venues to publicize the great outcomes that the new system or process was producing. If a new process or system is reducing friction, improving quality, increasing throughput, and advancing worker satisfaction, it would be foolish not to use these positive outcomes as a key element in your change strategy. Enterprise inertia is strong; promoting visible results creates momentum.

Visibility Is Key

In a lean or agile environment, the concept of visible results goes much deeper. Visual controls, such as product roadmaps, scrum rooms with posted backlogs, kanban boards, burndown charts, and interruption or "detour buckets" are more than simple promotion techniques; they are an integral element of the practice itself, and drive the improvements we seek. The visibility of the work the team has committed to, of feature cards as they move from "in progress" to "done," and of accelerating velocity of teams as they gain confidence and skill, enables any interested party to see with her own eyes the advancement of agility. Comparisons between projected and actual performance are no longer buried in a complex set of spreadsheets or obscure earned value calculations; the facts are right there in front of the team and its leaders.

© Rick Freedman 2016
R. Freedman, *The Agile Consultant*, DOI 10.1007/978-1-4302-6053-0_8

Visible results, in an agile context, are not simply celebrations and marketing campaigns; they are tools for exposing broken processes, unmet commitments, inconsistent performance, and centers of excellence. This is not to discount their importance in building momentum. It is, instead, a reminder to the agile coach or consultant that, in our lean, agile domain, visible controls enable us to show, rather than merely tell, the success stories and challenges that the enterprise is experiencing in its agile journey. Visibility is a central ingredient in the transition to agility, and skilled agile consultants use its power to keep the thrust rising against the gravity of culture and tradition.

The migration to visible controls is a top priority of any new engagement I undertake. I'm often confronted, when starting up new agile teams, with an unstructured mess of tasks, project plans, and work streams that are disconnected and unprioritized, with no correlation between capacity and commitment. Tasks, roles, and responsibilities are hidden and undecipherable. Team members are overcommitted and beaten down. Dependencies are either unknown or uncommunicated, and heroic efforts, like working all night and every weekend, are common. The basic task of explaining to me what they're working on, and why, seems insurmountable.

In this scenario, my first action is to encourage the team to "throw it up on the wall." If I can get the team to simply enumerate the tasks or features it has committed to deliver, even if they're not formed as stories or features, to then categorize them roughly by customer, or project, or whatever grouping makes sense to the team, we've now got the foundation for the rest of our initial transition. Teams can learn, in a single backlog generation session, that their chaotic, overwhelming mess can, in fact, be sorted into something that is visible and structured. It will not, of course, look anything like a proper scrum backlog, but it is the beginning round in an evolution that can then take them to prioritization, to effort-based sizing, to release and sprint planning, and to individual and team commitments.

A "show up and throw up" session, which typically creates a wall filled with undifferentiated tasks, projects, and features, can now be used as the basis for some grooming sessions that give agile aspirants the opportunity to learn by doing, rather than by lecture, and to show them how quickly simple visibility can have an impact. My first question when confronting an unstructured backlog with a new team is, "How can we sort and prioritize these?" Unfortunately, I frequently encounter teams whose work is so atomized that each member only sees his little piece, and the team has no visibility into the connection points, let alone the project vision. Including a product owner at this stage is critical. In many environments, only the business representative understands the vision of the overall product, and the manner in which the pieces integrate into a whole.

Every Picture Tells a Story

Categorization schemes can vary all over the map, but I'm primarily interested in how they fulfill a vision or roadmap. If time or feature commitments have been made to the business customer, the product owner can begin to articulate to the team how the pieces fit. A skilled product owner, whether her official title is Sales Executive, Delivery Manager, or Business Technology Liaison, should be able to help teams understand not only what's been committed but why. It seems like working backward, in the sense that agile teams will usually start with a vision, then create a roadmap, and build a backlog from there. In teams that are new to agile, however, it's unlikely that the agile advisor will walk into a greenfield. Even if we select a pilot project, my experience is that the project selected often comes with preconceptions, precommitments, and historical baggage that require untangling before a real agile effort can begin.

We start with the understanding that the concept of visible results has two meanings in agile: the visibility of success, in order to build enterprise momentum, and the visibility of the actual results of our work, so that accountability, status, progress, and value delivery are all evident in simple, readable form available to any interested party. The celebration and promotion of success lends credibility across the enterprise, but the visibility of backlogs, burndowns, "detour buckets" (lists of interruptions or other detours that impede the team's progress), obstacles, and other visual controls, are the mechanism of change. Agile is reality-based, and when the reality is visible to all, hiding places and broken processes become, well, visible, and subject to improvement. When the plan and progress are hidden in some spreadsheet or project plan that is available and decipherable only to a select few, we're back in the world of a product priesthood, with supplicants begging for information about the status of their work.

In sophisticated lean manufacturing enterprises, like Toyota, the number of visual controls can become overwhelming. Lean manufacturing facilities make visual charts for everything from "job by job tracking" to "priority-based hourly status charts" to "visual control for progression of work through an office process." When manufacturing intricate products with life-or-death implications, this granular tracking of everything from parts to documents makes sense.[1]

In agile we try to "maximize the amount of work not done," and so we tend toward the least number of visual controls required for the work at hand. If we're developing software to control automated braking on an automobile, we may have to behave like a manufacturer and track every detail. If we're building an app that lets users simulate tossing a wad of paper into a trash bin,

---

[1] David Mann, *Creating a Lean Culture: Tools to Sustain Lean Conversions*, Second Edition (New York: Taylor & Francis Group, , 2010).

not so much. The level of visual control should adapt to the project at hand, but it should also reflect the maturity of the team. For beginning agile teams, visual controls that display the product and sprint backlogs, the blockages and impediments, the progress from work-in-progress to completion, and the beginnings of a burndown chart (even if we're only counting items moved from backlog to done) are essential, but the visibility of a "detour bucket" of interruptions, or the introduction of individual kanban boards for certain members, might also be useful. As always, we inspect and adapt our use of visual controls to the situation at hand.

One of the traps of visual controls, especially in traditional or formal organizations, is more emphasis on the look of the charts than on their utility. I've attended countless debates about whether charts should burn up or burn down, for instance, or whether all kanban boards in the organization should have the same columns. This misses the theme completely; visibility is designed to stimulate action, not to look pretty. Charts that demonstrate whether improvement and progress are being made are not ornamental; they expose action or inaction on the migration of culture and behavior. I don't care if teams burn up or burn down. My question, especially with rookie teams, is whether they are burning at all. Detour buckets have no meaning if no effort is made to lessen and eventually end unscheduled interruptions that impede sprint progress.

In many enterprises that have yet to accept agility, a core problem is the disconnection between capacity and commitment. Sales teams and client managers are incentivized to go out and sell more and more, with ever-rising quotas and associated compensation. This encourages the executive and sales teams to push product or projects out to customers, with no visibility or correlation to the actual capacity to deliver. Sales teams make commitments that have no relationship to the delivery team's capacity to deliver, and get rewarded for doing so. Because sales and delivery are often siloed, if not actively feuding, delivery objections to unrealistic commitments often sound like mere grousing. Visual controls give product delivery teams the ability to come to the conversation with data. If, for instance, a long-term burndown chart demonstrates that teams have capacity to burn through 200 story points in an iteration, and sales commitments add up to 500 story points in that period, the disconnection becomes visible and data-centered, rather than just some narrative that "we're always overloaded." "Complaint without data is whining" is a common management theory, which the adherence to a visual control discipline can disarm.

No Blame, No Shame

Traditional organizations are often prone to using data to chastise and punish, rather than to improve. Beginning agile teams are often reluctant to make their commitments and results visible, in fear that their managers will then use performance against plan as an opportunity to hector and scold rather than as an indicator of process or management failures. In command enterprises, where dissent and "excuses" are discouraged or punished, the tendency to sweep issues under the rug, and to protect managers and blame employees, is ingrained and powerful. Agile consultants need to apply some of the Zen attributes I've encouraged, and realize that these inclinations will not disappear overnight. We need to display the agile mind-set to which we hope to guide the enterprise. "No blame, no shame" must be our guiding principle in every interaction, and we must role-model thoughtful root cause analysis, and select appropriate improvement efforts based on the organizational reality. It's easy, as an immature consultant, to get frustrated with broken processes, punitive managers, and "blaming and shaming" as a management technique. The simple discipline of visual control is the best mechanism for incrementally discovering and exposing counterproductive practices. By taking the emotion and speculation out of the conversation, visual controls (eventually) make it obvious that improvements are necessary, even if they rub leadership the wrong way and discourage comfortable blindness.

With all the preceding warnings, it may sound like visual management is too much of a hassle to be worth doing. Despite all their possibilities for resistance or misuse, visual controls, or, as they are often called in agile, information radiators, are indispensable for true agility. Visual controls that are easily legible, even from afar, that use physical representations, like scrum cards, that use color to indicate different states, and that are as simple as possible to interpret, quickly establish their value. Most project or product teams are accustomed to tiny lines on a project plan, or to an unconnected series of e-mails instructing them to prioritize this task over that, rather than a shared, visual work control system. Managers also value detailed spreadsheets containing hundreds of granular details that are usually privileged information, shared only within the executive suite. When these are replaced by multicolored scrum cards on a wall, it takes some getting used to. As Toyota and hundreds of other lean enterprises have demonstrated, physical tokens on the wall, easily read and interpreted, are much more likely to result in behavior changes and process improvements than are lines on a screen.

You may have noticed that I've stayed away from the term *metrics*. That's deliberate; metrics is old-school language, bringing up the ghost of punitive performance reviews and unhelpful comparisons between teams and individuals. I prefer the language of visibility, by which we uncover and improve on defects and deficiencies in the process and culture, and celebrate successes that all can see, rather than dry measurements that threaten and divide.

Visualizing the queue of work that has been committed is the first key objective of visual management. Queues are often invisible, residing in a salesperson's forecast or a "top secret" portfolio management system, until they suddenly become urgent as their due dates approach. Beginning agile teams consistently tell me that their queueing system is "the sales guy sells something, puts it into his forecast, and then runs down with his hair on fire when he realizes the date is near." Delivery teams will frequently hear through the grapevine that some major project is on the horizon, but they won't get the details until it's too late for them to plan and prepare. In other words, the organization's lack of a disciplined queueing and work control system creates a constant state of emergency for the delivery team.

By helping teams institute visual controls, we empower them to begin resisting ad hoc requests, to stay focused on the commitments they've made for the current iteration, and to self-manage their work flow. From scrum cards, easy to move and reprioritize, to kanban boards that clearly illustrate the work-in-progress stream, teams have not only made their successes visible, as cards move to the "done" column, but they've also been empowered through visibility to make a data-centered case for resisting interruptions and distractions. "Your lack of planning does not make my emergency" is a cute saying I've seen on many office coffee cups, but, with information radiators, teams now have the capability to walk their colleagues up to the wall and help them understand why that is true. As usual in this book, I won't be going into the technical details of how and when to apply visual controls, as any agile consultant should be familiar with the mechanics. For a more detailed breakdown of the granular techniques of visual controls, or information radiators, there are plenty of resources online.[2]

Every organizational change methodology emphasizes the importance of promotion as a potent method of enhancing momentum. Way back in 1995, John Kotter called the lack of short-term wins, and of their visibility, one of the top ten reasons for failure in organizational change. Importantly, he stresses that we're not just hoping for successes[3]; we're actively making the quest for short-term wins, and promoting them in a structured manner, like a campaign. This makes the quick development of visible controls critical; without data, success promotion is just talk. It also places the burden on agile consultants to be judicious in the selection of projects for pilots or first-time team efforts. Taking on behemoth, previously unsolvable problems the first time through an iteration is probably not wise. Agile advisors should make sure that the work teams take on early in the transition includes some "low-hanging fruit," some elements that the team can deliver successfully, and that can benefit from an agile approach quickly. Prioritization of backlog items must be judicious, not only driven by the customer's perceived urgency but also by size, complexity, and visibility. If the team has to work through a multitude of iterations before delivering anything of value, we're not far from the dreaded "we tried agile; it didn't work" conversation.

---

[2]www.netobjectives.com/files/VisualControlsEnterpriseTeams.pdf.
[3]https://hbr.org/1995/05/leading-change-why-transformation-efforts-fail-2.

A promotional campaign for organizational change should be structured and planned, and not consist of random acts of visibility. The successes we promote must have meaning to the organization; very few executives or associates will care that we ran regression testing on 49 new builds. If, however, that regression testing led to higher-quality products and delivered to customers faster and with higher satisfaction, that will garner some attention. I'm an advocate of a campaign that builds slowly, as the teams become more adept at agility, since early attempts will include as many failures as they do successes, and our visibility makes those apparent as well. As teams gain confidence and skill, the number and importance of our successes will grow, and the promotion of them will be increasingly persuasive. Persuasiveness is the key; the successes we promote would not just highlight the content of what we built but the importance of the agile practices we used to get there.

It's great when leaders call out the successes of agile teams and practices, but it's even better when the team stands up and describes its experience, from initial reluctance and trepidation to acceptance, mastery, and triumph. One of the indicators I like to track is simple team happiness, on a Likert scale. I ask team members to rate their happiness, not just with agile, but with their organizational life, on a whiteboard, with a simple 1-to-5 scale, and track that over time. Making increasing happiness visible is a powerful persuader. Everyone wants to be happier in their work, and every progressive manager should value team satisfaction.[4]

Other promotion techniques include "agile safaris," as recommended by Mike Cohn[5], in which teams that have not yet experienced agile sit in with an agile team and watch them work, and scrum room tours, in which agile teams walk their managers and associates through the scrum room and explain how the visible artifacts help them achieve their objectives. E-mails, newsletters, and banners are far down on my list; they smack of the multiple failed change campaigns that every enterprise has experienced, and become mere background noise to already skeptical associates. In lean and agile, teams don't want to be lectured or mandated; they want to observe, experience, and learn. They want to be persuaded, not hectored.

The obvious success of lean manufacturing and lean enterprises, with their abundant use of visual controls, illustrates beyond debate that these methods work. I want to emphasize that visual controls are only one element of the lean or agile enterprise. If they don't stimulate corrective action, they are ornaments, destined to turn dusty and forgotten in some remote corner. The agile consultant has the unenviable job of highlighting the dysfunctions

---

[4]https://en.wikipedia.org/wiki/Likert_scale.
[5]Mike Cohn, *Succeeding with Agile: Software Development Using Scrum* (Boston: Addison-Wesley, 2010).

and disconnections that these visual artifacts expose, and guiding teams and leadership to act. The results of visibility are far reaching; they shine a light on, for example, broken sales intake processes, invisible queues of projects, absent or erroneous prioritization schemes, and myriad other flaws in the culture, value stream, and process chain. As noted previously, there are players in every enterprise who make their living hiding in the cracks and aren't thrilled when those cracks are repaired. The skilled agile consultant doesn't only encourage teams to use visual controls to track their own work; she also works across the enterprise to help the entire organization recognize and address the problems they reveal. This is a distinction between agile coaching and agile consulting. Practice-focused agile coaches can help bring teams toward agile methods, while agile consultants focus on the holistic picture of the entire enterprise, and have the consulting skill and experience to diplomatically and persuasively propagate the agile and kaizen mind-set throughout the enterprise.

Summary

Visibility and transparency are central to lean philosophy, and drive many of our agile practices. The scrum board, with its categories of visible tasks, the burndown charts that show our progress as we go, the retrospective insights that we collect and post—all of these are visible so that action can be taken in real time and there's no hiding place for dysfunction. We transition to agile when the hidden dysfunctions bred within our culture, processes, and relationships threaten to overpower our ability to succeed. By bringing failures and issues to the light, we drive improvement. By making success visible, we drive momentum toward agility.

Evolve the Enterprise

Agile evolution within the enterprise is often visualized as ripples in a pond. The agile champion, coach, or consultant throws a stone into the pond by assembling the initial agile teams and using agile methods to deliver a pilot project. The pilot teams start to experience improved results, and to make them visible. The successes and challenges of that initial pilot expose obstacles and broken processes. These discoveries cascade through the enterprise and focus improvement efforts on identified roadblocks. Incrementally, as each new challenge is uncovered, the ripples of change and agility reach into further corners of the organization, eventually washing across the entire enterprise and up to the executive level. Executives eventually acknowledge the power of agility, and change their mind-sets and their management techniques to employ agile practices across the enterprise. Lean, agile thinking permeates the organization. Productivity, innovation, and happiness multiply. The enterprise achieves the nirvana of agility.

That's the "happy path," as project managers like to say. But what is the "sad path," and what can agile consultants do to steer their clients toward safe harbor and away from the shoals? Failed agile transitions abound. Many agile consultants make their living cleaning up after poorly executed agile migration projects. As with Total Quality Management (TQM), Business Process Engineering (BPR), Six Sigma, serial reorganizations, and myriad other "programs of the month," initial implementation may be challenging, but sustainment is nearly impossible. The weight of history, legacy, culture, and personality

© Rick Freedman 2016
R. Freedman, *The Agile Consultant*, DOI 10.1007/978-1-4302-6053-0_9

all conspire to pull the new initiative back to earth, and, when the consultants leave and the next big problem arises, the enterprise goes back to the "do whatever it takes" mentality, workarounds and shortcuts are applied, things drift back to the old ways, and skepticism grows while morale deflates.

I have a stack of books on agility a yard high, and each one has unique insights. They teach us how to follow an agile process, use visible charts, and help teams coalesce and perform. They offer guidance to coaches, developers, managers, and executives on the meaning and practice of agile. Scaling agile software development across the enterprise is a topic frequently raised, with varying degrees of formality, ranging from Dean Leffingwell's highly structured Scaled Agile Framework for the Enterprise (SAFe)[1] to Scott Ambler's Discipline Agile Delivery (DAD)[2] method, and from Larman and Vodde's Large Scale Scrum (LeSS)[3] to the common "Scrum of Scrums" approach found in Cohn's[4] and Schwaber's[5] works.

We'll take a quick walk through some of these frameworks, and look at some of the adherents and critics of each. Whether, as an agile consultant, you agree or disagree with these methods, you must be aware of them. Each, either in part or in whole, has elements that you can adapt and apply to the enterprise situation you find on the ground. Your clients, if they've researched agility at all, will be familiar with these ideas, and therefore so must you, for credibility if nothing else. Different techniques fit different circumstances, and the broader your knowledge the more value you can add.

The debate over the scalability of agile software development is settled. Agile development has been scaled successfully in hundreds of enterprises worldwide, and the techniques offered by these agile pioneers are prudent and proven. And, of course, these innovators and hundreds of their "certified" followers roam the globe, coaching teams and enterprises in the use of these techniques. Why, then, do so many agile transitions fail to evolve, or to stick? First of all, existing frameworks are almost primarily focused on software development. Ambler's DAD framework and Leffingwell's SAFe are explicitly information technology (IT)-centric. They present processes and practices that prescribe techniques for scaling agile IT, but they don't address adequately, to my eyes, the deep and ingrained cultural and management barriers to their visions, let alone offer realistic goals and techniques for agile advisors to help leaders evolve.

---

[1]http://www.scaledagileframework.com/.

[2]http://www.disciplinedagiledelivery.com/introduction-to-dad/.

[3]http://less.works/.

[4]Mike Cohn, *Succeeding with Agile: Software Development Using Scrum* (Boston: Addison-Wesley, 2010).

[5]Ken Schwaber, *Agile Project Management with Scrum* (Redmond, WA: Microsoft Press, 2004).

Agile Management Required

The exclusive focus on rules, ceremonies, and rituals applied by many coaches is actually counterproductive. Adopting agile practices can result in such rapid local progress (in the software development function) that the enterprise doesn't believe it needs to push further. What's the missing piece that would enable these initial, local successes to permeate the enterprise? To answer this question, let's go back to lean fundamentals. David Mann,[6] describes the missing element this way:

> Why is it that so many attempts to convert to lean end in retreat and disappointment? It is a paradox: So many lean implementations fail because lean is too easy! It's too easy to implement the physical trappings of lean while failing completely to notice the need for a parallel implementation of lean management.

The basic practices of agile are simple to learn and implement. New scrum teams can often absorb these techniques, and begin to profit from them, in a few sprints. These teams are successful in implementing rudimentary visual controls, in uncovering wasteful practices and processes in their retrospectives, and in developing long lists of blockages, detours, and wait-states that are impeding their momentum. They remove the obstacles within their teams, and start to exhibit stable, or even increasing, velocity, as their collaboration and problem-solving skills mature. After a number of sprints or releases, however, they plateau; the systemic problems, entrenched dysfunctions, and flawed processes that are not easily solved within the team become increasingly intractable, and the obstacles, detours, and defects pile up on lists but are never addressed or repaired. As the challenges ripple through the enterprise, they bump up against vested interests and legacy procedures that reach into the management and executive level. Their complexity and tenacity become unmanageable. Every process we touch affects dozens of others, with unpredictable results. Without the ability to improve the enterprise value chain, legacy processes, hierarchical organization structure, or the predictive, sequential mind-set of leaders, agile efforts lose their momentum, and gravity prevails.

In agile theory, as noted in the idealized example mentioned previously, scrummasters and agile coaches would guide teams to uncovering the obstacles and challenges that impede agility, leaders would use the big, visible controls and improvement backlogs to prioritize and enable change, and kaizen action would be taken every day to remove roadblocks and empower teams. Much

---

[6]David Mann, *Creating a Lean Culture: Tools to Sustain Lean Conversions*, Second Edition (New York: Taylor & Francis Group, 2010), p. 5.

of the agile literature recommends that these things happen but doesn't delve into the details of creating an agile leadership structure to ensure that they do. Again, from David Mann:

> *Without a lean management system in place to support the new arrangements, people are left to rely on their old tricks for fooling the system, using familiar workarounds to get themselves out of trouble. It's a path that leads swiftly away from a successful conversion. The promising lean system becomes one more sad entry in the roster of failed change projects.*[7]

This is where the role of agile consultant becomes arduous. It's often great fun to work with teams on a grassroots agile adoption, as they learn new, powerful techniques and gain enthusiasm and confidence. As the visual controls and agile practices start to reveal difficult, politically charged obstructions, and the team looks to the scrummaster and agile advisor to help them clear their path, engagements swiftly shift from fun to funk. Complex structures, systems, and tools; intransigent and self-focused leaders; habits of evasion, avoidance, and blame—agile consultants must now bang their heads against all of these, and find a path through. If we expect to evolve the enterprise to agility, we'll need to guide the organization through the fractious, controversial, and unyielding dysfunctions they've been avoiding for years. We'll have to leave in our wake a robust agile leadership culture, not just a set of practices and charts.

This leads us to another paradox. The Agile Manifesto reminds us to value "individuals and interactions over processes and tools," yet lean theory tells us that process focus is the pillar of lean management. To square that circle, remember that the lean processes referenced are those very practices that we've been instilling in our agile teams, namely, visual controls, accountability meetings, and kaizen reflection and action on obstacles, wait-states, and other forms of waste. These processes are miles away from the multistep, impersonal swim-lane processes that have evolved over time in many organizations, based on the theory that if you document every possible step of a process even an unskilled worker with minimal oversight can walk through the steps and produce a result. This is called the "so simple a monkey can do it" theory of process management, and, of course, it produces the result intended: unthinking, uncritical and mind-numbingly repetitive activities suited for monkeys but not for creative, intelligent humans. Managers in these sort of process-driven organizations "manage by exception," meaning that every error or missed expectation results in a reprimand to the team or individual, a heaping on of additional controls, or a public shaming for the team and manager that "missed their numbers."

When agilists talk about creating a lean or agile leadership structure that focuses on process, we mean the exact opposite. Our practices, like the backlog, the stand-up, and the retrospective, are the catalyst for collaboration,

---

[7] Ibid. at 16.

analysis, and action, not blaming and shaming. The real-time focus on assessing the problems uncovered by agile methods, discussing them with openness and honesty, and solving them with courage, discipline, and urgency differentiates our style of process management. This kaizen process doesn't violate the spirit of the Manifesto; it embodies it.

It also doesn't happen automatically, and this is where many agile advisors lose the plot. In order to evolve to agility, the enterprise must embrace the challenge of discarding what's broken and searching for new solutions. The development of an agile leadership culture that enforces improvement action, rather than mere list-shuffling, requires agile consultants to engage, and change behavior, across the enterprise. That takes many agile coaches and scrummasters out of their comfort zone, if not out of their level of competence. This is not a knock on anyone; engaging at the management and executive level requires a completely different skill set than guiding agile practices. Successful managers and executives have learned a set of beliefs and behaviors that have produced results and led them to their positions. The disruptive force of agility now requires them to modify, or even extinguish, the successful techniques of the past. This is a tough pill to swallow, and an even tougher one for the agile consultant to administer.

I don't think anyone who has worked for a traditional corporate enterprise would argue that their enterprise's management systems are lean or agile. Management decisions are made based on obscure reports, which often travel through multiple layers of the hierarchy before landing on the desk of the decision maker. These reports are often contradictory, as department managers massage their numbers to give the best impression. Meetings often devolve into either endless debates about which numbers are accurate or rote recitations of fictional outcomes that afford no questions or analysis. The rearview focus means that the problems addressed either have already been fixed by workarounds on the ground or have been repeatedly exposed in meetings spanning multiple years but have never inspired any action. Critically, from an agile perspective, these meetings are usually closed and exclusive, and both the results reported and the actions promised are often invisible to the rest of the organization.

One of the myths about agility is that it's just a disguise for an undisciplined work environment, in which teams make it up as they go along, with no planning, tracking, or accountability, and then leave behind an unsupportable mess. While anyone who has worked in a well-functioning agile organization knows this is nonsense, we must also acknowledge that the potential for this outcome is there. Every agile coach has encountered teams that believe that agility is an excuse for shedding discipline and resorting to "cowboy coding." We've all encountered managers in whom the report-driven, management-by-exception mind-set taught in their MBA programs are so familiar and comfortable that the idea of relying on visual controls scattered around the workplace, and on self-managed teams that make their own decisions, seems risky and unworkable. To delivery teams, discipline, even in an agile context, can feel like a brake on creativity. To managers, agile leadership looks like "the inmates running the asylum." Our primary task, as we take on the evolution to agility, is to reorient both groups to the real meaning and methods of agility. Our second task is to help them evolve to both a disciplined production process (like scrum) to deliver the product and an adaptive leadership culture to ensure that delivery processes are optimized, monitored, improved, and, most important, responsive.

To be clear, I'm not recommending that we replace one hierarchical, top-down management structure with another, "more agile" one. Agility requires adaptive leadership, not top-down management. Teams are self-managed, with the daily allocation, prioritization, and production work of traditional line managers now entrusted to teams, their scrummasters, and product owners. My thesis is simple: kaizen-style continuous improvement doesn't happen in a vacuum, and, at the enterprise level, simply leaving improvement to each individual team replaces hierarchical, process-bound management with a different type of dysfunction, that of suboptimization. Each team optimizes for its own specific needs, whether by project, function, product, or client, with no connecting thread between these local optimizations. Without some form of overarching agile leadership structure, the enterprise is at risk of atomizing into an agglomeration of independent units, each of whose optimizations contradict or even impede their colleagues' ability to deliver. Suboptimization, or local "centers of excellence," whose reforms are not guided by a vision for enterprise improvement, can be as disruptive to enterprise unity as the old, secretive, and hierarchical styles from which we're trying to evolve.

Agile Scaling Frameworks

With all of this said, what are the practical, on-the-ground actions that agile consultants can take to guide the enterprise to their own optimized version of agility? In summary, we need to create agile teams and visual controls, as we've discussed previously, and to encourage an agile leadership culture that ensures that those controls translate into quick exposure of issues, rapid and collaborative analysis, and immediate action to eliminate root causes, not just work around roadblocks. In-sprint burndown charts, for example, enable teams to spot production problems during the actual delivery cycle, not afterward, when the faulty product or missed deadline has already occurred. Retrospectives enable us to immediately apply the learnings of the iteration just completed, while they are fresh and their pain is still apparent, rather than waiting for eons while reports are generated, massaged, reviewed, analyzed, and then, in too many cases, ignored.

The works of Cohn, Adkins, and many others have documented the roles and responsibilities of scrummasters and product owners. In short, the scrummaster is there to train, guide, and help the team to apply the agile processes properly, and to help them deal with roadblocks and impediments that might put their commitments at risk. The product owner represents the interests of the ultimate consumer of the product, with the authority to guide the delivery team in building and prioritizing the backlog, to respond to changes and communicate their implications to the client, and to help teams make decisions about the features and functions required to satisfy the client's expectations. Here, we'll address their place in an agile leadership culture, and emphasize why their *actions*, rather than merely their roles, define the ability to extend agility across the enterprise. We'll see how the command-driven management style of the 20th century can evolve into an adaptive leadership style that suits agility and responsiveness.

As agility has progressed, the focus has shifted from team practices to enterprise scalability. When organizations first experimented with agility, scrum became the most popular agile framework. Similarly, Dean Leffingwell's Scaled Agile Framework has become the de facto standard in enterprise-level agile scaling. As illustrated in Figure 9-1, SAFe offers a structured, disciplined approach to scaling agility that defines roles and processes for four levels of the enterprise: the portfolio, value stream, program, and team levels. The diagram looks complicated, but, when decomposed, it presents a clear mechanism for solving some of the problems of scaling, such as misaligned strategies and dependencies, unsynchronized schedules, and the coordination of multiple, independent backlogs. Firms like Lego, Intel, and Accenture have applied SAFe to their agile efforts with great success.[8]

---

[8]See their case studies, and many more, at www.scaledagileframework.com/case-studies/.

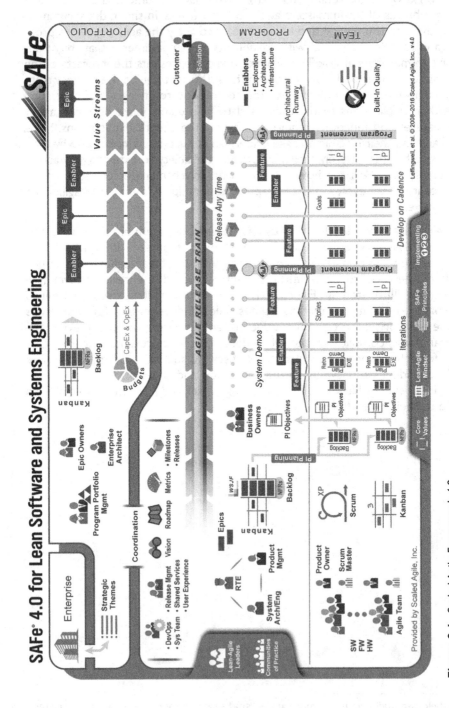

Figure 9-1. Scaled Agile Framework 4.0

At the Portfolio level, SAFe describes a process that is triggered by the strategic decisions made by enterprise leadership. As in most organizations, strategic themes are then refined into a portfolio of programs designed to achieve the strategic objectives. Epic Owners and Enterprise Architects collaborate, based on their budgets and commitments, to create a portfolio backlog that then drives the program and team backlogs at the next levels. At the value stream level, firms organize their delivery of value into Agile Release Trains, to coordinate large sets of programs and deliverables into a synchronized and integrated stream of delivery. Enterprise roadmaps, metrics, release management, and DevOps are managed at this level. Program-level participants, like the release train engineer, the system architect, and product management, focus on the features of the product, the epic-level components of that feature, and the synchronization of the architecture and the release schedule, while the teams perform the familiar scrum activities of iterating through the sprints to actually develop, build, test, and integrate the products that realize the strategic objectives set forth at the portfolio level.

SAFe has a large community of proponents and practitioners, and has been endorsed by many of the leading agile tool companies, like Rally and VersionOne. It's easy to see why this framework is so appealing. It shows enterprises how to take their successes in agile at the team level and scale them to fit the strategic goals and initiatives that executives care about. It presents a coordinated, synchronized, and disciplined approach that sets out clear roles, responsibilities, and time frames so that teams are not suboptimizing, improvising, or floundering. For executives who are accustomed to predictable, organized delivery, led by strategic decisions made at the leadership level, it offers an agile alternative that is comparable to existing portfolio-program-project hierarchies, and can correlate to the predictive models they're used to.

For critics, that's the rub. Many agile experts, including signatories of the Agile Manifesto, like Ron Jeffries[9] and Ken Schwaber,[10] have published critical reviews of the method. Most of the criticism revolves around a few ideas; that SAFe is not really agile because it imposes a top-down line-of-command structure, that its very structure and discipline make it less adaptable and agile, and that it assumes that big, portfolio-level programs should be tackled at all, versus breaking them down further and allowing teams to self-manage their division of work. I won't try to adjudicate these questions here; I recommend especially Ron Jeffries article, as it presents a fair-minded appraisal of the good and bad elements of SAFe from his perspective. For a laugh, check out Mike Cohn's lampoon of agile scaling frameworks, The LAFABLE (Large Agile Framework Appropriate for Big, Lumbering Enterprises) process.[11] As we've noted, this

---

[9]http://ronjeffries.com/xprog/articles/safe-good-but-not-good-enough/.
[10]https://kenschwaber.wordpress.com/2013/08/06/unsafe-at-any-speed/.
[11]www.mountaingoatsoftware.com/blog/introducing-the-lafable-process-for-scaling-agile.

book is not intended as a tutorial to agile techniques, so I'll refer you to the deep training material on the SAFe site,[12] or, if you're so inclined, to the certification opportunities available there as well.

DAD[13] is another structured enterprise-scale framework. Intentionally IT focused, and promoted as more of a "process decision framework," DAD is less prescriptive and hierarchical than SAFe, and is agnostic about the team-level practices applied. Billing itself as a hybrid model, DAD advocates using different methods, from scrum to kanban, and from Lean Software Development to XP, to create the perfect mix for the situation. Scott Ambler, the force behind DAD, describes it as risk-focused, goal-driven and enterprise aware. DAD has gained some traction in the agile community, but has not achieved the acceptance of SAFe.

Craig Larman and Bas Vodde[14] have made the most explicit connection between agility and lean concepts. Focusing on the lean concepts introduced at Toyota, and the lean manufacturing ideas that sparked Japan's rise as a quality leader, they bring us back to first principles in our agile thinking. They remind us that lean and agile are about different ways of thinking, not just different practices and behaviors. By reminding agilists that lean techniques are really intended to encourage us to apply systems thinking to the problems we encounter, and to learn a new, lean mind-set, they've developed a process for scaling agility that remains true to lean principles and doesn't support predictive, framework-focused recipes for agility. The ideas they express in the book have been compiled into a scaling process they call LeSS. Larman and Vodde emphasize that LeSS is a scaled-up version of regular, one-team scrum, and doesn't require lots of new processes or structures. Rather, LeSS recommends that all teams in an enterprise are working in a common sprint to deliver a common shippable product. LeSS adds a few more ceremonies—for example, breaking sprint planning into an enterprise-level "big room" session in which teams self-organize the entire product backlog—and a separate sprint planning session for each team. More than practices, LeSS concentrates on applying the principles of lean mind-set, such as systems thinking, transparency, continuous improvement, and a whole-product focus. For those agilists who frown on the highly structured and somewhat hierarchical concepts behind SAFe and DAD, Larman and Vodde's ideas are closer to the "Scrum of Scrums" concepts promoted by Cohn and Schwaber.

The Spotify scaling example,[15] the result of a long-term, experimental journey at the company, has become a model for scaling without an overarching

---

[12]www.scaledagileframework.com/guidance/.
[13]www.disciplinedagiledelivery.com/introduction-to-dad/.
[14]Craig Larman and Bas Vodde, *Scaling Lean and Agile Development: Thinking and Organizational Tools for Large-Scale Scrum* (Boston: Pearson, 2009).
[15]https://labs.spotify.com/2014/03/27/spotify-engineering-culture-part-1/.

framework, based instead on clear definitions of principles, roles, and alignment strategies. By defining a unique set of roles and principles, Spotify has created an agile culture that addresses many of the difficulties of enterprise-level agility. Spotify has created new definitions of teams and their collaborative roles, and defined the interaction between leadership and those team structures in thoughtful and imaginative ways. Organizationally, Spotify has modified the typical scrum team and instead created agile squads, with the ability to select their own methods and practices rather than mandating all-scrum or all-kanban, for example. Squads, once they've demonstrated that they've grasped the agile mind-set and can self-organize, can adopt or reject any of the typical ceremonies of scrum or XP. For example, some do daily stand-ups, some don't. They focus on principles rather than practices: autonomy, alignment with company mission, high motivation, and community trust building are some guiding ideas. Each squad is focused on a particular feature or function of the Spotify platform, like search or playlists, and so can build expertise in their area.

The next unit of collaboration at Spotify is the tribe, a collection of squads with a similar mission. Tribes periodically gather to discuss and minimize dependencies, and to ensure that all squads are working toward the same mission. Most collaboration sessions are impromptu and situational, rather than enforced on a specific schedule.

To keep team members connected with their discipline, a capability that is often compromised when functional silos are replaced by cross-functional teams, Spotify introduced chapters and guilds. Chapters are cross-team groups of those within the same discipline, such as coders or testers, who meet regularly and ensure that all are up to date on the latest techniques, that learnings are shared, and that nobody is reinventing solutions that already exist. A guild is a less formal and more inclusive group. A testing guild, for example, may include a wide collection of testers, but might also include coders who want to better understand testing or contribute to guild knowledge.

This is, of course, a brief fly-by of the concepts developed at Spotify. To dig more deeply into this model, access the resources cited.[16] The cited references go much deeper into the challenges of autonomy versus authority and the technical elements of this model, than I can include here.

My personal preference is toward the less prescriptive, less hierarchical models, like the Spotify or "scrum-of-scrums" approach. The prescriptive models, most notably SAFe, are easier to sell to command-based organizations, as they offer the perception of predictability and control, and seem like a one-stop solution to the enterprise scaling problem. In exchange for that corporate comfort level, however, I believe enterprises sacrifice some of the core

---

[16]https://ucvox.files.wordpress.com/2012/11/113617905-scaling-agile-spotify-11.pdf; Henrik Kniberg's "Crisp's Blog" http://blog.crisp.se/ is a great resource for keeping up with developments at Spotify and other enterprises using this model.

concepts of lean and agile. In high-structure models like SAFe, programs are defined at a high level and "roll downhill" to the teams, which start to resemble, in my view, an agile assembly line of developers working to spec, with less autonomy and ownership of the outcomes they produce. Tightly defined release trains can drive teams to imposed deadlines and arbitrary time boxes, and budgets created at the portfolio level resemble, to me, arbitrary estimates defined before the understanding of the requirements are known and understood. These models constrain the autonomy and creativity of the teams, and fail to acknowledge some of the hard-won lessons of agility, namely, that hierarchical and predictive program management doesn't work, and that innovation occurs closest to the work.

In the Spotify model, principles, not practices, rule. Through the creative use of organizational structure, and enterprise acceptance and reinforcement of a few core principles, squads, tribes, chapters, and guilds retain their autonomy and collaborate to define their own methods of solving problems and delivering solutions. This model is necessarily evolutionary, as teams gain maturity in self-organization and collaboration. It's also a more difficult sell to traditional hierarchical enterprises, as it requires executives to trust that teams will perform successfully and manage themselves to mission-based outcomes. The "high-autonomy, high-alignment" model at Spotify reflects the ideals of lean and agile most accurately, as it enables executives to set enterprise mission, goals, and objectives, and to focus on encouraging motivation and alignment, while allowing teams to organize, innovate, and manage themselves to come up with the best methods and practices to fit the mission and their team culture.

Opinions differ, of course, and I present all of these models so agile consultants can draw their own conclusions. Different organizations, depending on the existing culture, the maturity of teams, the architecture in place, and the company's business niche, will benefit from different scaling approaches. It's obviously easier for a disruptive, innovative startup to embrace a Spotify model than it would be for a large bank or insurance company with dozens of projects in flight at the same time and regulatory compliance issues that require traceability and audibility. The ability and experience to discern the client enterprise's legacy, culture, and marketplace, and recommend the appropriate scaling approach, is a consulting, not a coaching, skill. The further up the ladder we move, and the more we need to change executive mind-set and management styles, the more critical mature consulting and advisory skills become.

Evolving to Agile Leadership

Whether we recommend that enterprises adopt the SAFe framework or the Spotify model, we're making big assumptions about the organization's ability to adapt. SAFe requires managers to embrace disciplined portfolio management, to adopt a kanban approach to that portfolio, to invest in changes in the technical architecture to enable agility, and to migrate to agile metrics and concepts. The Spotify model expects managers to step back from their traditional "how to do it" roles and apply a more hands-off, trust-based, mission-oriented management style, allowing autonomy at the producer level. Whatever enterprise scaling philosophy we apply, we aren't just touching some isolated groups of technicians in a small agile pilot team. We're evolving way beyond the "Agile 101" activities of guiding and coaching individual teams, and instead tackling the entire edifice of management style, philosophy, and organization. We're advising the enterprise on its entire structure, and asking managers and executives to migrate from the ingrained styles they've applied to a completely new set of beliefs and practices. Every experienced agile coach or consultant has seen the challenges and gyrations many teams go through to adapt to agility. Project managers, client representatives, sales teams, operations teams, and developers, testers, and solution designers all initially struggle with their changing roles as agility evolves and they encounter unfamiliar territory. I've said before that agile practices, like scrum, can be taught in a day and start showing results in a few sprints, but that doesn't mean that agile is easy. The deeper you go, the harder it gets, and the evolution to enterprise agility must go broad and deep to generate the results the enterprise expects.

The most important work on agile leadership comes, unsurprisingly, from Jim Highsmith at Thoughtworks. Highsmith's paper on Adaptive Leadership,[17] and his associated talk on this topic,[18] are the most sophisticated representations of the challenges facing the executive and management layer of the enterprise as it transitions to agility. With a hat tip to Mr. Highsmith, I'll outline and interpret some of his key ideas, and then apply the unique perspective of the agile consultant to guide our advisory path at enterprise level.

Let's start at the strategic level. What strategic questions should enterprise leadership contemplate in our increasingly turbulent and disruptive business environment? In the contest between efficiency, the holy grail of 20th-century business, and responsiveness, the mantra of the 21st, where should we focus our strategic intent? Efficiency and low cost are, of course, constant drivers of competitive advantage, but, for many firms, from Google to Amazon and from Gap to Ford, responding to the concerns and desires of the marketplace has become the key differentiator. Those retail stores, from Gap to Uniqlo, that can respond quickly to the trends on the street and keep pace with rapidly changing customer demand, use responsiveness as *the* key attribute of success. Internet-based businesses respond daily with new features, and quickly dispose of the ones that don't work. Responsiveness is the key, and simply creating a few agile teams in IT can't achieve that; only enterprise agility can.

---

[17]https://assets.thoughtworks.com/articles/adaptive-leadership-accelerating-enterprise-agility-jim-highsmith-thoughtworks.pdf.
[18]https://youtu.be/EEj6zVipqq0.

Every business leader should be considering the benefits that responsiveness can bestow in his particular marketplace. When organizations, from Salesforce[19] to Capital One,[20] recognize and exploit the idea of agility as a business strategy, not just a software process improvement technique, and disrupt entire industries by achieving enterprise agility, competitors and other businesses must take note. As difficult as enterprise transition may be, the benefits of applying an agile mind-set to the entire business are manifest. The difference between doing agile, following the practices in isolated product development teams, and being agile, enabling the entire organization to respond continuously to changes in market needs and trends, is the foundational idea of enterprise agility. As Highsmith reminds us,

> *Adaptive leadership is the work of energizing, empowering and enabling teams to rapidly and reliably deliver business value by engaging customers and continuously learning and adapting to a continually changing environment.*

Focus on value, rather than on tasks or activities, is a core lean and agile philosophy. Executives and managers who aspire to agility must also make the transition from managing and monitoring activity to measuring, through customer feedback and collaboration, the value delivered. The Triple Constraint, or Iron Triangle, taught in traditional project management programs, consisting of scope, time, and budget, is still important in agile work, but it is viewed as a set of constraints and boundaries, not as the marker of success. All experienced project managers know that projects can deliver on scope, cost, and schedule and still deliver zero value to the customer, especially in these turbulent times. It's a central part of the agile consultant's role to help leaders understand this concept, guide them through the change in mind-set, and persuade them that it's value, not activity, that requires measurement and oversight. Agile consultants often encounter managers who continually refer back to the traditional management style, as in "agile doesn't allow me to estimate like I'm used to" or "agile doesn't fit into my traditional strategic plan process like traditional project management." They are presenting current conditions as if they are ideal, and it's the consultant's job to remind them that these techniques are not working, so we're not contending with a comparison between a perceived ideal and an unsure and unfamiliar future. We must remind them that studies consistently show that half of the features they deliver are not valued or used by customers. We have to educate them on the success rates of agility versus predictive methods, as illustrated by the Standish Group studies cited earlier. When sponsors compare every aspect of agility to their traditional practices, the obvious question is

---

[19]https://developer.salesforce.com/page/Transforming_Your_Organization_to_Agile.
[20]www.capgemini.com/resource-file-access/resource/pdf/capital-one-doing-business-the-digital-way_0.pdf.

"How's that working out for you?.'" Of course, experienced consultants will phrase it diplomatically and with sensitivity, but it's important to remind them that these techniques, though familiar, are ineffective and uncompetitive.

Many executives seek to migrate to agile due to a perception that "we'll get stuff faster." Speed-to-value is, of course, a desired effect of iterative, incremental refinement, but the perception of speedy delivery by the client is equally critical. Many leaders don't realize that most customers would prefer a minimum viable product (MVP) that meets their core needs in 3 months, rather than an omnibus, all-in project that delivers their entire visualized scope in 12 months. They often assume that because the client delivered a 400-page Business Requirement Document (BRD), with field-by-field specifications and validations, they must deliver everything in the BRD exactly as specified. They don't consider the possibility that clients don't need, and frequently don't even want, everything they've requested. Clients often throw everything they've ever dreamed of into the spec because they've been trained to believe that they have one chance only, and that, even if they don't need specific features now, they better throw them in because there's no "phase 2." Agile consultants need to walk enterprise leadership through this chain of logic explicitly, so they grasp that it's OK, in fact it's required, that we have an MVP conversation with the ultimate customer and help the customer define the core problems the enterprise is hoping to solve, and the core features that will achieve that goal. Both the sponsoring executives and their customers require a transition to an agile mind-set, and only the agile consultant and her agile colleagues can guide them there.

In the evolution to agile, many consultants engage with teams that are running an endless race with commitments that exceed the capacity to deliver. Executives encourage sales teams to sell more and more, and then throw those commitments over the wall to already overloaded teams. This cycle of pressure inevitably leads to burnout and despair, which inevitably leads to poor quality, since something's got to give. The agile terminology for this is technical debt, meaning we'll hack though some parts of the product with less-than-craftsman-like code, with the false idea that we'll come back around later to repair the damage, or, in agile language, to refactor the code to repay the technical debt. Of course, in these pressure environments, day 2 never comes and product quality starts to impact the customer, creating an endless cycle of support, revision, repair, and patch. The lack of connection between commitment and capacity is a common dysfunction in many enterprises, and is a large impediment for agile evolution. Quality declines, technical debt multiplies, and teams are detoured from their goals to support and maintain poor-quality products, leading to more pressure to deliver. As Highsmith notes, only management can solve this problem, and again it requires a mind-set change. One of the techniques I use for making this disconnection between commitment and capacity visible is Big Room Planning, in which every team exposes its portfolio of pending projects and available resources to the entire enterprise, including leadership. When leaders have to make the uncomfortable priority decisions themselves, and are confronted with a quantitative analysis of commitments versus capacity, they often begin to realize the conveyor belt of pain they are inflicting on their teams. Again, from Jim Highsmith:

> *Do less: cut out or cut down projects, cut out overhead that doesn't deliver customer value, cut out or cut down features during release planning, cut out or cut down stories during iteration planning, cut down work-in-process to improve throughput. At the same time, focus on delighting the customer by frequent delivery of value.*

Our goal as agile consultants is to ensure that the client understands the imperative for change, realizes that just because techniques are familiar and comfortable doesn't mean they are adequate, and rises to the challenge of adopting an adaptive mind-set. It's ultimately leadership and culture that will enable agile to stick, or to become unstuck. Agile consultants also need to help the leaders adapt, by assuring them that we're not here to impose anything, that hybrid mixes of traditional, waterfall, scrum and other practices should be introduced if their environment calls for it, and that our goal is to help them inspect their current environment and challenges and adapt to the right mix of agility that addresses their unique situation.

Summary

There are many enterprise-scale agile frameworks available, from SAFe to LeSS, and each has features that can help organizations in their evolution. We've reviewed many of them, and addressed their benefits and drawbacks. Agile consultants must be familiar with these, as our work migrates from team-level coaching to enterprise-level consulting. Ultimately, at the executive level as well as at the team level, achieving agility is a human exercise, and it requires that agile advisors can address the fears, myths, and dislocations that agility brings, and can persuade leaders and teams that the evolution, even with some associated pain, is worth the journey. From Spotify to Thoughtworks, agile advisory shops are looking beyond the "Agile 101" practices and considering the strategic and organization requisites for turning agility into a competitive advantage. To evolve from practice-based coaches to strategic advisors, agile consultants must take the next step beyond scrum or kanban and devise a strategy for persuading and guiding leaders to the adaptive mind-set that truly embodies the agile ideal.

Engaging at Enterprise Level

Agile Strategy

> *Reasonable men adapt themselves to their environment; unreasonable men try to adapt their environment to themselves. Thus all progress is the result of the efforts of unreasonable men.*
>
> —George Bernard Shaw

Early in my consulting career, when I worked for one of the "Big 5" global consulting firms, I was invited to attend a three-day Strategic Planning workshop. Consultants from around the world gathered in a ritzy hotel and worked through a proprietary planning methodology, with the expectation that we'd be selling lots of strategy engagements. The beginning phase of this planning process was titled "Planning to Plan." We were instructed that consultants, upon engaging with a new client, should spend a few weeks doing a cultural analysis, performing individual interviews with key decision makers, assessing the organization's readiness to plan, clarifying the goals for the planning process, selecting a planning team, identifying stakeholders, and then producing a "Planning to Plan Assessment."

In subsequent stages, we were taught to perform an Environmental Scan, a Values Scan, and a Mission Workshop, and use those findings as input to our Strategic Business Model. We were then advised to facilitate the client through a Current State Capabilities Audit and a Future Capabilities Analysis, and then use those learnings to develop a Capabilities Gap Analysis. The Gap Analysis would then be decomposed into a portfolio of Action Initiatives and run through a Risk and Contingency Scenario model. Finally, with all the action plans decomposed into projects and assigned to the appropriate department heads, we'd advise the client through the implementation phase. The leaders of

R. Freedman, *The Agile Consultant*, DOI 10.1007/978-1-4302-6053-0_10

our consulting organization were quite enthusiastic about this methodology, for a couple of reasons. First, it placed us in the "strategic conversation," as my manager repeated like a mantra. Second, every manager gushed, it would be a profit machine, as it would institute a multiyear "relationship" at "strategic-level rates," as we planned, analyzed, implemented, and then started all over again, conceivably for the rest of our lives.

You can tell from my tone, and the quotation marks I used, that I am now a skeptic. At the time, however, I couldn't have been more enthusiastic. I was selected by my firm to engage at the executive level, strategizing my way through the Fortune 500 and making a positive impact on both the client and my firm! What could go wrong?

Then I went out into the world and tried to apply this model. What I quickly discovered was that, for most client firms, it was an exercise in futility. It typically consisted of weeks or months of preparatory activity, "planning to plan" and other discovery efforts, culminating in a leadership-only retreat for a couple of days to hammer out a draft of a Strategic Plan. That plan was then reviewed by stakeholders, the board, and other interested parties such as major stockholders, which then initiated a further round of debate and nego-tiation, as each stakeholder tried to protect its silo from disruption and tilt the field in its direction. After weeks or months of to-and-fro, we produced a com-promise document, often watered down to a thin soup so as not to offend or disrupt. This document was then passed out to managers to implement. Each manager, of course, interpreted the by-now ambiguous directions, and flew off on different paths, with little coordination or collaboration. The leadership team, the author of these plans, went back to the pressing demands of running the business, and provided little oversight or alignment. The enterprise spent tons of money on a set of disjointed initiatives, and delivered a fragmented and ineffective set of results. And then, of course, the consulting firm was waiting in the wings to develop a new and improved version of the Strategic Plan.

I'm not suggesting that strategic planning is useless, or that it can't provide value. I'm also not implying that most firms still do it this way; this sort of planning is an artifact of a set of dead assumptions, and many enterprises have moved toward a leaner, more inclusive, and more iterative model. Remnants of this static style of rigorous strategic management still remain, however, and many firms I've advised still suffer from the "three-year-plan" model. This model assumes that the marketplace will wait for them as they work through their strategy.

It won't. Turbulence in the marketplace invalidates the long-term strategy model, because there is no long term in today's environment. In a few short years, Amazon killed Borders, Apple decimated Blackberry, Google hobbled Yahoo, and Uber upended the taxi business. The assumptions behind tradi-tional strategic planning, that the past was predictive, that markets were sta-ble, that competitive differentiation was lasting, that enterprises could conceal their "secret sauce" and profit on it indefinitely—all of these core strategic ideas are now obsolete. Technology, globalization, instant communication, and universal Internet access are some of the forces that have changed business strategy forever, as we've discussed throughout. Static, exclusive, and long-term strategic planning, like predictive project planning, is no longer relevant.

Instead, firms must evolve to lean, agile strategies in the executive suite, and migrate to an adaptive, change-friendly, and participative planning model. As in project planning, strategy must stop attempting to predict from the past, and instead adapt to the reality of the ever-changing now. In Chapter 2, we reviewed the contrasts between the hierarchical command structures of the postwar period and the autonomous, adaptive, mission-driven enterprises that are arising in the wake of the Internet and technology revolutions. We identified the changes that are forcing organizations to rethink their business models, like rapid technological change, price and product transparency, and digital disruption. It's one thing to identify the challenges of the new, unstable marketplace, and quite another to devise a planning process that can give managers a window into what might be coming, without committing to specu-lative and unrealistic predictions. As agility is increasingly viewed as an enter-prise-level initiative rather than simply a software process improvement, it behooves agilists to consider the ways in which strategic thinking must change to accommodate lean, agile practices and ideas.

Faulty Assumptions in Strategic Planning

When I say that the assumptions of traditional strategic planning are obsolete, which beliefs am I talking about? There are quite a few premises that are no longer valid:

- **Managers know best**: One of the key lessons that lean has taught us is that those closest to producing the actual, customer-facing value are most familiar with their con-straints, struggles, and challenges, and are as likely as senior managers in the executive suite to have practical improve-ment ideas. The exclusivity of the traditional strategic plan-ning model is one of its fatal flaws. Disconnection from the teams in the enterprise, the customers outside, and the reality of the dynamic, disruptive marketplace killed Kodak, and tolls the bell for all those who only face inward.

- **Strategies can be built without input and feedback from the customer**: In the traditional planning model, the executive team members strategize in isolation from their own customers, proceeding under the assumption that the past is predictive, that their read on the mar-ketplace is correct, and that they know better than their own customers what the market values. Rather than getting out of the building and collaborating with customers, traditional strategic planning occurs in an off-site conference room or executive boardroom, with only internal players involved.

- **Strategies can be long term**: As noted previously, the long term gets shorter every year. As new entrants, new technologies, and new business models emerge on a faster cycle, plans become outdated quickly. As we've learned from waterfall software development, by the time the customer has a chance to react to the product, the market has evolved, and the product addresses last year's needs. Adaptability trumps predictability every time. The idea that we can foresee the shape of our marketplace two years or even six months ahead is a fallacy.

- **Experimentation and risk are dangerous and should be avoided**: Traditional strategic planning, especially at old-line firms that believe new ideas will endanger their brand image and reputation, often relies on "brand extension" rather than innovation. Cherry Coke is a brand extension, but Red Bull is an innovation. Cherry Coke may incrementally improve results, appealing to a narrow segment of cherry lovers, but Red Bull creates a whole new category. Innovative companies, like Google and Amazon, aren't afraid to try new ideas, test them in the marketplace, and retain or discard them based on customer reaction. The failure of the Amazon smartphone didn't damage its brand, and the resounding rejection of Google Wave didn't stop Google from learning about its customer's preferences and trying again with Google+. Experimentation and failure, as long as it's not existential, is a learning experience, and learning from prototypes and customer feedback loops turns out to be less dangerous than not venturing at all.

- **It's all about the data**: The image of the 20th-century executive brings to mind a man in a mahogany-lined office, poring over a stack of green-lined computer paper and examining the data from last quarter, or last month. Sales numbers, year-over-year comparisons, competitive analysis, trend lines: these were the driving factors for the man in the gray flannel suit. Data was difficult to obtain, required large investments in computing power, and was thought to hold the key to competitiveness and success. Now data is ubiquitous, much cheaper and easier to get, and instantaneous; the problem becomes separating and analyzing the meaningful data from the dross, in real time. The "big data" problem is too much data, too fast, and too cheap, and competitive advantage is drawn from quickly figuring out which data to act upon. Google and Facebook give away the service to capture the data, and then build their strategies around what they've gleaned. Strategies based on last quarter's data can only address last quarter's problems.

- **Stick to the plan**: In the traditional model of project management, success meant on time, on budget, and within scope. Customer value wasn't part of the equation, and the highest good was building a plan and sticking to it. Variance from the plan was a signal of failure. With the ascent of lean and agile thinking, we now understand that cost and schedule are constraints, but value is the goal. The same is true in strategic planning: those who stick to a plan are likely to be left behind in the value race, as customer needs and desires change. Adapting the plan, delivering minimum viable plans incrementally, getting rapid feedback, and letting that feedback drive your subsequent iterations is the new normal in strategic thinking.

In short, most of the assumptions and beliefs that were handed down from the military strategies of World War II, and became the basis of corporate strategy during the 20th century, are in question in our current business environment. Everything we did to gain efficiency and guide execution in the command-and-control organization is being challenged by the innovation and transparency brought by technology and the Internet. Migrating the dynamism of agility to the static domain of long-term, top-down strategic planning is the next step in enterprise evolution.

Adaptive Strategy

We've identified ideas and assumptions that no longer apply, which begs the obvious question, what does? What works in strategy today, and how is it related to the agility to which we're guiding our clients? When the past is not prologue, and certainly not predictive, looking back on the successes and failures of the past loses its value. The deluge of data, generated in real-time by every transaction and every click, makes the selection and recognition of pertinent information more critical than trend lines and rear-view reports. The hierarchic command structure, with orders flowing down and compliance flowing up, does not result in the best outcomes. Each of these foundational ideas of strategy now must be questioned and adapted, based on the markets we play in and the customers we hope to attract. As in agile software development, strategies emerge, as leadership engages with the marketplace, the customers, the technology, and its own teams.

In Chapter 2, we noted that Alfred P. Sloan, the archetype of 20th-century management, believed companies would die if they didn't "provide procedures for
predicting change." Venture capitalist Maxwell Wessel advises enterprises to
"Predict the Future of Your Business."[1] Wessel counsels businesses to ask three
simple questions, and then, through scenario planning, think about how your
answers to these questions change your markets, create new opportunities, and
render old ideas passé. The questions are simple, but their analysis can reveal
risks and options that smart, innovative enterprises can capitalize on:

- What's changed?
- What business assumptions become irrelevant?
- How could new models take advantage of the change?

Wessel then enumerates some examples of clearly visible changes on the
horizon, and speculates on how their inevitable evolution might present risks
and opportunities for those who look forward with foresight. Machine learning, for example, has obvious implications in the practice of "big data" analysis,
but it also presents the risk of massive dislocation as machines learn to do
the jobs of professionals and other knowledge workers. Current software
can predict the actions of hackers, for example, in order to prevent fraud but
can also predict the likelihood that an individual will become a hacker in the
first place. Everyone from Google to the U.S. Government uses algorithms
to predict our predilection to purchase a product, or to engage in terrorism.
How can enterprises steer their way through these scenarios, positive and
negative, and navigate toward new business models that create value without
unleashing chaos? From technology changes like the Internet of Things and
Smart Cities, to cultural changes like resurging urban density or "the death
of location" due to the ubiquitous grid, wise companies build future vision
into their firms by asking, analyzing, and answering the three simple questions
proposed by Wessel. This is an activity to which agile consultants can add significant value; facilitating planning teams to consider plausible future scenarios,
and their ramifications to the firm, enables agile consultants to migrate up the
chain from practice-focused consulting to strategic value.

Scenario planning, or "strategic foresight," as it's often called in the academic
world, is not new. Back in 1967, Royal Dutch Shell began an experiment called
"long-term studies." Ted Newland, a company veteran, describes the inauspi-
cious beginnings of this initiative. "I was placed in a little cubicle on the 18th
floor and told to think about the future, with no real indications of what was
required of me," he reported to Angela Wilkinson and Roland Kupers for
their *Harvard Business Review* article.[2]

---

[1] Maxwell Wessel, "Predict the Future of Your Business," *Harvard Business Review*, https://
hbr.org/2015/04/predict-the-future-of-your-business, April 13, 2015.
[2] Angela Wilkinson and Roland Kupers, "Living in the Futures," *Harvard Business Review*,
https://hbr.org/2013/05/living-in-the-futures; May 2013.

A small team began considering alternative futures, from different oil-price scenarios and their implications to the firm to the analysis of various economic and geopolitical shocks that could potentially impact the marketplace. This approach, according to Newland, helped to prepare the company to survive and prosper through the OPEC (Organization of the Petroleum Exporting Countries) embargoes of the 1970s and the cataclysmic events of the 1980s such as the collapse of the Soviet Union.

It's not only Shell that applies this future-planning practice; according to a 2013 study,[3] scenario planning adds to the innovation capabilities of firms, and helps firms avoid missed opportunities and unrecognized threats. Using interdisciplinary teams that are highly networked within the firm, and in the broader marketplace in which the firm competes, can help "spot signals that are relevant ... explore them, filter out noise ... pursue opportunities ahead of the competition, and recognize early signs of trouble."[4] This sort of strategic thinking, according to the study, helps enterprises achieve some key aims:

- Enhanced capacity to perceive change,

- Enhanced capacity to interpret and respond to change, and

- Enhanced capacity for organizational learning.

In the 2015 version of Bain & Company's annual "Management Tools and Trends" report,[5] the top two findings, agreed upon by 75% of responders, were that the following:

- Our ability to adapt to change is a significant competitive advantage.

- Innovation is more important than cost reduction for long term success.

Bain's definition of Scenario Planning tells us:

> *Scenario Planning allows executives to explore and prepare for several alternative futures. It examines the outcomes a company might expect under a variety of operating strategies and economic conditions. By raising and testing various "what-if" scenarios, managers can brainstorm together and challenge their assumptions in a nonthreatening, hypothetical environment before they decide on a certain course of action.*[6]

---

[3]René Rohrbeck and Jane Oliver, "The Value Contribution of Strategic Foresight: Insights from an Empirical Study of Large European Companies," http://papers.ssrn.com/sol3/papers.cfm?abstract_id=2194787&download=yes, December 30, 2013.
[4]George S. Day and Paul J. H. Schoemaker, "Scanning the Periphery," *Harvard Business Review*, 83(11) (2005).
[5]http://www.bain.com/publications/articles/management-tools-and-trends-2015.aspx.
[6]www.bain.com/Images/BAIN_GUIDE_Management_Tools_2015_executives_guide.pdf.

The advantages of this approach, according to Bain, is that it allows planners to challenge implicit and widely held beliefs, test the impact of key variables, and identify the key levers that can influence the company's future course. The unfortunate news is that only 18% of Bain's survey responders worldwide reported applying scenario planning as a key element of their strategic planning process. Maybe this is why Bain analysts report that the following:

> We see a significant risk in 75% of respondents believing that they have a competitive advantage relative to their peers. Statistically, it doesn't add up. (A more realistic number is probably 25%.) Executives who believe that their companies are more competitive because sales and profits are rising in the midst of a recovery risk making wrong moves due to complacency.

The results of scenario planning, according to these surveys, illustrate its connection to agility. Perceiving, interpreting, and responding to change is at the heart of agile development. The scrum cycle of development is specifically designed to respond to changes in a turbulent business environment; bringing that mentality to strategic planning through scenarios is a proven technique to enhance change readiness and responsiveness. When agile teams develop the solution to a customer problem, they engage in tactical scenario planning, in such conversations as the following: "If we change this, what happens to the rest of the product?" or "What's the impact of moving this feature earlier in the release cycle?" This informal, tactical scenario planning is an implicit element of innovation, as teams think through the implications of various decisions. Evolving this sort of future thinking in the strategic process enables strategic planners to scan and evaluate the world outside their office, visualize the changing landscape, analyze the effects of various plausible future states, and make plans based on where the puck will be, not where it is now or was in the past.

Agile Strategic Thinking

Scenario planning is, of course, just one tool in a toolbox that includes other instruments like benchmarking, customer relationship management, and big data analytics. The tools applied are less important than the mind-set through which we approach strategy. Agile strategic planning accepts the foundation ideas that experimentation and innovation are more meaningful than predictions based on past events, that recognizing and acting on patterns in the data is more helpful than looking at data in the rearview mirror, and that planning and execution are better served by inclusion, participation, and consensus than by top-down edicts from an exclusive team of executives.

Agile or adaptive planning is, of course, inextricably linked to the adaptive leadership we discussed in Chapter 9. For adaptive planning to work, leaders must shed their need for predictive plans and budgets and become accustomed to the uncertainty and mutability of reality. The model of management before the advent of lean was based on executives dictating that certain projects be executed, in a prioritized order, connected to a set of static objectives negotiated behind closed doors and handed down in a long-term plan. Budgets were assigned, completion dates were mandated, and any changes to date, budget, or scope were subject to lengthy negotiation processes, and seen as "deviations."

When strategic planning is adaptive, and the enterprise embraces mutability, everything is a deviation. Scopes, dates, and budgets emerge from the circumstances we encounter by reading the market, reading our performance, reading the customer, and constantly deviating from our plans to create new, reality-based designs. Strategy becomes a series of 3, 6, and 12-month visions, each subject to many variables and open to changes based on the forces of the marketplace and the circumstances of execution. I'll reiterate that this is far beyond the capacity of the practice-oriented coach; the capability to explain, persuade, and guide leaders to this new way of thinking about their business requires mature consultative skills. We must, as agile consultants, be able to persuade reluctant leaders and teams to let go of their comfortable habits of false predictability and ride through the waves of uncertainty and change that are the norm in today's business environment.

An Agile Strategic Framework

Back in 2012, I had a lengthy conversation with Tom Conrad, a member of the founding team at Pandora. We chatted about agile development, and how that approach had influenced strategic planning at Pandora. I've included that full interview[7] at the end of this chapter. Here's a quote from Conrad that outlines Pandora's current style of strategic planning:

> Every 90 to 120 days, we'd build a list of new opportunities. . . . We'd generate a list of maybe 60 different product ideas. . . . Then we passed the list to the engineers who articulated the resources required to deliver, but certainly nothing like a full specification. Then we'd bring all the executives together, hang all the sixty or so ideas on the wall, and I'd give a walkthrough, describe who supported them and what revenue might be tied to them...the CEO, myself, every exec would walk around and vote for the ideas they supported...at the end we'd have about 10 to 15 ideas that were fully supported...we'd hand off 10 or 15 initiatives to the engineering team and let them run with them for 90 days, and at the end of that time we'd go through the process again.

---

[7]www.techrepublic.com/blog/it-consultant/agile-strategic-planning-and-innovation-at-pandora/.

Conrad illustrates a real implementation of some of the ideas I've been outlining here: short time horizons, inclusiveness, minimum viable plans, as opposed to the 152 objectives I've seen some organizations commit to (and never deliver), with the understanding that some of the initiatives might work and many might not, and the commitment to revisit the whole process on a quarterly basis to keep pace with the market reality outside their doors.

Many of these ideas have now migrated into a planning process known as "big-room planning," which, in many agile organizations, has all but supplanted the traditional executive off-site that was the accepted planning model. In both Pandora's process, as described by Conrad, and in the big-room planning sessions that are becoming ubiquitous in agile enterprises, plans and ideas are made visible to the entire organization, priorities are set by consensus rather than edict (although executives still reserve the right to manage the priorities and flow of work), and, critically, a connection is established between commitments and the capacity and capability to deliver.

I want to emphasize this element; many organizations accustomed to traditional planning often generate their portfolio of projects based on wish lists and political bargaining, with no thought to the teams' actual capacity to deliver their dream list of projects. By focusing on the limited list of initiatives that the enterprise can actually deliver, minimum viable plans keep the focus on high-value efforts and avoid the trap of starting many projects and finishing none.

Tom Conrad's description is a rough outline for a big-room planning session, but the idea has evolved and become more consistently applied. These sessions typically include a representative selection of executives, managers, customer-facing experts, technical experts, and other leaders, managers and "do-ers." They often cascade, from the full organization (if that's reasonable based on size) to the individual program teams, and even to the actual delivery teams if their initiatives are broad enough to require a strategic approach. Every enterprise that decides to engage in big-room planning designs its own participation program, with the caveat that we want to avoid exclusivity and make these as participative as is reasonable and productive.

In preparation for big-room planning, executives should understand their priorities and expectations for the planning period but must also come prepared for surprises, adaptation, and negotiation. Managers and their teams should have thought about their real capacity and capability to deliver, and should also have their planned work mapped out and prioritized for the planning period, usually one quarter. It's also critical that teams have thought about their risks, dependencies and resource gaps, as big-room planning is the perfect venue for negotiating and trading for resources and deliverables to ensure that commitments that are made are feasible and properly resourced. Agile consultants should be adept at the planning and execution of big-room planning sessions.

Deep and careful planning is the key to emerging with a reasonable and valuable set of initiatives to which the enterprise can commit.

A typical agenda for a big-room planning session begins with an introduction by a senior leader, setting the stage for expectations from the session, and encouraging the teams to be open and collaborative. For command-oriented organizations evolving to agile, it's important for executives to ensure that there will be no repercussions from conflict or debate, and that the session is reality based, even if commitments have been made. Each delivery team then has a short window, typically five or ten minutes, to present its current plan for the quarter, any new ideas or requests that have emerged this planning period, and any high-level risks or dependencies of which the entire population should be aware. Teams are often encouraged to rank their projects in order of risk, with initiatives that have heavy external dependencies or resource needs listed in red. It's typical, after these introduction presentations, to give the teams an hour or so to update their plans based on what they've heard, as this visibility into their peers' plans can often trigger other questions, concerns or ideas.

The next stage is often called a "marketplace," in which all teams have an opportunity to meet with the other teams attending, to negotiate for resources, ensure that dependencies are considered and can be achieved, and generally to make sure that everyone's plans and needs are synchronized, and that commitments are made to satisfy requirements for deliverables and resources. This session is the core of the exercise; it enables teams, which often work in isolation in large agile enterprises, to collaborate, not just within teams but across the enterprise to ensure that their planned work is feasible and resourced, and that risks are mitigated. It also gives, finally, a holistic view of the organization's overall goals and priorities, both to the executive team and to the actual team members or their representative leadership.

Is this really strategic planning? Where are the long-term visions and objectives? There's a common misconception that objectives, like "Dominate the market in shoelaces" or "double our penetration of the robotic vacuum market" are strategic, when, in fact, these are objectives only and don't address the core elements of a comprehensive strategy. As in chess, saying "I want to win every game" is not a strategy, it's an objective, and it misses the key element of a plan to achieve that ambitious and ambiguous goal. Strategy, in chess or in business, requires us to think about components such as timing, approach, where to compete, what our unique tactical advantages might be, and how we intend to sustain our execution. The beginning chess player won't achieve her winning goals by competing with grandmasters, and the small enterprise won't achieve its strategy by competing in saturated markets dominated by giants (unless they're Tesla). These strategic ideas probably won't emerge from a big-room planning session, although they will inform, and be informed by, its outcomes. There is still a place for executive vision in an agile strategic planning process, but without big-room planning as an input and output of that high-level strategizing, plans risk becoming disconnected from reality, from the market and the customer, and from the teams doing the work. Strategies tend to fail when the enterprise doesn't understand both the holistic strategy and the means and tactics to get there, and are not bought in through participation in their framing.

The agile consultant engaging at the strategic level is undertaking a monumental task, far beyond the practice-based coaching that occurs at the grassroots level. The concepts we've discussed essentially tell the executive team that everything they've learned, and practiced throughout their careers, is wrong. This message is difficult to transmit, and difficult to swallow, especially for hierarchical command organizations that are accustomed to leading from the top and avoiding risk and experimentation. The ability to meet executive teams where they are, to avoid proselytizing and instead persuade through results and data, and to incrementally build the understanding of the benefits of the agile approach, are core competencies of the effective agile advisor. As we succeed in developing agile teams, and they begin to display their successes, the migration to agility across the enterprise becomes an imperative. Agile teams can't survive if the enterprise, through stubborn adherence to outmoded techniques, works against them. No agile coach or consultant can be truly effective in creating an agile enterprise without understanding this strategic and human challenge, and devising strategies to guide the strategic process in an adaptive direction.

Summary

We've looked at the typical strategic planning processes of the 20th century and examined some of the outmoded beliefs that drove that approach. The speed of digital disruption and market change, the changing tastes and requirements of customers, and the visibility of formerly secret information are all drivers of a new approach to strategy. Those organizations that can let go of false ideas of predictability and sustainable advantage, and migrate to adaptive leadership and adaptive planning, are more likely to succeed in our turbulent environment, to innovate, and to foresee market challenges. We've reviewed some approaches to adaptive planning, such as the Pandora model and the big-room planning approach, and reviewed the importance for agile consultants of engaging at the strategic level to ensure that agility at the team level is sustainable.

Interview: Agile Strategic Planning and Innovation at Pandora

Pandora's CTO and VP Tom Conrad describes how the company's agile strategic planning process diverged from the traditional, annual, all-hands product planning session.[8]

I recently had an extended conversation with Tom Conrad, Chief Technology Officer and Executive Vice President of Product at Pandora, the Internet radio pioneer. Tom was a user interface designer for Mac OS at Apple, held posts at Pets.com and Documentum, and was the Technical Director for the You Don't Know Jack line of video games before joining the founding team at Pandora.

My interest in chatting with Tom was not in the "so you're doing agile development" vein; rather, I'm interested in innovative companies that have migrated from agile development to agile strategy, and Pandora is a prime example of this wave of management philosophy. As many organizations have discovered, agile development can help add flexibility and responsiveness to their development cycle, but these improvements only go so far when the rest of the organization has not evolved to a more agile approach.

Tom began our conversation by poking a hole in one of the foundation ideas of the IT revolution of the past few decades: the suggestion that the rapid changes we've seen have been due mostly to rapid technological advance. He said:

> *If you'd asked me during the first 12 years of my career, what were the biggest innovations, I wouldn't have said laptops, or the Internet, I definitely would have said that the massive changes in the way that we write software was the single most disruptive thing I'd seen to that point.*

This is, in my view, an important insight; as critical as new hardware, software, and connectivity technologies have been to the IT revolution, none of these developments have been as meaningful as the migration to more iterative, collaborative, and change-friendly development techniques. I'm in vehement agreement with Tom on this point; these new development approaches have enabled the rapid, responsive release of products that solve customer and consumer problems, and that have facilitated the evolutionary release cycle we've all become accustomed to, with new iPads and iPhones, new versions of cloud-based software, and new generations of digital cameras and microprocessors every few months. While many of these new capabilities are delivered in hardware, they're based on software, and iterative, incremental evolution focused on the needs of the marketplace has been the real enabling technology of the revolution.

---

[8]Originally published on TechRepublic.com, by Rick Freedman, August 29, 2012. Used by permission.

Tom next reminded me of the restrictions of the "bad old days," even at a company seen as the poster-child of innovation:

> At Apple we couldn't change a single byte without a year-long certification and release cycle. When I was there, that cycle was, pragmatically speaking, closer to two or three years. We did a little better than the automotive industry, in terms of innovating and getting to market quickly, but not much.

Tom and I chatted a bit about how these agile ideas have manifested at Pandora. He started by describing how traditional, multi-year strategic planning would handicap an innovative company like Pandora:

> Mobile systems, new advertising technologies, are all changing at a tremendous pace; we know more about the opportunities there today than we did 90 days ago. 90 days from now the world will be further fleshed out. It's important for us to react to new information. If the iPhone SDK becomes available, and 90 days later the apps store opens, if you're in a multi-year cycle, obviously you've risked missing an opportunity to react to critical new information.

Tom has defined in a brief comment the challenges that today's innovative companies face that Westinghouse or Proctor & Gamble, for example, may not have faced 20 years ago. While innovation and new products have always been an element of strategy for leading companies, the marketplace was significantly more stable and the product cycle much more deliberate and long-term than it is now. Maytag may have had to release new features and functions in its household appliances, but it was unlikely that entire new markets and platforms for their products were opening up and mutating month-by-month.

Tom went on to describe how these new conditions influenced Pandora's innovation cycle:

> Everything we do here has been based on a 90 to 120 day calendar. I can tell you, based on the marketplace reaction to our products, where we might be 90 or 120 days out, but for each month beyond that it gets foggier and foggier. What that allowed us to do is be reactive to new opportunities as they come along. This planning philosophy informs how we perform all the way to the CEO level, and we have great support for this approach from the CEO.

I asked Tom how the strategic planning process at Pandora diverged from the traditional, annual, all-hands session that often ended up with a 100 item project list of initiatives that never got prioritized or acted upon because it was so large and overwhelming.

For six of the years since we've launched, from 2005 to 2011, we used an agile version of the old-school, facilitated off-site approach. Every 90 to 120 days, we'd build a list of new opportunities presented to the business. This was a product-management facilitated process, with the advertising team bringing in ad opportunities that had come along, and the product teams speaking with the voice of the consumer. We'd generate a list of maybe 60 different product ideas. There'd be a single PowerPoint slide for each opportunity with a few bullet points fleshing it out. The only requirement for getting on the list was that there was some stakeholder somewhere in the business that thought we'd be foolish not to pursue that idea in the next 90 days. Then we passed the list to the engineers who articulated the resources required to deliver, but certainly nothing like a full specification. Then we'd bring all the executives together, I'd hang all the sixty or so ideas on the wall, and I'd give a walkthrough, describe who supported them and what revenue might be tied to them. We'd hand out little sticky notes, and everyone would get the same number of votes, and the CEO, myself, every exec would walk around and vote for the ideas they supported. There'd be some horse-trading and some reconfiguration of some ideas, and at the end we'd have about 10 to 15 ideas that were fully supported and the rest with a few votes here and there. So at the end of the process we'd hand off 10 or 15 initiatives to the engineering team and let them run with them for 90 days, and at the end of that time we'd go through the process again.

I think that Tom's description of the original Pandora planning process is instructive for a few reasons. Firstly, it's more agile and iterative than most corporate planning processes I've experienced, and is a great fit with an agile software development approach. The number of projects generated by the process is small enough so that they can be tried and either accepted or rejected based on real-world engineering or market results, rather than on politics and positional jockeying. The cycle is quick enough to frequently consider new developments in the marketplace or the technology. The realities of resource constraints are built in to the process, since under-resourced projects are bound to fail, and so will bubble up to the vision of the executive team at the next session.

The Leadership Commitment

Commanders know the objective; leaders grasp the direction. Commanders dictate; leaders influence. Controllers demand; collaborators facilitate. Controllers micro-manage; collaborators encourage. Managers who embrace the leadership-collaboration model understand their primary role is to set direction, to provide guidance, and to facilitate connecting people and teams

—Jim Highsmith (2000)

All of the agile practices we apply, from scrum and kanban to big-room planning, are just that—practices. They are the result of the incremental discovery, over decades, of challenges with prevailing methods, and of trying different solutions to address those challenges. As we've inched toward what we now call agility, we've tried, and accepted or discarded, many ideas that we thought might alleviate the issues we found with predictive, big, upfront plan techniques. We've codified certain sets of practices, like scrum or XP, often as a set of rules to follow. We've come a long way from the faulty ideas that held us back, like the hubris to think we could predict the future and put a firm fixed price on it. Many enterprises have evolved substantially toward a lean, agile set of methods that, taken together, lead them to believe that they've achieved agility.

© Rick Freedman 2016
R. Freedman, *The Agile Consultant*, DOI 10.1007/978-1-4302-6053-0_11

The application of methods and practices, even for teams that have evolved to agile strategic and big-room planning, is still "doing agile." Our teams and leaders have learned and internalized the techniques and tools of agility, and they are seeing results from their efforts. The enterprise is not truly agile, however, until both the leaders and the ultimate customers have made the transition from "doing agile" to "being agile." Agile theorists, from Mike Cottmyer and Michael Sahota to Jim Highsmith, have addressed this issue of migrating to an agile mind-set across the organization, and thus enabling the enterprise to truly be agile. As with any transition that is about more than just following a set of rules, and requires a change in attitude, behavior, and perspective, it's easier to learn the moves than it is to become adept. We've heard, from second grade on, that we need to learn the rules before we know enough to break them properly. Learning the rules, however, is necessary but not sufficient. To go beyond blindly following rules to the adaptive mind-set required for enterprise agility, executives and clients must abandon traditional ideas and embody a different approach to leadership. Leaders and customers, and the teams that deliver value to them, need to go beyond the "know how" and internalize the "know why." For the agile consultant, the ability to both coach the enterprise in the know-how required to begin the agile journey and then embody and transmit the know-why that enables agility to permeate the enterprise is the ultimate challenge.

Lean Leadership Basics

When thinking about guiding enterprises to agility, it's always my inclination to go back to first principles. In agile, my first principles are based on lean thinking. One of the key elements of lean, which we rarely see addressed in agile discussions, is the idea of "leader-standard work." While I don't believe that all of the lean ideas and processes included in leader-standard work, heavily weighted to a manufacturing climate, are applicable in agile, a basic understanding of the concept can add significant value to our discussion of the leadership role in agility.

Leader-standard work, in a lean manufacturing environment, is designed to solve a number of problems. In many organizations, every time a new executive, manager, or supervisor joins the team, his initial impulse is often to bring a new set of management techniques, new processes, new metrics, new teammates, and a new cultural style. David Mann,[1] whose work is the source of many of these ideas, calls this phenomenon the "new sheriff in town" mentality, and, as anyone who has spent time in a corporate enterprise knows, it can be an extremely disruptive and confounding experience. As an agile consul-

---

[1]David Mann, *Creating a Lean Culture: Tools to Sustain Lean Conversions*, Second Edition (New York: Taylor & Francis Group, 2010).

tant, I hear stories constantly about organizations that were in the midst of an agile transformation, only to be pulled back to waterfall when a "new sheriff" showed up in the executive suite. Thrashing back and forth from traditional to agile practices is common in many companies, as different leaders and different silos either embrace or resist agile methods, and as the difficulties of migrating to agility start to emerge.

Providing a standard set of expectations for leaders helps protect teams, and the organization, from this sort of thrash. When we define the leader's set of responsibilities, from the immediate product owner and scrummaster to the executive suite, we set a baseline of behaviors and attitudes that are applied regardless of personality. One of the known wastes in any process is variability, which can subvert the gains made by lean and agile adoption. When new leaders know that the option of throwing the cards up in the air and starting over is not available, the risk of disruptive variability is diminished.

Leader-standard work also has the advantage of making agile leadership qualities visible. As with our big visible indicators in agile team practices, leader-standard work provides transparency at the executive and management levels. Existing managers who are unwilling or unable to make the transition from predictive, hierarchical styles to adaptive, collaborative styles will be recognized quickly, and can be trained, reassigned, or managed out as required. The whole point of agility is to evolve from a "hope and wish" corporate mentality in which we wait for leaders and teams to "get it", to a transparent, reality-based conversation that enables kaizen and action. The clear expectations of leader-standard work allow executives to make quick decisions about their talent, address them, and avoid the risk of delay and confusion that can result from active or passive resistance.

Leader-standard work is based on a few foundation ideas. The first is that leaders work in a complementary fashion, with the leader at the team level managing execution of each task, the supervisor spot-checking work periodically throughout the day, the value stream manager managing daily accountability and managing resource capacity and issue resolution, and executives reviewing trends, performing Gemba walks (management walkthroughs of the work site), taking ownership of quality produced by the entire value chain, and leading kaizen efforts. The second key idea is that this work is driven by a neatly defined set of processes that drive the daily activities of each leader in the chain, with the intention of developing a set of best practices for leaders to follow.

The language applied in lean manufacturing differs greatly from the agile lexicon, but many of the basic concepts remain. Leader-standard work typically refers to supervisors, value stream managers, and plant managers, while we talk about scrummasters, product owners, and executives. Leader-standard work refers to things like shift changes, Gemba walks, and buzzer-to-buzzer spot-checks, while we use velocity, detours, blockages, and big-room planning sessions in agile leadership practices. Despite the differences in language, lean concepts still apply. We still measure daily progress, but instead of buzzer-to-buzzer meetings we use stand-ups. We still manage progress across the iteration or cycle, but we do it in sprint planning and demo sessions instead of Gemba walks. We still collaborate to improve blockages and inefficiencies, but we do it through retrospectives and scrum-of-scrum sessions, rather than supervisor "tier 2" sessions. For more detail on the fundamentals of leader-standard work refer to Mann.[2]

From Lean to Agile

Lean thinking is the basis for agility, but agile was designed for software development, and has mutated significantly from original lean concepts. While collaboration, customer focus, self-managed teams, and kaizen originate in lean, the Agile Manifesto and Principles originally evolved to correct deficiencies in predictive software development. Enterprises have now discovered that these ideas can go far beyond the software team, but the original principles addressed technical architecture, iterative development, working software, and changing requirements. Many of the artifacts of lean manufacturing don't apply in agile, and agile has simplified lean practices significantly. While "simplicity"—maximizing the work not done—came from lean, a walkthrough of many lean manufacturing enterprises can look anything but simple, with dozens of charts, checklists, sign-ins, and pitch charts scattered around the plant. While the same can be said of scrum rooms and kanban boards, the process focus of lean manufacturing has been replaced by a less prescriptive "inspect and adapt" mind-set, less likely to focus on multiple daily quality and progress spot-checks, and more likely to vary widely in implementation based on local conditions and decisions. Agilists would much rather talk about the expected behaviors and mindsets of executives than about leader-standard work. So where does the twain meet? The opening quote from Jim Highsmith can be applied equally to lean or agile, but the practices required for effective agile leadership differ. Let's take a look at the roles and mindsets expected of different leaders in the agile enterprise, and see how those can be both harmonious and divergent from lean practice.

Every agilist knows that scrummasters and product owners each have defined areas of responsibility, with the scrummaster owning the process of scrum or agile, and the product owner representing the client's interests in developing the product. Undefined in the Scrum Guide or in most other agile literature is the equivalent of leader-standard work. We've looked at various scrum scaling frameworks, some of which, like SAFe (Scaled Agile Framework 4.0), attempt to address the question of leadership standards by prescribing a clear set of roles and responsibilities, from the Portfolio to the Team level. In this

---

[2]Ibid.

scaling strategy, as illustrated in Figure 9-1, roles from Portfolio Manager to Epic Owners at the Portfolio level, through Value Stream Engineers, Solution Architects, and Release Managers at Value Stream level, Release Train Engineers and System Architects at the Program level, and down to the product owner and scrummaster at the Team level, are designated by the framework. As we've discussed, many agilists find this prescriptive model too similar to a corporate hierarchy for their taste.

On the other end of the spectrum, Ken Schwaber[3] describes an organic scaling strategy in which one agile team begets others, which then multiply and scale further, rearranging the product backlogs so that subsets can be assigned to new teams. The original team now becomes an integration scrum team, with the mission of taking responsibility for all the new scrum teams and integrating their efforts into a quality product. New scrummasters report to the original scrummaster, and new product owners report to the first product owner. This becomes a natural hierarchy, in which the original team spawns new teams, new scrummasters, and product owners, and those teams in turn generate additional teams, with responsibility for overall product conformance and quality reaching up the chain. Nowhere in Schwaber's description is any role defined for executives, whom, it is assumed, focus on strategic direction, and on exhibiting the collaborative qualities outlined in Highsmith's quote opening this chapter.

Somewhere on this spectrum lies the appropriate vision for leadership in a particular enterprise. It's the agile consultant's job to help the enterprise determine the suitable model for its unique circumstance. As noted in Chapter 9, SAFe is a great choice for large, complex organizations migrating to agility from a predictive, hierarchical model, while still exercising some control from above, and still performing some predictive budgeting and strategy alignment. Enterprises that are already more focused on egalitarian, participative management, and have experienced some success with grassroots agility, might prefer Schwaber's organic model. In either case, the mind-set and behavior of managers and executives will still need to evolve. Again, to go back to lean principles, let's take a look at the criteria for lean leadership set by James Womack, the original popularizer of lean ideas through his bestselling study of Toyota lean culture[4]:

Lean leaders:

- eagerly embrace the role of problem solver.

- realize that no manager at a higher level can solve a problem at a lower level—problems can only be solved where they live, by those living with them.

---

[3]Ken Schwaber, *The Enterprise and Scrum (Developer Best Practices)*. Redmond, WA: Microsoft Press, 2007.
[4]James P. Womack Daniel T. Jones, and Daniel Roos, *The Machine That Changed the World: The Story of Lean Production* (New York: Free Press, 1990).

- believes that all problem solving requires experimentation.

- understands that no problem is solved forever. The introduction of countermeasures will create new problems at some other point in the organization. The critical, probing mind of the lean manager stays active in the pursuit of perfection.

These overarching principles apply in agile as well as lean. Let's examine them with a bit more focus on agile language and practice.

Eagerly Embrace the Role of Problem Solver

Too often, in my experience, managers and executives play the role of problem creator, rather than problem solver. They drive sales teams to sell more and more, while starving delivery teams of resources. They commit to unrealistic and overly aggressive dates and budgets, forcing teams into "death march" projects that sap morale and disappoint customers. They remain remote from their organization, hiding in mahogany suites on the executive floor with little contact or interaction with the enterprise. As noted in Chapter 2 management resistance and cultural norms are often the key barrier to agile adoption. The traditional, hierarchical style of management we explored in Chapter 2 often leads to counterproductive, adversarial relationships across the enterprise, as individuals jockey for position and hide bad news for fear of reprisal or corporate shunning.

The lean or agile leader displays the opposite of these behaviors. In agile, every bit of bad news is a lesson to learn and an opportunity for improvement. Rewards and incentives are focused on team achievement rather than adherence to discipline and corporate conformance. Executives and managers exist to enable teams to achieve and to remove barriers to that success, not to manage the daily tasks of their teams. Teams self-manage the details of their work, and management creates the environment for them to perform to their highest potential. Leaders address broken processes, lacking skill sets, and ineffective leaders or employees, rather than kicking the can down the road. They manage intake, ensuring that the organization doesn't commit to more than it can reasonably deliver. The concept of service leadership is key in this context. Agile leaders work for the team, not the other way around.

Problems can only be Solved where they Live

This may seem in conflict with the previous statement, but they're actually complementary ideas. There are local problems and global problems within an enterprise. Agile leaders must be problem solvers at the global level, working on the repair of broken corporate processes and norms, and must also have the proper amount of Zen to leave the local problems to the local teams and resist the temptation to jump in and prescribe a cure. We've learned from decades of lean practice that only the local team has the intimate understanding of the sources of their challenges and obstacles. We also know that ownership of those issues is a key component of team dynamics and enablement. I've advised too many teams, disheartened by repeated frustration, that have adopted a posture of "learned helplessness," learning from repeated failed attempts that any ideas they come up with will be shot down or overruled by management. These demoralized teams will simply wait to be told what to do, and how to resolve their concerns, by managers, always staring upward in the hope that some direction will rain down. This learned passivity is a powerful obstacle to team empowerment, and is especially tangible in organizations that have run the cycle of organizational panaceas, only to repeatedly devolve to previous patterns.

While successful agile leaders want to avoid prescription, that doesn't imply disengagement. Leaders can provide the forum for collective problem solving, applying big-room planning sessions and "Gemba walks." The concept of Gemba walks, mentioned earlier, is a central element of lean, and is, I believe, a missing element in many agile transitions. By simply walking around, visiting teams and uncovering their concerns and challenges, executives can project an attitude of caring and concern and encourage teams to let go of the fear of reprisal and blame. They can gently remind team members of their commitment to agility, and provide coaching and direction that improves strategic alignment, without digging down into prescriptive management. MBWA (Management by Walking Around) is an old idea, but it is institutionalized as the Gemba walk in lean organizations, and is an overlooked tool in enterprise agility.

All Problem Solving Requires Experimentation

The enterprise is, by its nature, a conservative entity, utilizing proven methods and processes to achieve a consistent and repeatable result. Typical organizations have two key fears: risk and change. The transition to agility exacerbates both of these concerns. Agilists embrace disruption, while enterprises avoid it. Experimentation and emergent outcomes are key to agility; predictable results drive corporate planning, with experimentation confined to the research and development function. The continual feedback and improvement loop of any kaizen enterprise makes the basic assumption that feedback will result in change; otherwise, what's the point? We also assume that we can speak freely and point out deficiencies and inefficiencies without censure. Many executives forget that the proven methods to which they cling became "tried and true" through decades of trying, and cannot be sacrosanct as markets evolve. Strong agile leaders also recognize that kaizen efforts can never reach their goal, which is perfection. Only consistent experimentation in an open, collaborative environment enables improvement. The hierarchical idea that only constant pressure from the top can motivate workers to achieve has been discredited for years, but it is still the ruling philosophy in many enterprises. Agile leaders must be encouraged to drive fear and reprisal from their mind-set and behavior, and accept the reality that risk and change are essential elements of improvement and innovation.

No Problem is Solved Forever

Agile theorists often talk of enterprises as complex adaptive systems (CAS). According to an MIT paper,[5] "Complex Adaptive Systems are dynamic systems able to adapt in and evolve with a changing environment." In a CAS environment, everything we touch touches something else, and every change spreads across the system, creating unforeseen circumstances that we then need to iteratively adjust. Systems thinking, a core precept of both lean and agile, reminds us that, as with technology, the bug we fix here has the potential to blow up something there. This is one of the reasons that legacy-bound organizations fail; they fall in love with, and, worse, enforce their own history and culture while the world sweeps by at exponential speed. Those who favor stability over change make the fundamental flaw of believing that the universe cares what they want. Complex adaptability requires us to go beyond merely anticipating the implications of the changes and experiments we undertake. It also requires us to acknowledge that we'll be wrong most of the time when we try to foresee unforeseen consequences. Kaizen is eternal and systemic.

The cited MIT paper also notes that "complexity results from the inter-relationship, inter-action and inter-connectivity of the elements within a system and between a system and its environment. This implies that a decision or action by one part within a system will influence all other related parts, but not in any uniform manner." It's this interactive influence that disrupts predictability, and upsets predictive managers. In the predictive corporate world, one of the worst things a manager can do is keep coming back to the same intractable problems. This is perceived as a sign of incompetence and failure, in the traditional view. Agile managers grasp the idea that yesterday's solution will soon become tomorrow's problem, and that challenges, especially in evolving complex enterprises, will circle back around numerous times as circumstances change.

Agile Leadership Responsibilities

The point of this discussion is clarity of roles and responsibilities. Agilists understand the accountabilities that product owners, scrummasters, and teams take on in agile practice, but more ambiguous is the commitment of

---

[5]http://web.mit.edu/esd.83/www/notebook/Complex%20Adaptive%20Systems.pdf.

leaders. To ensure that clarity, I've assembled the following list that lays out, in my view, the actions and behaviors that leaders, from executives to managers and team leads, must assume:

Executives:

- Determine and communicate enterprise strategy.
- Empower and encourage team achievement and ownership.
- Ensure that enterprise-level commitments match capacity and capability to deliver.
- Practice service leadership, understanding that they work for the teams and not vice versa.
- Leave the executive suite to go, see, encourage, and guide.
- Take on the hard challenges of enterprise improvement that create the environment for success.
- Encourage enterprise-level collaboration, and break down silos and barriers.
- Embody the Agile Principles.

Managers:

- Communicate corporate strategy and guide team alignment to strategic objectives.
- Understand their teams' capacity and capability.
- Protect teams from unreasonable demands and expectations.
- Influence executive strategic planning by building a robust feedback loop.
- Create a kaizen atmosphere in which dissent, disagreement, and concerns can be freely discussed and solved.
- Respect the autonomy of their teams while ensuring alignment with enterprise priorities.
- Be a leader and coach rather than a foreman.
- Embody the Agile Principles.

Team leads, including scrummasters and product owners:

- Respect the agile processes: don't succumb to the temptation to change the process rather than addressing the dysfunction.

- At the same time, inspect and adapt both the product and the process through kaizen methods.

- Encourage and sustain evolutionary gains in productivity and quality.

- Fearlessly call out unforced errors and gaps.

- Create a feedback loop to ensure leaders stay connected to customer-level realities.

- Take problems to the team rather than prescribing remedies.

- Encourage team-level collaboration, and break down silos and barriers.

- Embody the Agile Principles.

Of course, these lists are not complete; whole books can be written about the commitments of agile leaders. While not conclusive, agile leaders who exhibit these qualities will have a head start on evolving their organizations to agility, and to transforming themselves and their companies into open, fearless, honest, responsive, and continuously improving enterprises.

Customers Are Leaders Too

After all this discussion about internal leadership, it's important to remember that customers have leadership responsibilities as well. In the customer-centric world of agile, it is customers, and their representatives, the product owners, who determine what we work on, how we prioritize it, and whether or not we've achieved their vision of the product. When we evolve from an internal-facing, product-led strategy to a customer-focused, market-led view, the role of the customer transitions from a passive consumer of new products, created based on internal needs, research, and metrics, to the central figure in the entire enterprise value chain. We move from the push of a marketing-led product cycle to a customer-pull model, offering new versions and features based on feedback from our clients. We shift from an internal clock of product cycles and upgrades to a customer-focused and market-led cadence. "The customer is king" has been a business motto for 100 years, but in the agile world, the customer is more than king; he is collaborator, innovator, product designer, partner, and judge.

Many customers of information technology (IT), whether internal users of enterprise systems or external customers using technology systems or products, have adversarial relationships with their IT providers. Projects or products are late, buggy, unfriendly, and obsolete. IT support and delivery teams talk in technical jargon and don't understand the business's needs. Specifications are thrown over the wall, and are often incomplete and obscure. Expectations are missed, promises aren't kept, tempers are frayed, and mistrust escalates. The daily interactions between delivery teams and customers become tense, fraught, and unproductive, and the pressure mounts with each new defect or miss. The vicious cycle of technical debt leads to increased defects and support, which leads to further pressure and mistrust, and around we go with no exit in sight.

When the enterprise begins the journey to agility, it's not uncommon for the customer to be negatively impacted. Their list of committed fixes, changes, and upgrades are often wildly out of sync with the team's capacity to fulfill, sales teams are out selling more and adding to the pipeline of commitments, and executives are exerting pressure to fill the 200-pound bag of capacity with 500 pounds of work. The mandate to get things done does not change the capacity to deliver, except by forcing teams to sign up for death march projects, further sapping morale and quality. In the end, someone has to transmit the bad news to the customer that commitments previously made, totally out of whack with capacity, will need to be reprioritized, rescoped, and in many cases delayed or dropped. This is not a happy message, on either side of the conversation, which often leads product owners and executives to avoid it, thus exacerbating the vicious cycle even further.

Not a happy picture for anyone. Coaches can train small teams in agile practices all day long, but unless the ultimate customer is engaged in the conversation, and persuaded to adopt an agile mind-set that's ready to accept experimentation and sustainable development, agility will falter and fail. As important as it is to guide teams and leaders to agility, failure to also guide the customer on this path will undermine our efforts. On the positive side, a customer who grasps the advantages of agility, understands that change can mean disruption but can also drive improvement, and is willing to take the journey with us and accept the uncertainty and experimentation that come with agile, is an invaluable partner. These customers can back off the intransigent expectations and relationship tensions and give the team some space to get itself sorted and try the agile approach.

For the agile consultant, the job of helping our sponsor's enterprise bring its customers into the agile fold is decisive. We need to elevate our focus from just the team and its practices, and convince leadership, marketing, and sales teams that their customers are not only at the end of their value streams but also at the beginning, driving their product direction with their needs, desires, and expectations. We need to help them understand the difference between a push system, with its focus on ever-new methods of marketing and promotion, to a pull system, in which the focus is on responding to the market and partnering with the customer to understand their expectations and challenges. We must help sales teams learn to throttle commitments to fit capacity, a difficult chore when their compensation is based on selling more stuff. Finally, we need to convince leaders that the traditional metrics, like sales quotas and advertising impressions, must be combined with disciplined intake processes and customer feedback loops. These systemic organizational adaptations are as important as the agile behaviors of delivery teams, and far more difficult to coach.

It should be clear that, in addition to the grassroots activities we undertake with delivery teams, we must have a parallel top-down effort that persuades and educates. When I take on an agile evolution project, one of the first things I focus on is discovering an internal agile advocate at the executive level. Sometimes it's the sponsor who engaged me, but often the directive comes from further up the leadership chain. Agility has been the subject of much publicity lately, from the *Harvard Business Review* to *Forbes* and *Fortune* magazines, and there often exists a level of curiosity, or even commitment, in the executive ranks. If we're to change the attitudes and perceptions of the ultimate customer, we need to have sponsorship from the top, as all the incentives and metrics we've discussed run against the grain of the message we intend to send. As discussed previously, we first need to help leaders understand and embrace their roles before we can start realigning customer expectations.

How Agile Consultants Encourage Change

In Chapter 1 we discussed the change management techniques recommended by Mike Cohn and John Kotter. From Cohn's ADAPT (Awareness, Desire, Ability, Promotion, Transfer) framework to Kotter's XLR8 principles, there are proven methods for guiding enterprises through major change. In simple terms, we educate and persuade, create awareness of the need to change, develop a sense of urgency through a Big Opportunity or idea, build a supporting coalition or team, and encourage an evolution of values, culture and practices across the enterprise. These theoretical ideas simplify into the techniques that I use when persuading both leaders and customers to work in a different way.

I'm a believer in social proof, the idea that it's easier to persuade people and organizations to change when they see others successfully adapt. I therefore am an advocate of both evidence, like the Standish Group agile success metrics we saw in Chapter 2, and anecdote, like the voluminous case studies available on the Web. I often start my engagements by compiling a bibliography of articles and studies that demonstrate the potential benefits of agility. While we can't make anyone read a study, we can provide them for those who might want to dig deeper. I've developed many training programs, from "Agile Basics" for teams and product owners to "Agile for Executives" to "Agile for Customers," and I've presented them worldwide to both sponsors and their clients. I've invited previous clients to recount their journeys, triumphs, and struggles, to help prepare my new client for the road ahead. All of these methods of social proof can be helpful with both sponsors and customers, to allay their fears and truthfully prepare them for the challenge of wholesale transition.

Visibility is a key agile value, and also a potent change enabler. I've observed that it often takes beginning scrum teams a few months to grasp the basic practices and put them in motion, but, once my initial teams start to experience success and generate consistent velocity and quality, I want to make them visible to both the leaders of the enterprise and its customers. I find that seeing a well-functioning team in the act of planning a sprint, refining a backlog, or presenting a demonstration can go a long way toward getting all parties on board with the migration. It's important to wait until these practices are running well; we don't want to expose too many warts in front of our audience. However, some challenges should be visible, such as the reality of the team's capacity and the technical challenges that are holding the team back. "Waiting for customer" is an area of blockage that may be beneficial for the end client to see, and "stuck due to technical issues" might motivate leaders to put some urgency into those eternal system fixes.

In our discussion about Exploration and Engagement, in Chapter 4, we emphasized the importance of knowing your sponsor and her organization. I begin engagements by seeking out the advocates of agility, from the executive to the business analyst, so that I know where the resisters and supporters might lie. Consultants with the persuasive and personal skills to build a supporting coalition of agile believers, to help guide and encourage the enterprise in its evolution, are more likely to lead a successful transition. When the team gets into the inevitable trouble, the teammate who encourages them to push on, who picks up the agile ideas and reinforces them with the team, is invaluable. Likewise at the executive level, the leader who understands that organizational transition is hard, and can send a positive message through the enterprise to keep the momentum going and allay fears, is an essential partner for the agile advisor.

The same is true on the customer side. The agile consultant who can educate the client, understand the history of the relationship, their concerns and disappointments, and can paint a compelling picture of benefits to come, has a greater chance of alleviating some of the pressure and mistrust that has built up over years. When agility starts to show some results that benefit the customer, it amplifies our message and begins to reform the adversarial relationship, slowly and over time, into one of enhanced trust and collaboration.

Summary

The key, of course, to both executive and customer acceptance and participation in agility is successful results. Once we persuade sponsors and clients to trust us to make things better, we must do so. We must provide the metrics and visibility that illustrate our successes. We must truly collaborate, and hear the sponsor and customer when they are faced with challenges, or have improvement ideas. We must, as always, demonstrate our understanding that transition is difficult, and that there will be many bumps and detours before we reach agility, and that kaizen is eternal. We're now on the hook to deliver the results that customers value and that our sponsors expect. Our skills as facilitators, persuaders, educators, advisors, guides, and mentors will be tested to their limits. Finally, we must embody the agile principles and model the behaviors so that we train, coach, and mentor through our own behaviors rather than simply with words and theories.

The Agile Enterprise

As an agile consultant, it's gratifying to see the evolution within teams under your guidance. Delivery teams begin to communicate and collaborate. Managers make the transition from foremen to leaders. Executives begin to understand that enablement, encouragement, and service leadership is more effective, and more human, than mere power. The enterprise begins to untangle some of its faulty processes and legacy dysfunctions, and begins to accept the simplicity and honesty of agility. The agile advisor who guides the enterprise to the edge of substantial improvement in process, culture, and leadership can rightfully have pride in that accomplishment.

It's great to celebrate, but don't revel in your success for too long. The evolution to a real-time, responsive, and agile enterprise is not complete. With the threats of digital disruption and changing technology always present, agile advisors will have to dive even deeper to get to that ultimate goal. We'll have to develop strategies to enable our sponsors to examine and improve their business processes, their customer relationships, and their core business model. We'll need to advise them on the technical architectural enhancements they may need to make, in order to provide a firm foundation for the responsive enterprise. They may have to change the way they store, disseminate, and analyze the reams of data that are thrown off by every transaction in the digital marketplace. Their "innovation engine" may be broken, or they may lack one altogether. Marketing, sales, manufacturing, distribution, customer interaction—all may need to evolve significantly for the enterprise to benefit

© Rick Freedman 2016
R. Freedman, *The Agile Consultant*, DOI 10.1007/978-1-4302-6053-0_12

from the agile ideas we've been championing. From the business model to the technical architecture to the way products are marketed, delivered, and supported, to reach true enterprise-level agility, the agile consultant must inspire the organization to push further, past team practices, past lean principles, and past executive behavior change, to an enterprise-wide transformation that touches every element of the business model.

Not every organization wants or needs to go this route. Many of our clients will be happy when they reach agility in their product development function, or when their executives migrate from hierarchy to collaboration. Many will be thrilled to do agile, and lack the desire or will to go through the disruption required to be agile. That's fine; as consultants, we are servant leaders ourselves, and must put aside our personal preferences and desires in order to help the enterprise achieve its goals, not ours. Still, when agile coaches and consultants gather, I often hear the "one that got away" stories, of enterprises that made significant strides, which could have gained much more but decided that they had reached their limit of tolerance or aspiration. These rueful conversations of what might have been may be inherent in the consultant's role, but they leave a tinge of regret all the same. "If only . . ." we consultants lament, trailing off with knowing looks.

I won't extol the benefits of agility, or highlight the risks of the disruptive economy, any longer. Let's focus instead on the destination of responsiveness and adaptability, and the traits and behaviors the enterprise needs to adopt, to evolve toward agility across the entire organization.

Agility = Responsiveness

According to a report by Tata Consulting Services (TCS),[1] the responsive enterprise can "shift rapidly to where customers want it to go next—the next buying experience they want, the new innovations they desire, or the new way they want to do business with your firm altogether." My favorite definition, however, comes from Responsive.org, a member-run organization that believes the following[2]:

> *Responsive Organizations are built to learn and respond rapidly through the open flow of information; encouraging experimentation and learning on rapid cycles; and organizing as a network of employees, customers, and partners motivated by shared purpose.*

---

[1]www.tcs.com/consulting/related-insights/Pages/Responsive-Enterprise-Operations-Evolution.aspx.
[2]www.responsive.org/.

The consistency with agile and lean principles is clear. We exchange information quickly and openly, without regard to rank or title; we "fail fast" in order to learn what works and what the marketplace values; we work as a collaborative network, including our customers, teammates, and partners, to deliver the most value to the ultimate consumer as quickly as is feasible.

Responsive.org has, through experimentation, developed a simple set of sliders that help enterprises diagnose their own level of responsiveness.

The elements of responsiveness versus efficiency depicted in Figure 12-1 should be familiar by now. The beauty of this scale is that it simplifies the components of responsiveness to a few traits, and allows the enterprise to grade itself, rather than having some outside consultant come in and make a pronouncement. Clearly organizations that are still following the Industrial Revolution model, in which predictive planning, economies of scale, and risk avoidance drive the business, will, if they are truthful, place themselves on the left, efficiency-focused end of the spectrum, while enterprises that have adopted an agile model across the organization will trend toward the responsive side.

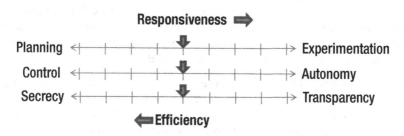

Figure 12-1. The Responsiveness scale (Source: Responsive.org)

As an agile consultant, I'd use this scale to lead a facilitated session with the leadership of the organization, use a survey to gauge the opinions of the entire enterprise, and then compare the two. This simple consulting exercise will yield invaluable information. Is leadership deluding itself about their level of responsiveness, or are their views in concert with those of their employees? Do certain teams perceive different levels of responsiveness? Do agile teams score their company differently than waterfall teams? The discussions driven by this dialog may be fraught, especially if leaders are defensive and hierarchical, but they are important to the consultant who must devise a plan for evolution.

Zara: A Case Study on Responsiveness

To illustrate the elements of responsiveness, let's look at Zara, a "fast fashion" company that has upended its market with a responsive model. Highlighted in Responsive.org's video "The Responsive Organization,"[3] Zara focuses on one of the most competitive niches in the world, and one in which fashions and trends change and mutate daily. If a pop star wears a certain kind of leggings, all other leggings can go out of style in a week. I'm writing this chapter during the week that we learned of the death of pop star Prince, and I have no doubt that purple will be the color of the season, at least for a while. The typical fashion retailer has a six- to ten-month turnaround, from the catwalk or the street to the design, fabrication, and delivery of apparel to stores. By that time, sadly, the nostalgia and celebration of Prince will be over, and purple apparel will likely be overexposed and out of style.

Zara, on the other hand, has the unheard of turnaround of weeks, rather than months, to go through the entire cycle. As outlined in *The New York Times*,[4] Zara uses a combination of human interaction, technology, empowered teams of designers, and a sleek supply chain to deliver its designs to a worldwide network of stores. The human interaction comes in the form of store managers who are trained to initiate conversations with their customers about why they select certain items of apparel, and why they return or shun others. This information is widely and quickly communicated to autonomous teams of designers, empowered to change style elements, like zippers and lapels, as well as colors, and order them into production and delivery.

Although some proportion of its garments are made in typical low-cost countries like Bangladesh and India, all of its design, and most of its manufacturing, is done in Europe or nearby Turkey. This a critical element in its speed to market; rather than shipping designs to China and waiting months for the turnaround, Zara can design, ship, and test-market a limited number of items to its many stores and see how customers react. Only when its feedback loop confirms that each item resonates with customers does Zara move to bigger batches.

The trendier the garment, the closer to its Spanish headquarters it's produced. Due to its agility and customer intimacy, Zara can ship out the right number of garments to fit the demand, thus avoiding the "specials" and sales that most retailers must resort to to get rid of unwanted merchandise. Because of its fast turnover, and its cheap prices, customers buy on impulse, thus challenging the high-price, high-street brands like Gucci and Prada. Masoud Golsorkhi, the editor of *Tank*, a London magazine about culture and fashion, says, "With

[3] https://youtu.be/jnmr8zvomE8?list=PLFPUGjQjckXFlCxcqpeWjbFd8BeKQ0-sn.
[4] "How Zara Grew Into the World's Largest Fashion Retailer," www.nytimes.com/2012/11/11/magazine/how-zara-grew-into-the-worlds-largest-fashion-retailer.html?_r=0, November 11, 2012.

Zara, you know that if you don't buy it, right then and there, within 11 days the entire stock will change. You buy it now or never. And because the prices are so low, you buy it now."

A web search for "Zara responsiveness" will turn up thousands of master's theses, magazine and newspaper articles, and case studies, as well as the *New York Times* article I cited. The reclusive owner, Amancio Ortega Gaona, is one of the world's richest people, displacing Warren Buffet in the list. Zara uses no advertising, marketing, or promotions to power its brand; it expects its customers, and its street presence, to speak for it. Zara has become the world's largest fashion retailer by following an innovative business model that exemplifies all the characteristics that agilists esteem. Zara is not a technology company, but it uses technology to enable the high-touch, data-driven, team-autonomy model that every enterprise seeking responsiveness should emulate.

Moving Toward Responsiveness

A business model like Zara's doesn't evolve overnight. It requires a mission that generates enthusiasm in both customers and enterprise teams. It requires a firm technological foundation, simple and effective processes, and an 'innovation engine' that enables the firm to refresh and adapt both the products and the business model. An efficient supply chain is also key. Zara moves the sliders away from predictive planning, hierarchical control structures, and secrecy or exclusivity of information. Experimentation, autonomy, and transparency are all inherent in Zara's model, and agile consultants should be leading every willing enterprise to evolve in that direction.

As an agile consultant, I've seen successful and failed transitions. Even in transitions considered successful, each enterprise threw up unique challenges and deficiencies. One of the elements that derails many attempts at transition is disjointed, disconnected, and cumbersome technical architecture. I've lived through sprints in which every team member sincerely committed to delivering backlog items, and dove in head-first to create the promised products, only to be derailed by systems that were constantly failing. If the team can't load its test cases because the quality assurance (QA) server is down, or can't run its tests because the core database is not responsive, it's pretty hard to commit to delivery. I've also seen organizations whose technical architecture is solid but which have so many process hoops to jump through, ostensibly to mitigate risk, that innovation, creativity, and speed are all discouraged.

The native Internet giants, like Google and Facebook, are in a constant development cycle, rolling out incremental changes in a continuous stream. Google developers, during peak times, make a code change every second.[5] For this

---

[5] YouTube, Tools for Continuous Integration at Google Scale, www.youtube.com/watch?v=KH2_sB1A61A, August 27, 2012.

to occur, they need an IT architecture that enables the business, system development, and IT operations to partner, removing silos and providing an integrated, robust, and holistic technological foundation. DevOps,[6] the effort to bring development and operations together, is a great start down this path, but, for many rookie agile organizations, it's an ambitious goal. Even for those who realize this ambition, it only solves part of the problem. While developer and operations teams may achieve better collaboration and a more coherent vision and mission, the problems of architectural agility and business participation can be left out of the conversation.

Tata Consulting Services, in the paper cited in footntote 1, recommends an approach it calls "BizDevOps."[7] This approach strives to include all corporate players in the IT development and rollout function, from business leaders to process designers, security experts, and quality assurance, as well as the developers and operations teams. In this scenario an agile enterprise transitions to an integrated approach along a path that TCS calls "Initiate, Walk, Run." In the initial stage, teams adopt agile practices and some automated tools for testing and build environments. As the enterprise gets ready to "Walk," teams have internalized the agile mind-set, and have developed their skills to the point that they can be the "generalizing specialists" that agility requires. They've begun on their DevOps journey, and have built a robust toolset that enables quick build, test, and integration. When ready to "Run," they've achieved integrated teams, blown up remaining silos, and adopted a kaizen attitude to improvement. Their technology is an integral element of their competitive advantage, and their processes evolve to meet the needs of the customer and market.

It should be obvious that guiding enterprises to the objective of a "BizDevOps" structure is an incremental, iterative project, and that the path will be long and daunting. Our previous discussions regarding the agile mind-set required of leaders and customers, and the differences between development and operations, should remind us that mind-set and practices come before enterprise agility but are not the end goal. Ever-closer collaboration and integration in the IT team, leavened with a kaizen attitude, is the destination.

Simplicity: Maximizing the Work Not Done

Most large enterprises with which I have engaged are anything but simple. From complex and obscure processes and overly broad product lines to complicated organization structures, enterprises, as they grow, build empires that

---

[6]For a tutorial on DevOps, see www-01.ibm.com/common/ssi/cgi-bin/ssialias?sub type=BK&infotype=PM&appname=SWGE_RA_VF_USEN&htmlfid=RAM14026USEN&attachm ent=RAM14026USEN.PDF.
[7]www.tcs.com/consulting/related-insights/Pages/Responsive-Enterprise-Operations-Evolution.aspx.

reinforce the siloed, process-bound hierarchies of old, and then add extensions every time they sense an opportunity or detect a problem. Processes grow to encompass every move or error an employee could possibly make, entrenching a risk-averse culture that stifles innovation. New departments spring up to address every trend of the moment, from chief digital officers to chief social officers to chief innovation officers, and then each C-level hire proceeds to create his own empire and process rulebook. At the end of all this expansion, the company often can't get out of its own way, as every decision needs to run up and down an endless flagpole, smothering morale and decision speed.

Surely the key driver in any movement to simplicity is the threat of small, nimble startups like Uber or WhatsApp that can gain billion-dollar scale with a few hundred employees and a smartphone app. Companies that are getting sucked dry by constant investment in legacy architectures, or by support and marketing of too many products across too many segments, are striving to simplify their operations by divesting certain assets and reinventing many of their processes. The last few years have seen a large uptick in corporate divestitures,[8] as companies from Weyerhaeuser and Roche to Proctor & Gamble[9] and HSBC have decided to sell off brands. When Jack Welch, celebrated chief executive officer (CEO) of General Electric (GE), took over the reins at that venerable company, one of the first moves he made was to sell off businesses in which GE could not compete. In January 2016, GE continued the trend started by Welch; it divested its $157 billion GE Finance business in what current CEO Jeff Immelt called a "pivot" to a "simpler, more valuable GE." GE also sold off $27 billion in GE real estate assets. Immelt also notes, as we've been arguing in this chapter, that "as we build the next industrial era, customer focus is more important than ever."

Simplification is about more than divesting assets. For most enterprises, process and business model innovation plays a larger role in simplification than do asset sales. Traditional functional departmentalization, designed to enhance industrial efficiency, now inhibits work flows and has become a barrier to responsiveness. This is the problem that the Business Process Reengineering (BPR) movement of the 1990s[10] was trying to solve, but that was before the wholesale disruption brought by the Internet. Still, the base idea is the same: reduce costs and increase quality by radically rethinking the entire set of organizational structures, processes, and technologies that drive the business. Although the "radical" element of the BPR movement became self-defeating in

---

[8]https://hbr.org/2008/10/how-the-best-divest.
[9]Serena Ng and Ellen Byron, "P&G Faces Up to Mistakes in Beauty Business," *The Wall Street Journal*, July 9, 2015, accessed from www.wsj.com/articles/procter-gamble-agrees-to-sell-beauty-businesses-1436444762, July 13, 2015.
[10]https://en.wikipedia.org/wiki/Business_process_reengineering.

many enterprises, some of the ideas are directly compatible with agility, such as customer focus, cross-functional teams with ownership of the complete product, and the use of IT to rebuild outmoded processes. These ideas, revolutionary in their time, are now just a standard tool in the pursuit of a different objective, simplicity or, as Bain & Co. call it, "complexity reduction."[11]

Agile consultants who are engaged at the enterprise level often find that their sponsor companies are shackled by intricate processes, which often have evolved from decades of workarounds or process-checks that resulted from errors or personalities long gone. I engaged at a large bank that had built its reconciliation process around the skill set of one individual, relying on faxes and phone calls rather than technology because "Charlie's not a technical guy."

At Charlie's inevitable departure, these inefficient processes lingered on because they became "the way we do it." Mature consultants, with their objective eye, are in a perfect position to observe these legacy dysfunctions and diplomatically call attention to them. This, of course, is just the opening move in the drive to rethink the process and work flows of an organization. The consultant who can convince her sponsor to invest in a process management professional, or can herself map and optimize processes for responsiveness, can have a larger impact than simply building agile teams. Again, our intention is not to offer a tutorial, so check the bibliography for some great resources on BPR and process reengineering.

Moving from the theoretical to the pragmatic, the migration to simplicity requires the enterprise, and its agile advisors, to address four key elements of complexity:

- **Organizational**: The complex organizational structures, siloed departments, and complicated value chains of many organizations must be analyzed and simplified.

- **Product proliferation**: The breadth of offerings, if too wide and varied for the enterprise to manage, and outside its core competencies, is a critical target for simplification. While agile consultants probably won't have much influence in this area unless they're engaged at the highest levels, our drive toward agility in the rest of the organization can make these challenges more visible and encourage lean thinking.

- **Process Improvement**: The legacy processes, that attempt to standardize and channel work flows and actions, must be revisited to ensure that they aren't stifling innovation or treading worn cowpaths that exist because they exist.

---

[11] www.bain.com/Images/BAIN_GUIDE_Management_Tools_2015_executives_guide.pdf.

- **Leadership**: Leaders are often enablers rather than resisters of complexity. Multiple detailed reports that require too much information and too much time, rather than simple dashboards that focus on the key indicators, can waste hours of time for employees who should be delivering customer value rather than digging out obscure numbers; agenda-less meetings that reach no conclusion; empire building rather than collaborative behavior. All of these managerial predilections must be driven out if the organization is to simplify.

For experienced consultants, the tools for these efforts are well known. The redesign of organizational structures is a common consulting practice, with principles, from the McKinsey "Seven S" organizational design framework[12] to Jay Galbraith's "Star Model,"[13] to guide us along the way. Process mapping and optimization tools, from simple flowcharts to swim-lane process mapping to task-on-arrow diagrams and other techniques, are all useful to help visualize the bottlenecks that restrain effectiveness and responsiveness. The tools of lean, which we[14]'ve been reviewing in regard to their relevance to agile, are also a set of diagnostic tools. DMAIC (design, measure, analyze, improve, control), provides an improvement and simplification roadmap to start the journey away from complexity.

Innovation: From the Product to the Business Model

Is innovation a flash of brilliance, a nagging idea that springs forth in a dream or a flash of insight, or is it the outcome of a process that can be defined and managed? Is it possible to create an enterprise "innovation engine," an extension of the research and development department that encourages the entire company to develop new ideas for products, processes, and even new business models? Is innovation a core competency only of companies like IDEO, the vaunted Silicon Valley design firm, or is it a value that can be instilled across an entire organization, or even automated?

When I think of innovation, the process that comes to mind involves a group of smart people in a room with a whiteboard, tossing ideas around to solve a specific problem or to improve a process or business model. The classic demonstration of this type of interactive brainstorming is illustrated in this video

---

[12]www.mckinsey.com/business-functions/strategy-and-corporate-finance/our-insights/enduring-ideas-the-7-s-framework.
[13]www.jaygalbraith.com/services/star-model.
[14]www.wikihow.com/Document-a-Process.

from Ted Koppel's Nightline episode,[15] which examines the creative process employed at IDEO. In a large group setting, designers tackle the problem of creating a "new wave" shopping cart, defying all the common knowledge about what a cart is to completely revamp a familiar object.

Management theorists, from Joseph Schumpeter and his "creative destruction"[16] concept to Michael Porter and his theories of strategic advantage, have stressed the importance of innovation. Porter suggests that firms have two main mechanisms of competition: innovative differentiation or high efficiency. In our current business environment, many firms are looking for ways to systematize innovation, rather than the anonymous "suggestion box" of yore or hoping for the random brilliant insight.

The agile twist on innovation is that it's neither a lone genius and her flash of insight nor an internal activity performed by a group of "creatives" but rather an interactive process that requires sensing the changing market, listening to customers, watching the competition, and then innovating toward a specific strategic goal. We all know the story of Post-it notes, the poster child for an innovative idea that came from a failed attempt to solve a completely different problem. In the new world of innovation, firms, like Apple with the iPod or Amazon with its cloud services, make a strategic decision to tackle a defined new market and then innovate deliberately to get there. The ubiquity of data, and the analytic resources available, enable the responsive enterprise to pay attention to signals emanating from its employees, its customers, and the social media channels that explode with valuable feedback all day.

I recently interviewed my friend Ludwig Melik,[17] who told me that he was investing in an innovation management software platform, Planbox. My immediate reaction was, "How do you automate innovation?" Innovation management software, Melik educated me, is not a replacement for the "team swarm" approach of brainstorming employed by IDEO and many other firms.

> Our client enterprises still want to meet in small teams, to innovate in many different ways, but if you don't have a process and community to develop these ideas they just walk out the door. It's not about some individuals submitting random ideas, but instead a sustainable source of great ideas that can transform the business. Innovation management is about creating a central repository where ideas are kept, and then developing a consistent process and community to test and execute the right ideas.

---

[15]www.youtube.com/watch?v=taJOV-YCieI.

[16]http://economics.mit.edu/files/1785.

[17]https://dzone.com/articles/can-innovation-be-automated.

Melik also made an explicit connection between innovation management and agility:

> There's an obvious connection between innovation management and agility. Many of our corporate clients want to apply an agile process, iteratively prove out the concept, and fail fast, to ultimately become more successful and innovative. The output of the agile experimentation loops directly back into the innovation management tool, so you track the results and plan subsequent iterations and funding for the right ideas. If you don't have a feedback loop that cycles from ideas to experimentation to iterative development, you won't be successful in the turbulent market environment we live in.

The agile consultant needs a special set of skills and experiences to advise the entire enterprise on these revolutionary practices. In Chapter 13, we'll explore the consulting skill set required to facilitate, persuade, and guide firms in their pursuit of the responsive, agile enterprise.

Summary

From product to business model innovation, the responsive enterprise is monitoring the signals from the entire environment, from internal teams all the way to the ultimate customer, and all the social channels in between. Responsive companies have the ability, from their IT systems to their supply chain, to respond to those indicators, innovate and develop new products, target unique niches, and stymie the competition. New business models, like Uber, or the improvement of existing models, like Amazon's AWS self-provisioning cloud offering, are examples of strategic, targeted innovation that promotes creative destruction, which pushes traditional businesses to extinction but creates valuable new enterprises that displace them.

The Agile Consulting Model

Evolving the client's enterprise to agility is our mission as agile consultants. We help clients grasp the agile practices and mind-set, and, if we're lucky and effective, we guide them to a leaner, more responsive, and more human way of working. Partnering with both the executive suite and the grassroots delivery teams, we help them transition from a predictive "big-bang" approach, to a nimble, iterative, and collaborative culture and value chain. Talented agile consultants can have a significant positive impact on the client's ability to shed the familiar tenets of predictability, risk aversion, and control and adopt the agile values of transparency, creativity, and empowerment. The belief that we can specify, predict, and estimate the scope, schedule, and cost of a complex project is discredited; in its place we can leave an enterprise that embraces change, risk, and openness.

Ironically, however, one of the last holdouts of the predictive mind-set is the consulting business. In my 15 years of advising professional services firms, I've seen every possible business model. The predominant model by far, even now, is based on a one-time-through, big, upfront plan methodology that mirrors the software development life cycles of old. This is the case for many reasons. Primarily, it's because that's what the consulting client wants. How nice for the client if the consultant is willing to take all the risk, presenting an "estimated" price and schedule based on a vague and indecipherable requirements document or, sometimes, just a conversation.

© Rick Freedman 2016

R. Freedman, *The Agile Consultant*, DOI 10.1007/978-1-4302-6053-0_13

The estimate, presented with many caveats and contingencies, becomes fixed and eternal in the client's mind. Then, on beginning the work, the consultant discovers all the unseen complexities, personalities, and cultural obstacles, and learns to his dismay that his tentative "rough order of magnitude" estimate has been perceived as a firm bid. Clients have become accustomed to playing one firm against the other in order to get the best price, and to shift the risk of uncertainties and unknowns to the consulting firm. Some consultants even go so far as to sign up for the dreaded "not to exceed" price, in which the client gets the benefit if the project comes in underbid, and the consultant eats the overage when the inevitable risks manifest.

Prediction Is Unpredictable

The predictive planning model is dangerous when we're doing a standard consulting gig, like installing packaged software or building a data center. The practice of analogous estimating, in which we look at similar projects of like duration and set a price with some built-in buffer, neglects the fact that no projects are alike. As all experienced consultants learn, it's not the technology that gets you, in most cases; it's the humanity. Change resistance, difficult personalities, the unsaid and unknown make each engagement unique, no matter how "analogous" the specification may be. Engaging for a consulting gig is risky because the customer wants certainty and predictability in an uncertain and unpredictable domain. The client's two big questions, how long and how much, are the exact questions we can't answer in a predictive, big, upfront scope regime.

If estimating and planning a packaged software implementation is tricky, negotiating a consulting engagement that applies agile techniques is downright treacherous. We don't know, before we engage, the state of the client's culture, business model, or value chain, let alone the personalities we'll be dealing with. The depth of their dysfunction is purposely disguised, in order to entice, rather than repel, the consultant. We don't know, until we explore, the enterprise's familiarity with agility. As difficult as it is for the client to articulate expectations for a packaged software implementation, guiding the client through an iterative engagement in which requirements will be emergent and evolving is much more demanding. As the hype cycle around agility has accelerated, many consulting firms claim the agile mantle, and many executives have formed their ideas about how agile works. Applying agility to the consulting relationship requires us to dispel myths and misconceptions, and employ all of our persuasive and educational skills to help our prospects understand how an agile consulting engagement would work, and why it would be to their benefit.

Consider a typical Big 5 consulting project from just a few years ago. The prospect sends out a number of requests for proposals (RFPs) to their vendor list of consulting firms, or calls in a sales rep. Through a mix of business and technical language, the client tries to articulate the current state, the desired state, and the solution it expects the consulting firm to deliver. RFPs are rarely phrased in a way that enables the consulting firm to apply creativity or innovation; they're more likely to state things like "the system shall have ..." or "the end user will see ...," and the consulting firm becomes simply a fulfillment agent of a preconceived project, often with an preset due date. It's not uncommon for the solution proposed to be unworkable, infeasible, or outright ridiculous. Even if prospects have actually devised an elegant solution, they rarely can communicate it precisely, thus leaving the consultant to make many assumptions, most of which will be wrong. The prospect, if we are lucky, will offer a "bidder's conference," in which we get to ask a few questions along with all the other potential competitors. This often becomes, rather than an opportunity to uncover the devilish details, a jousting match between bidders, who strategically try to avoid giving away to their competitors either their solution ideas or their confusion.

After attending the bidder's conference, most firms will huddle in a conference room and map out their reply. In responding to prospects, it's common for consulting organizations to amplify or even distort their experience and expertise. They usually don't feel they're being dishonest; instead, those around the table tell each other, "If we get the work, we'll figure it out." So the guy who goes out for coffee becomes a "Java expert," and the intern who managed the school carnival becomes a "Senior Project Manager." Even without these distortions, the RFP response process is risky; many experienced consultants won't even bother with them, heeding the old adage that if you have to respond to an RFP you're already too late. We're typically developing a solution to an imperfectly stated and poorly understood problem, or the wrong problem altogether. Once the solution is devised, the consultant's proposal is delivered to the prospect with a nice glossy cover, and then the firm sits back and waits.

If the firm loses the work, it has invested a significant number of potentially billable hours on a failed bid. This may seem an inseparable part of the business, but I've seen firms that jump at every opportunity, literally proposing themselves out of business as they devote all their hours to long-shot bids that never come through. Like a bad-luck gambler, they go into every roll of the dice thinking "this could be the one!" Failing to qualify opportunities leads to bad behavior such as inflating credentials, pulling in "talent" off the street without proper vetting, and grossly mispricing deals due to lack of experience, or desperation.

If the firm wins the work, it typically finds, once it engages, that the consultant and the client have very different ideas of what was signed up for. In the big, upfront plan model, the consultant and the client begin the first phase, Requirements Definition, and, as they dig into the details of the broadly sketched scope outlined in the RFP, they find that each has visualized a completely different process and outcome than proposed, and that the boundaries of the project are far more elastic in the client's mind than they are in the consultant's. The consultant discovers first-hand all the ills of predictive planning that we've been discussing; the client has a vague and undefined vision of the outcome, and can't articulate it in ways that we can decipher. Many stakeholders believe that they can add or subtract features based on their role, rank, and perspective, regardless of the scope defined in the proposal. All the vagaries of human and cultural personality manifest themselves and resist or block progress. Many deals that were celebrated as save-the-company coups turn out to be profitless death marches.

In the traditional consulting engagement, both the client and the consultant are focused on the so-called Iron Triangle, the constraints of scope, budget, and schedule. The client, in a bid to limit risk, typically focuses on constraining the schedule and cost by fixing the budget and timeline. Consultants, to protect their interests, concentrate on fixing the scope, to avoid the dreaded "scope creep" that plagues fixed-bid projects, thus constraining the customer to the features and functions they specified at the beginning of the engagement. Unfortunately, as we've learned from experience, neither of these strategies work. If consultants allow the client to fix the price and schedule, they often end up "eating" the overage, or disappointing on delivery date, when they discover the intricacies of delivering the client vision. If clients allow the consultant to fix the scope, anything that changes their requirements, such as shifting market conditions or new ideas about the project, enters an onerous change-control process that is designed to protect the upfront specification, rightly or wrongly. We set up an adversarial relationship from the start, as the client maneuvers to get the most for the least and the consultant jockeys to give the least for the most. The predictive, big, upfront plan consulting model is death on the relationship, hitching the client to a rigid specification that has no flexibility to bend with the circumstances, and dooming the consultant or firm to eternal hostilities, with the customer serially disappointed and the consultant marching to an arbitrary and impossible cadence.

Moving to an Agile Consulting Model

It's easy to delineate the failings of the traditional consulting model. Failed projects, consulting industry consolidation, plus the spectacular market flameouts of the many Internet consulting shops that exploded during the market euphoria of the late 1990s and fell to Earth in the dot-com bust of 2000, illustrate that success in the consulting industry is hard to achieve and difficult to maintain. Even with its failings, however, those left standing, from the prestige firms like Bain and McKinsey to the hundreds of small IT consulting shops scattered around the country, have the opportunity to earn substantial fees and deliver high-impact projects. Like those industrial firms that have embraced lean and agile ideas to remain relevant, both the renowned global giants and the successful local players have revised their engagement models to leaner, more flexible, and more client-focused methods.

Search for "agile" on McKinsey's[1] web site and you'll find hundreds of thoughtful and valuable articles, case studies, and presentations that illustrate the firm's deep experience, and deep thinking, on the agile transformation. Visit McKinsey's Digital Labs[2] site and you'll see that the firm itself now engages using an agile model, touting its "app in a day" and "client capability" workshops that mention agility as a key component of their offerings. Open the May 2016 issue of *Harvard Business Review* (HBR),[3] and you'll see an article on "Embracing Agile." Look further in HBR's archives and you'll find dozens of articles on agility, including discussions of agile strategy, agile marketing, agile adoption, and agile workforce management. The management theory cycle, from the major consulting firms to the academic management journals, is in full swing around agility. Still, all of this talk is about using agility within the enterprise. In terms of migrating the consulting firm itself to an agile model, available advice is scant.

For consultants and firms that see the value of engaging in a new way, the migration to agility is not that mysterious. I've seen many consulting firms that make an incremental evolution toward agility, even if starting from a waterfall model. The traditional model, delivered incrementally rather than as a "big bang," with separate scope, schedule, and budget for each phase, is the first step toward agility for many consultants. In this evolution, consultants, rather than proposing a once-through, all-encompassing omnibus project, propose a detailed discovery process first, with its own scope, time box, and "cost box" (or budget), and with a clearly defined deliverable consisting of a findings document and presentation that reviews the unique needs, constraints, and circumstances found through our exploration. I sell this discovery phase as a valuable outcome of its own, helping the firm understand the implications in terms of possible risks, inherent constraints, and stakeholder expectations. While still structured as a traditional 4D engagement, we now have the opportunity to assess for ourselves the circumstances we're walking into, and we enable the client to cap its investment, mitigate the risks of a new project, and determine whether the project is worth the investment, disruption, and risk. While we're not in the business of discouraging clients from hiring us, we should be in the business of avoiding work that adds no value or drags us into dangerous waters.

---

[1]www.mckinsey.com/.
[2]www.mckinsey.com/business-functions/mckinsey-digital/how-we-help-clients/digital-labs.
[3]https://hbr.org/search?search_type=search-all&term=agile&loaded=1.

The same theory applies to the other phases of a 4D engagement model. After completing the separately scoped discovery phase, we can propose a more informed design phase, present our solution ideas, and introduce our client to the concept of collaborative participation, and to its ability to make changes as its circumstances change. We can iterate through this phase until the client accepts a design, then scope and price the development and deployment phases in turn, each with an agreed timeline and budget. Each phase is entered with a more complete and realistic understanding of the situation, and each decision, for both the client and the consultant, is more informed and deliberate. We never get too far ahead of the planning horizon, and the client has the opportunity at every step to stop a low-value or problematic effort, thus avoiding the "project that wouldn't die" scenario.

While not yet a true agile, iterative model, this phase-by-phase approach has many advantages for clients accustomed to the fixed-price, fixed-date, fixed-scope approach. They can still budget for these individual phases as projects, and so not dramatically upset their procurement and financial models. They begin to understand that they must participate iteratively to ensure they get what's needed, and we start to break them of the habit of "over the wall" specification documents. They see incremental value and have the chance to redirect the project if it strays from their expectations or requirements. We grant them visibility into our consulting process, so we can mutually determine whether we're a good fit. We can progressively advise them toward a minimum viable product, and so start to guide them to lean project thinking, and wean them from the kitchen-sink style of specification. As in an agile environment, we're evolving from a one-pass, big, upfront plan approach to a collaborative, iterative, flexible, and transparent relationship, without blowing up either their existing mental models or their enterprise procurement processes. I'm often presented with this challenge to agile consulting; "How can I sell the engagement without a project estimate?" With this approach, we can range-estimate each phase, stay within our planning horizon, and incorporate our learnings into each subsequent proposal. We're constantly discovering and adapting as we go, thus giving us a better chance to estimate each phase from knowledge, and to propose a more suitable approach. This simple evolution from big-bang to distinctly proposed phases integrates agile thinking and benefits into a waterfall-style methodology, without radically changing the consulting engagement model.

Figure 13-1 is an example of a range estimate, by phase, for an actual merger project in which I engaged. Note that this is not a project about agility; rather, it's a project in which I applied some basic agile ideas to executing a non-technical project for a client with no agile experience. A quick glance reveals that this is an interim step between a big, upfront plan engagement and an iterative, incremental project in which the client commits to a piece at a time and has the right to change, adjust, or stop that project at any phase. Notice also that within each phase is a list of high-level features, each of which will have multiple tasks. This makes this sort of engagement amenable to an agile delivery approach, as we decompose features into epics and stories, and apply our agile practices to iterate toward an end result. While we are proposing to the client in the planning language the client understands, we're also preparing ourselves to apply agile practices to the project, building a backlog and a series of sprints to incrementally deliver each phase.

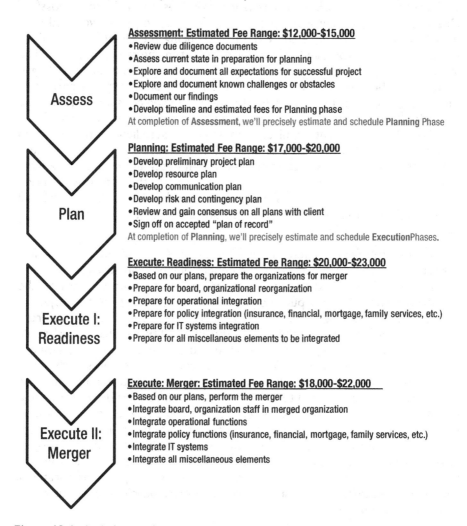

Assessment: Estimated Fee Range: $12,000-$15,000
- Review due diligence documents
- Assess current state in preparation for planning
- Explore and document all expectations for successful project
- Explore and document known challenges or obstacles
- Document our findings
- Develop timeline and estimated fees for Planning phase

At completion of **Assessment**, we'll precisely estimate and schedule **Planning** Phase

Planning: Estimated Fee Range: $17,000-$20,000
- Develop preliminary project plan
- Develop resource plan
- Develop communication plan
- Develop risk and contingency plan
- Review and gain consensus on all plans with client
- Sign off on accepted "plan of record"

At completion of **Planning**, we'll precisely estimate and schedule **Execution**Phases.

Execute: Readiness: Estimated Fee Range: $20,000-$23,000
- Based on our plans, prepare the organizations for merger
- Prepare for board, organizational reorganization
- Prepare for operational integration
- Prepare for policy integration (insurance, financial, mortgage, family services, etc.)
- Prepare for IT systems integration
- Prepare for all miscellaneous elements to be integrated

Execute: Merger: Estimated Fee Range: $18,000-$22,000
- Based on our plans, perform the merger
- Integrate board, organization staff in merged organization
- Integrate operational functions
- Integrate policy functions (insurance, financial, mortgage, family services, etc.)
- Integrate IT systems
- Integrate all miscellaneous elements

Figure 13-1. An Agile consulting engagement proposal

Contracting for the Unknown

Let's start this conversation by acknowledging that most consulting contracts, even if they explicitly agree to a fixed scope, budget, and schedule, are leaps into the unknown. We include the fixed elements for the convenience of the client, which wants to devote a specified budget to its project, have a guarantee of a complete deliverable, and know when its outcome will be ready. These are all reasonable goals, but their reasonability does not make them possible. One of our initial challenges as we migrate from these predictive, fixed contracting models to an agile approach is convincing the client that the fixed approach doesn't work, and, furthermore, is not in the client's interest. The Standish Group statistics on failed waterfall projects versus successful agile projects may be persuasive but they are not usually convincing. The corporate client has great pressure to stay with the waterfall, fixed consulting model. The strategic planning approach, the procurement standards, financial processes, and the risk-management impulses of most corporate clients tether them to a fixed model that is perceived as enabling a predictive budget and schedule, thus protecting the enterprise from unforeseen costs and delays, and a fixed scope, preventing the consultant from deviating from the enterprise's stated requirements. Our job becomes the exposure of the risks of this model, and the education of the benefits to a consulting client of a collaborative, incremental, and change-friendly regime.

While citing the Standish statistics is an important part of the conversation, the real goal is to help clients grasp the benefit of embracing change as a competitive weapon in our turbulent environment, and to educate them on the increased level of choice, input, and guidance they can exert on the project as the result emerges. Clients will often insist on the fixed-contract model from one side of their mouth and then decry the inflexibility and change-resistance of their consulting partners from the other side. It's the consultant's responsibility to make the connection for them between the constraints of the fixed model they insist on and the ills they condemn. To migrate them to an agile engagement model, we need to connect in their minds their desire for a fixed scope with the change-avoidance regime that results. We need to remind them that the fixed budget and schedule that they insist upon rarely protects them from overages once they have sunk major investments into project development. Critically, we need to demonstrate to them that agility works, through an incremental exposure to the benefits of engaging collaboratively, with an exploratory mind-set and an eye to the real developments out in the world and the market.

It's a fantasy to believe that an agile-naive client is going to contract for a "let's see what happens" engagement with open budget and schedule. The consultant's next challenge in migrating clients to an agile model is figuring out how to introduce them to the agile engagement without freaking them out.

I often offer to give away, or refund when engaged, the initial discovery element of the engagement, especially with clients new to agile consulting, to illustrate that we can discover in short iterations, demonstrate our findings as we uncover them (with the caveat that further learnings may change our determinations), and add value immediately even in the discovery phase. Clients are often pleased to learn that, rather than waiting months for the outcome of our exploration, they can incrementally learn what we're finding and then end up with a complete, contextual review based on our final determinations at the end of the effort.

Rather than contracting and delivering the discovery, and the subsequent phases, as fixed bids or ranges, we can now take the additional step toward agile by proposing to bid actual time expended for the discovery phase, with frequent presentations, similar to iterative demos, that not only show what we've discovered but also keep the client informed on the expenditures to date and the expected schedule, which evolves as we proceed and learn. The same approach is, of course, also applied to the design, planning, development, and deployment of the project outcome. Our evolution from a predictive to an agile consulting model is itself iterative and incremental. We begin by transitioning from a complete, fixed bid for the entire engagement, to a set of smaller ranged bids for each phase of the 4D model, and then incrementally move to decompose each phase into a series of iterative deliverables, with client collaboration and change-readiness built in. Eventually, of course, we hope that the client will completely adopt an agile model internally to correspond with the way we engage, and we dream that our example of agile engagement will awaken them to the benefits of agility. The rate of migration to this model, however, will be highly variable and subject, naturally, to the client's culture, aspiration, and adaptability.

Summary

Helping our clients evolve from a predictive model to truly agile consulting engagements is an exercise in trust and relationship building. The separately phased approach, as noted, is not a true agile engagement. We can migrate even closer to an ideal agile relationship when the client is ready. This is a revolutionary transition for most corporate entities, as procurement, relationship, and financial norms are overturned. When the client requires a new software application, for example, we can apply an agile scrum process very similar to the one we utilize when we develop internal applications in an agile shop. We can collaborate with the customer to create a vision, a roadmap, and a set of features or epics to work from, and then decompose those epics into user stories that we can prioritize in a backlog. We can iterate through delivery as we're accustomed to, demonstrating an incrementally advancing model of the client's vision, modifying and reprioritizing as we go, and billing the client on a strictly hourly basis. This, of course, is the ultimate level of collaboration and trust, and requires, in my experience, a history of migration from predictive planning to staged phases, and then to an increasingly agile engagement based on proven success and escalating trust. The path from predictive planning to a true agile engagement model can take years, as we illustrate through results that the enterprise will get what it needs without being gouged on price or compromised on schedule.

Running the Agile Consulting Practice

The Agile Consulting Skill Set

There's a significant difference between a consultant and a contractor. While consultants may work on contract, their focus and intent should be distinct from that of a contractor. Contracting is transactional, while consulting is relationship-oriented. A technical contractor, such as a database expert, can come into an engagement for a few months, apply her technical expertise to a particular situation, and then go on to the next contract, with everyone satisfied. A consultant, on the other hand, must develop a relationship with the client to be effective. Experienced consultants understand that technical or domain expertise in their field is the price of admission, but mutual trust, respect, and honesty are the factors that enable impact. This is not a value judgement: both roles are important. The difference is in the mind of the client; the client's expectations of each role diverge. The difference is also in the way we engage; consultants are more likely to require a set of skills that go beyond the domain, and enter into the realms of facilitation, negotiation, persuasion, and strategic thinking. Consulting is an advisory relationship, while contracting is typically a utilitarian transaction.

© Rick Freedman 2016
R. Freedman, *The Agile Consultant*, DOI 10.1007/978-1-4302-6053-0_14

There are, of course, no absolutes implied. The spectrum from contractor to consultant is wide, and many domain experts also must diagnose problems, devise alternative solutions, and persuade their clients to adopt one course or another. Similarly, many who call themselves consultants are often just domain experts looking for a raise. For each of these roles, the attributes of mature players fall somewhere on the spectrum, with a mix of domain and advisory skills. I believe, however, that there is a distinct code of conduct, set of ethics, and expectation of results that define consulting. While a contractor can bring his skills and await direction from the client, a consultant must bring experience, initiative, creativity, problem solving, and executive relationship skills to the engagement. The contractor owns the outcome of his particular component, at the direction of the client; the consultant owns the business result.

Again, with no absolutes implied, this is the distinction I make between agile coaches and agile consultants. Agile coaching is often transactional; "Come in and spin up these three scrum teams." While many agile coaches defy this and engage at the enterprise level, I've seen dozens of situations in which a coach comes in, teaches and guides teams through agile practices, and then calls it good and moves on. Again, no value judgement implied; teams benefit from lean and agile practices, and practice-focused coaches have helped organizations make great strides toward efficiency and effectiveness. When we engage as agile consultants, however, we are signing on to a deeper level of commitment and relationship. We're proclaiming ourselves as advisors to the enterprise, not agile domain experts addressing teams. We're taking on the challenge of making dysfunction visible, and having the candor and gravitas to persuade organizations to evolve from long-honored practices. We're looking at the enterprise holistically, and creatively inspecting and adapting to the prevailing conditions, personalities, and culture. We shouldn't be satisfied to see some teams adopt agile practices. Instead we should be striving to make agility pervasive and sustainable. The clients, of course, will determine how far toward that goal they will evolve, but enterprise agility should be the agile consultant's aspiration.

In Chapter 1, I reprised my "five fundamentals" for consultants, first presented in my 1999 book *The IT Consultant.*[1] As a refresher, those five fundamental ideas are:

- Focus on the relationship.

- Clearly define your role.

- Visualize success.

- You advise, they decide.

- Be oriented toward results.

---

[1]Rick Freedman, *The IT Consultant: A Commonsense Framework for Managing the Client Relationship* (San Francisco; Jossey-Bass, 2000). Available at: www.amazon.com/ Rick-Freedman/e/B000APKF5U/ref=dp_byline_cont_book_1.

These are foundation ideas for the consultative mind-set but are not the specific skills that consultants must apply to fulfill these concepts. Let's dig a bit further and uncover the capabilities that combine to make a competent agile advisor.

Foundation Skills for Agile Consultants

The skills of a mature consultant fall into three categories. Consultants require advisory skills: the capability to engage with the enterprise at all levels, diagnose problems, diplomatically and sensitively explore solution options, persuade clients to make informed decisions, and build a trusting relationship that enables productive interactions. This includes our ability to communicate effectively, facilitate teams and organizations to decisions, and influence decision makers to follow a fruitful path. We also obviously require the agile domain skills to lead clients to those informed decisions. The latest agile theory from a book or article is available to anyone; the experience and wisdom to fit the solution to the circumstances is a deeper level of advisory capability. Business skills are the final component. Every business model is not amenable to the same set of practices and techniques, and every enterprise has a distinct language, market, culture, and set of processes. Our agile mantra of "inspect and adapt" should make it clear that one size does not fit all, and that business context skills are a differentiating factor for consultants. We've addressed business skills throughout this book, and we'll look at agile domain expertise in Chapter 15. Here, we'll focus on the advisory skills that ensure consulting competence.

Advisory skills cover a wide gamut. Everything from communication to facilitation, and from negotiation to persuasion and influence, falls into this category. Communication is at the center of this group of competencies. Our ability to understand what the client means rather than merely what she says, to listen with our whole mind rather than formulating our rebuttal while the client speaks, to speak in the client's language and in the language of her business—these are the central skills that form the foundation for our advisory capabilities.

In the interactive and human framework of agility, the need for communication skills is elevated. The many different perspectives within our teams and the enterprise pose a challenge to our capabilities. Can we communicate with the product owner, who brings a business mind-set to the conversation, as well as the coder, who is thinking about the technical issues? Can we explain to the executive and client why they should adopt agility, and also stand in front of a team and train in user story writing or relative estimating? Can we engage in the give-and-take of a cultural evolution without expressing frustration, blame, or surprise when the client is resistant or its processes are clearly counterproductive?

Communication has long been a challenge for the information (IT) professional, and the jokes about the introversion and "geekiness" of computer specialists are legion. From the programmer hiding in the "glass house" of the 1960s data center to the Star Wars nerds of Silicon Valley, the stereotype of the uncommunicative techie is pervasive. The migration from the mainframes of the 1960s, hidden in the basement, to the computer on every desk of the client-server migration, required technical experts to learn how to listen to the client and help diagnose their problems and build the systems it required. The migration to agile has raised the communication stakes again. Now we must persuade our clients, and their customers, to speak in the language of user stories and to participate directly with our teams as they build and refine systems and products. We go from the remoteness of "over the wall" specifications and requests for proposal (RFPs) to the direct communication of story workshops and client demonstrations. We often have to bridge the gap from the project management language of traditional predictive programs to the agile language that rules today. Our tone and content must change as we navigate the enterprise, conversing with everyone from the chief executive officer (CEO) to the business analysts. From interviewing candidates to reporting on the team's progress, sharp, concise, and clear communication underlies all of the advisory skills we're advocating.

Discovery and exploration, for example, rely on our ability to ask the right questions, interpret the responses, and develop a theory based on what we hear. If we've been engaged to guide an enterprise or team through agile transition, we need to have clear and revealing conversations about their current practices, their exposure to agile, their organizational or team structure, and their pain points with their current methods. If we're applying agile consulting techniques to a technical project, the only way to understand the client's needs is for the client to tell us, as the giant specifications documents of the past give way to user stories. These conversations require delicacy, as we don't want to imply that the client is broken or "doing it wrong" before we understand the full circumstances. They require active listening, by which we gauge inflection and body language, and focus on the speaker to read between the lines of what we're hearing. Fran Lebowitz, noted wit, has said that "The opposite of talking isn't listening. The opposite of talking is waiting."[2] I would submit that the opposite of listening is often formulating a rebuttal, and that the struggle for many rookie consultants is shutting off the internal dialog and just hearing what's said. While I believe that every interview should be a conversation and not an interrogation, the consultant should be mostly listening, gently sparking the conversation rather than dominating or directing it.

In my years as a technical consultant (I managed global data center implementations for Intel) I witnessed many ineffective solution presentations that merely served to confuse the client and sabotage the sale or implementation. At Intel we called these "speeds and feeds" presentations. Of course, the domain specialists representing the client want to understand these technical details; executives, not so much. Solution definitions, pre-agile, were often communicated in the language of "Here's what we geniuses came up with.

---

[2]Fran Lebowitz, *Wikiquote*, https://en.wikiquote.org/w/index.php?title=Fran_Lebowitz&oldid=2092360, February 28, 2016.

If you're smart, you'll take it!" I've spent many hours mentoring and coaching technical specialists in the art of setting up the conversation by identifying the problem we're solving and why it matters, including the client in the conversation, offering options rather than mandates, and, especially, taking the ego and emotion out of the response to the client's decision.

The emotional element is often the hardest to overcome. Domain experts expend a lot of time and creativity developing elegant solutions to their client's problems. When the client questions or rejects them, immature advisors will often become defensive or demotivated. We become ego-attached to our own ideas, and then the client that rejects them becomes an enemy or a fool. Overcoming this emotional response and replacing it with a productive dialog is a crucial step in the journey to maturity for a consultant. In the agile environment, where every solution is experimental, negotiable, and temporary, emotional attachment to our ideas is a real obstacle to progress.

The Facilitative Mind-Set

Facilitation is a skill, but it's also a mind-set. Facilitative management rejects the concept that the best ideas come from the top down, from those in authority, or from appointed gurus. It's a cliché to say that the intelligence of the team is better than that of the expert, but, in my experience, it's accurate. The practice of facilitating teams to the most creative solutions, the best methods, and the appropriate adaptations to our practices is core to agility. The scrummaster is, essentially, a facilitator. She has no authority to order the team to any conclusion, and no power except that of the agile techniques. Every scrum ceremony is an exercise in facilitation. From the stand-up to the retrospective, the scrummaster is gently guiding the team members to their own conclusions. The facilitative role is one of neutrality, service, and clarity. Strong facilitators bring the Zen quality of emptiness to their practice. We have no stake in the outcome except to ensure that all voices are heard and that the team owns its decisions. We're there to try and bring order to the turmoil of conflicting perspectives, points of view, and ideas. We can attempt to capture, record, and gain consensus on ideas that arise in our sessions, but we can't prioritize or discard any ideas; that's up to the team.

It may seem obvious to anyone with exposure to agility that facilitation is key, but in fact facilitative management can be a revolution in the traditional enterprise. Managers and executives accustomed to issuing mandates must now engage in facilitated deliberations across the enterprise, and must let go of the idea that they have the sole keys to wisdom. Team leaders must migrate from a foreman role, enforcing diktats, and embrace a collaborative role as a servant-leader facilitating the team's own deliberations. Agile consultants must not only be strong facilitators themselves, they must be prepared to train and mentor facilitative skills across the enterprise, and encourage the entire leadership structure to migrate from a culture of authority and directive to one of participation and group ownership. Facilitative skill is at the heart of agility, from the team to the executive level.

To perform as a strong facilitator, agile consultants must adopt more than the mind-set. They must strengthen their facilitation skills. The beginning facilitator works to master the skills of active listening, paraphrasing, summarizing, and questioning. As the team begins to brainstorm or design a solution, the facilitator is ensuring that she is capturing the contributions clearly and accurately, consolidating ideas that coincide, and maintaining the momentum by following the flow of the conversation and gently probing to get to the underlying ideas. She must include everyone, even the back-row wallflowers, into the conversation, and respect the opinions of all. She must be completely focused on the entire room, noting expressions, silence, and enthusiasm level as well as verbal contributions. The skilled facilitator has a bag of tricks to apply in different situations, from brainstorming to matrix diagrams and from flowcharts to fishbone diagrams. She knows how to apply decision techniques such as multivoting, quadrant diagramming, and force field analysis.

As usual, I'll remind readers that this is not intended as a tutorial. To sharpen your technique in these areas I strongly recommend the books of Ingrid Bens,[3] the acknowledged expert in this domain. My intent is not to teach you the basic techniques but to make the connection between facilitation and agility. If the ideas and techniques I've described in this section are new to you, you'll struggle as a scrummaster, let alone a coach or consultant. If you are already an experienced facilitator, you should seek to expand your skills to the realms of conflict resolution, complex group dynamics, and the design of facilitated sessions for controversial or complex situations. The stronger your skills in facilitation, the more impact you can have, from the team to the strategic level. I commonly facilitate executive strategic planning sessions as well as standard agile practices, and the lesson is that anything can happen, and the more prepared we are with techniques and attitude, the more likely the success of the session. The ability to remain neutral, focus on your facilitation role, and avoid taking sides or allowing debate to degenerate into conflict or argument is a mature skill that requires experience and Zen. Like agility, the practices are easy to learn but hard to master, and similarly, as we advance our maturity the focus shifts from ceremonies to mind-set.

---

[3] www.amazon.com/Ingrid-Bens/e/B001JRXBLS/ref=dp_byline_cont_book_1.

Agile Negotiation

Agilists know that INVEST is the acronym that defines a well-formed user story: stories should be independent, negotiable, valuable, estimable, sized appropriately, and testable. In what ways is a user story, the atomic unit of agile requirements, negotiable, and in what other areas of agile practice is negotiation required? In any consultative engagement, negotiation is required throughout the process, from the initial rate and vision-setting conversations to the negotiation of a definition of done-ness. What's unique about agile negotiation, and what is the negotiation skill set required for agile consulting?

We're all familiar with the common ideas about negotiation; go for win-win scenarios, make sure all sides have a chance to express their needs and concerns, come in knowing your bottom line, iterate through a compromise process until all sides benefit, leave no "sore losers" in the aftermath. We're also familiar with the dark side of negotiation; the "used car salesman" who tries to con us into a bad deal, the imbalance of information, the tricks like "he who speaks first loses" or "good cop, bad cop." Negotiation can be a tool that ensures all parties exchange value and leave satisfied, or a scheme that manipulates us into a raw deal, triggering buyer's remorse and bad feelings. It all depends on intent, of course, but technique also plays a role. Let's leave the tricks of negotiation to the scammers and con artists. In the agile world, our intent is to ensure that all parties understand each other, achieve value, arrive on a solution that's fair all around, and can continue to collaborate without hurt feelings.

For those who need a basic foundation in negotiating techniques, I recommend reading *Crucial Conversations*[4] or *Getting to Yes*,[5] the classic primers on successful negotiating skills. These works focus on more than the "tips and tricks" of negotiating. They delve into the psychology of the negotiating process, and discuss the emotional as well as the substantive content of this stressful process. To illustrate the high emotional and ego content of negotiation, let's examine a well-studied phenomenon known academically as "The Bidder's Curse."[6] In the influential paper cited, the authors analyzed data from eBay auctions and found that "in the majority of auctions, the final price is higher than a fixed price at which the same good is available for immediate purchase on the same webpage." Why would buyers pay more at auction than they would to simply purchase the identical item? The answer, the paper suggests, is "competitive bidding, or 'bidding fever.'" Overbidders become emotionally attached to the item they've bid on, even if an identical item is

---

[4]Kerry Patterson, Joseph Grenny, Ron McMillan, and Al Switzler, *Crucial Conversations: Tools for Talking When Stakes Are High* (McGraw-Hill Education, 2011).
[5]Roger Fisher, William L. Ury, and Bruce Patton, *Getting to Yes: Negotiating Agreement Without Giving In*, Second Edition (New York: Penguin Books, 2011).
[6]http://eml.berkeley.edu/~ulrike/Papers/ebay15.pdf.

available at a fixed price. They become ego-involved: "I'm not going to let bidder 'USisBest479' beat me for that guitar I want!" Even if the bidder on the other side is an impersonal Internet handle, our competitive instincts kick in, and those of us most inclined to be concerned about "winning" actually lose by competing ineffectively. This effect illustrates precisely the challenges of negotiation. Once emotion is riled up, and competitiveness and ego flare, our worst negotiating behaviors kick into gear, and cause us to lose by "winning."

In agile negotiation, the only win is trust, collaboration, and mutual benefit. We negotiate to understand clients' needs, not to sell them something, or sell them *on* something. We negotiate to match our commitments to our capacity, so we can promote sustainable development. We negotiate to ensure that we are delivering what the client needs now, so that we can adapt as the marketplace changes. We negotiate to ensure that we are continuously improving both the product and the process. Most important, we negotiate with our ego and emotion in check, enabling us to reach mutual value without competitive instincts infringing on the process.

What do we mean, for example, when we say user stories must be negotiable? User stories aren't fixed, since we understand that, as we iterate toward a vision, that vision or the external circumstances will change. As these changes occur, we frequently renegotiate the meaning of individual stories, renegotiate the scope or backlog, and renegotiate the acceptance criteria to fit the new situation. While agilists agree that stories, once committed to a sprint, should remain constant, that doesn't mean that, during the sprint, the team won't discover new technical or functional obstacles or conditions that require internal negotiation to reallocate tasks and resources. Whether the agile team's customer is an internal department or an external client, the entire purpose of constant collaboration is to keep the door open to renegotiating every aspect of the project to ensure that it meets the needs of today, not yesterday.

Negotiation is a key element of the agile concept of variable scope. If product backlog items fall below the prioritization line and will not be delivered, due to time box constraints, budget constraints, or new learnings, we need to negotiate with the customer to ensure that we're still delivering the highest-value product. Those very constraints can also be renegotiated, if, say, the customer agrees to extend the timeline or budget to ensure that new or low-priority items are included. As we walk through these scenarios it becomes clear that the agile principles point toward deep negotiation skills as a key success factor for coaches and consultants, as well as product owners.

The idea of constant negotiation, like that of constant collaboration, is disruptive to many organizations. The common cry from the executive team is "I thought we landed on a solution. Why is this changing every time I look at it?" while the cry from the team is "scope creep." The agile advisor must be prepared to address these concerns, persuading executives on the benefits of participative decision making and change readiness, while helping teams understand that the built-in constraints of time box and cost box, and the idea of variable scope, enable us to deliver high-value projects without gold-plating or "just in case" features. The workday of the typical coach or consultant is one of constant negotiation, making these skills a core competency of the agile consulting role.

Influence and Persuasion

The foundational work in the science of persuasion and influence is *Influence: The Psychology of Persuasion.*[7] Dr. Robert Cialdini, a Columbia University-trained Ph.D. in social influence, has written an accessible and fascinating study that combines research and anecdote to uncover the factors that make us both persuadable by others, and persuasive ourselves. His thesis is that we are programmed by evolution and social structures to automatically respond to certain influences, and that these influences can be used for good or ill, to persuade us to make healthy and productive choices, or to lure us into traps for the benefit of others. Let's look at a list of these influencers, and then, rather than rehash the material from the book, we'll review how these ideas relate to agility.

Cialdini's six influential factors are:

- **Reciprocation** is the impulse to repay in kind what someone has provided to us, whether we asked for it or not. Cialdini cites the university professor who, as an experiment, sent Christmas cards to total strangers and received a reciprocal response from people who had never heard of him. He also cites a 1960 study by Alvin Gouldner[8] determining that all human societies follow this rule of reciprocity. From the free address labels in a charity solicitation letter, to the free samples at the ice cream shop, the expectation of reciprocity is built in to many of the conventional interactions of life.

---

[7]Robert B. Cialdini, *Influence: The Psychology of Persuasion* (New York: Harper Business, 2006). Also available online *as Influence: Science and Practice* at www.cfs.purdue.edu/richardfeinberg/csr%20331%20consumer%20behavior%20%20spring%202011/cialdini/robert_cialdini-influence-science_and_practice.pdf.
[8]Alvin W. Gouldner, "The Norm of Reciprocity: A Preliminary Statement." *American Sociological Review,* 25: 161–178 (1960).

- **Commitment and consistency** are powerful intrinsic motivators. Why do political attacks on "flip-floppers" work so well? For the same psychological reason as bettors at the race track become more confident in their horse's chances after they bet. We have an innate desire to be consistent with previous decisions or behaviors, and we prefer those who honor their commitments. Once we make a commitment ourselves, we're reluctant to repudiate it, even if it's not in our interests currently.

- **Social proof** is the psychological trigger that spawned the laugh track, the advertising meme "1 million clients trust our product," and the salted "tip jar" found in many restaurants and bars. When we see (or hear) others performing a behavior, like laughing at lame jokes on TV, we're more likely to exhibit that behavior ourselves.

- **Liking** the influencer is, unsurprisingly, a strong motivator toward compliance with his persuasions. What may be surprising is how often this trigger is used in our daily interactions. Liking, for example is one of the success factors of social networking. When we see an advertisement on Facebook, or read an article posted by a friend, we're more likely to click because we're surrounded or encouraged by "friends" we know and like. From Tupperware parties to the "chain of friends" sales technique, we're more likely to buy or comply when the influencer tells us "your friend Jim thought you might be interested in . . .". We know Jim, we like him, so the influencer invokes Jim's name in hope that some of that liking will stick to him.

- **Authority** as a motivator is familiar to every human being, from the first "because I said so . . ." response we get as kids to the "following orders" defense proclaimed in every war atrocity trial. The impulse toward responding to authority is inherent because it has worked for many species for millions of years. From the alpha dog to the silverback gorilla, and including the modern corporation, the variety of rewards, punishments, and incentives that authority figures can convey, and our inherent motivations, drive us to comply with authority even when, absent that authority, we would find their orders abhorrent or ridiculous.

- **Scarcity** is the persuader that leads to the perennial "going out of business" sales that have lasted many years, the velvet ropes at "exclusive" clubs, or the "Act now! Only 100 left!" ads that show up on late-night TV. It also is responsible for the propensity to keep old newspapers or record albums; they might be valuable someday because of their scarcity. Scarcity drives the club-goer seeking the status of exclusivity as well as the collector of baseball cards or comic books, because, especially when they are flawed and scarce like misprinted postage stamps or coins, their value soars without any intrinsic difference in value.

The triggers of authority and consistency are familiar to many consultants. Teams and individuals follow outdated and ineffective practices because they are told to, or because they always have. Command-and-control organizations use authority as the motivating factor to keep their employees compliant and obedient. "The way we do things here" is often cast in concrete by the desire to remain constant to the decisions we've already made, even when circumstances change drastically. These motivators have enabled the growth of the modern corporation and society, and contributed to some of the worst tragedies in human history. They also pose some of the biggest challenges to agile consultants as we encourage organizations to move away from command structures, with which humans are inherently comfortable, to participative cultures that seem fraught with uncertainty and risk. They challenge us to demonstrate the inconsistencies in seemingly consistent behaviors when they are counterproductive. Understanding the pull of these hidden motivators is a key differentiator for mature consultants.

Many of these persuasion factors are also immensely useful in agile consulting and agile practices. We work well as a team when we honor the idea of reciprocity; if a team member helps us in this sprint, we have an obligation to help her the next time. Once our team commits to the agile framework, its initial resistance and hesitation is often allayed, like that of the bettor or speculator who commits to a wager. The concept of visible success relies on social proof for its power; if those guys are doing it, and it works for them, maybe it'll work for us too. Liking, of course, is an integral part of team "storming, forming, norming and performing." As we get familiar with our teammates, and as they display reciprocity and commitment, we learn to like them more, thus reinforcing our motivation to cooperate and succeed together.

The wise consultant uses these motivators for good, not ill. We renounce the manipulation of these triggers to persuade our clients to do what we want, and instead use the positive elements to encourage behavior that is positive and sustainable. Social proof, as noted, is a great way to use the successes of one team to spread enthusiasm and belief in the power of agility. Commitment, rather than reward and punishment, is the driver of agile performance. The authority of the domain expert, earned instead of conferred by title, can be used to help teams push through technical challenges. The scarcity of accomplished agile consultants drives our rates to their market value, and our authority as domain experts can persuade enterprises to follow our advice.

One warning: persuasion can be a slippery slope. Unlike the huckster or con artist who uses our impulses against us, we must maintain the purity of intention that lies behind lean and agile concepts. We're not there, as scrummasters, coaches, or consultants, to persuade the client to do things our way (except for following the basic principles of agility). I've seen respected consultants become dictators, taking a "my way or highway" approach to advising, so sure of their superior knowledge, and so competent in their use of persuasion that they leave behind solutions that are inappropriate and unsustainable for the client's culture. We use our persuasive skills to help guide the client enterprise toward the right path for the client, not to demonstrate our mastery of manipulation or impose our own vision.

These advisory skills, mingled with the five fundamentals of consultative behavior, prepare us to navigate the tricky paths of agile evolution with the purity of intent and competence that encourages sustainable relationships. As our competence and maturity in these consultative behaviors grows, so will our usefulness to the clients and teams that engage us.

Summary

We've stepped out of the purely agile focus and looked at the consultative skills and behaviors that drive success. The advisory competence expected of a consultant must be applied to the benefit of the client enterprise, and not to impose the consultant's vision or preferences. By gaining control of our egos and emotions, and by displaying the neutrality of the facilitator, we enable teams to make, and own, their decisions and commitments. We use the power of persuasion to guide teams and enterprises to adopt the agile principles, and adapt them for their best fit. The agile consultant must demonstrate the openness, candor, and respect that they encourage in their clients, and must model the Zen qualities of emptiness and empathy that agility requires. Agility is a mind-set, and so is consulting; together, they inspire consultants and their clients to achieve things they never thought possible.

Agile Domain Expertise

Necessary but not sufficient–that's been our description of agile domain expertise throughout the book. We've explored all the components of agile consulting that augment our basic agile skills and enable us to bring more consulting value to our clients. Still, although not sufficient, agile domain expertise is necessary, and like the marketplace and the technology we've been describing, agile theory and practice is turbulent and constantly evolving. There was no Scaled Agile Framework for years after the Manifesto was written, no Spotify teaming model, no Project Management Institute certification for agile. Agility evolves continuously, and, as agile advisors, we must evolve with it or risk obsolescence. As many consultants have found in the last decades, through the migrations from mainframes to minicomputers, minis to client-server, then to networks, to Internet, and to cloud, staying the same means falling behind. How many highly paid COBOL programmers failed to move to structured languages like Pascal, to function and object-based languages, then on to Ruby, Python, and containers? Many of us chose this field specifically because there's always more to learn, and room to grow. With agile, we've picked a rapidly evolving field with lots of opportunity to expand our knowledge and take on new ideas, techniques, and strategies.

For the coach or consultant who wants to develop his agile domain competency, the options are many. From local agile communities to myriad certifications, and from droves of agile blogs to mountains of agile books, we can enhance our understanding of lean, agile, and enterprise theories and strategies every

© Rick Freedman 2016
R. Freedman, *The Agile Consultant*, DOI 10.1007/978-1-4302-6053-0_15

day. We'll take a look at some of the global and local communities, the books I've found to be foundational reading and the ones that supplemented and expanded my knowledge, and the certifications that enhance our credibility and demonstrate our passion, and our depth of agile knowledge. We'll talk about a development path for agile consultants and examine the levels of competence that mark the growth of our agile experience.

The Foundation

I learned most of what I know about agility from two sources: reading and experience. As I noted in the Introduction to this volume, a chance encounter as a journalist with Jim Highsmith, one of the signatories of the Agile Manifesto, started me on my passage from gung-ho traditional waterfall project manager to agile advocate. I started my journey by picking up Highsmith's book *Agile Project Management*, and then, as is my habit when an idea piques my interest, steamrolled though every agile book I could get my hands on.

At the beginning, since I was no longer a software developer, lots of the works out there that focused on agile as a development methodology didn't move me and ended up in my discard pile. Slowly, I developed a foundational library that I considered my basis for agile theory and practice. All of the agile books I reference in this volume are cited in the bibliography that follows, but there are a handful that stand out as the cornerstones of my understanding, and that I recommend to both new agilists needing guidance and experienced agilists who want to fill gaps in their fundamental knowledge.

Here are some of my top recommendations.

Agile Project Management, by Jim Highsmith

Highsmith's book lays out the agile case clearly, and helps us understand agile as a mind-set and a set of values, not just a set of practices and techniques. I'm thankful that I started here: I began my agile journey under the tutelage of the key original thinker in the agile world, and began from the correct place of mind-set and values.

Agile Estimating and Planning, by Mike Cohn

Where Highsmith taught me agile values, Cohn's book tutored me on agile reality. What do teams, coaches, and managers need to do every day to begin the agile transformation? How do traditional project managers and developers let go of the familiar practices of waterfall projects, functional silos, and magical belief in predictive estimation? If we acknowledge that we can't know the route, how will we reach the destination? Cohn's books guided me to the balance between a theoretical approach and a pragmatic, in-the-trenches understanding of how agile is really done.

Coaching Agile Teams, by Lyssa Adkins

Adkins has clearly lived the agile transition, and she talks about it with passion and clarity. She displays her hard-won migration, from a traditional project manager, thinking she owned every detail of the project, to an agile "adept," so infused with the agile mind-set that rather than merely becoming a scrum-master, Adkins became a Zen master of agility, helping coaches understand the personal voyage they must make before they can coach others.

Agile Project Management With Scrum, by Ken Schwaber

Schwaber, along with Jeff Sutherland, developed the scrum process, but this is not merely a methodology guide. Schwaber, like Highsmith, walks readers through the evolution of ideas and challenges that development teams faced, when the traditional methods kept failing and development teams were mistrusted and miserable, unable to deliver valuable products. While scrum-focused, this fundamental book helps scrum teams understand not just the methods but the evolution that brought us to agile.

Succeeding With Agile, by Mike Cohn

Cohn has two books on the list, because it's hard to become an effective agile leader or scrummaster without absorbing his step-by-step instructions for building, coaching, and mentoring teams, and sharpening their skills in an agile environment. Cohn has obviously encountered many permutations and combinations of challenges, issues, and resistors, and grants you the benefit of his experience in making the right choices on your agile path.

Other Books

There are tons, literally, of other agile books in which I've found great value, from Michelle Sliger's *The Software Project Manager's Bridge to Agility*[1] to Dean Leffingwell's *Scaling Software Agility*,[2] and specialized works focused on agile retrospectives, metrics, or testing, but these five are my touchstones as I go about the challenge of guiding enterprises as they evolve toward agility. As noted, check the bibliography for the entire contents of my agile library.

---

[1]Michele Sliger and Stacia Broderick, *The Software Project Manager's Bridge to Agility* Boston: Addison-Wesley Professional, 2008).
[2]Dean Leffingwell, *Scaling Software Agility: Best Practices for Large Enterprises* (Boston: Addison-Wesley Professional, 2007).

Experience

I mentioned both books and experience as my teachers. Books are easy to get your hands on; experience, not so much. Especially in the early days, after the Manifesto and Principles were released, agile shops were few, far between, and brimming with controversy. Getting the opportunity to introduce or experience agile in the business world often required stealth efforts, in which the word *agile* was never used, and we talked instead about "light" or "low-overhead" project techniques. Once I absorbed the idea that reams of paper trails and stage gates did not protect us from failures and overruns, I became increasingly obsessed with simplifying the project process for the consultants on my team. I stripped every project technique to its bare essentials and then stripped it again. I wouldn't call the project methods my teams employed at Entex[3] or Intel agile, but they were certainly leaner and more efficient than the 17-binder methodologies I learned during my Big 5 residency.

I was lucky; my early columns on agility for TechRepublic[4] got some attention and burnished my credentials as an agile consultant. I began to be approached by clients large and small to help them understand and implement these new ideas, and I got the chance to see many different cultures, business models, and personalities, and to learn the value of adaptiveness and empathy. I recognized the revolutionary nature of this change, and realized it was about much more than methodology. From small local information technology (IT) consulting shops to multinational companies, I was exposed to the myths, misconceptions, and concerns associated with migration to agility, and incrementally developed strategies to counteract resistance and fear (strategies I hope I have communicated in this volume). Because I started early in the migration cycle, I watched agility go from revolution and controversy to standard practice and learned hard lessons about cultural inertia and the momentum of new ideas.

Lucky for me, but what about the practitioner today? How does an aspiring scrummaster, agile coach, or consultant go about getting the exposure required to become a proficient agile practitioner or advisor? I'm not talking about certifications here; we all know that many are certified but few are chosen. While the path through certifications is not to be disregarded, all the certs in the world do not make an adept, and, as we learned in successive generations of certifications, from PMP to MCSE, and from CCNE to CISSP,[5] many folks are great at taking tests yet lack the judgment and maturity to perform the work. The real test of capability is in the doing, and the real training ground is in the real world, not a training course. So how do aspirants get that chance?

---

[3] www.nytimes.com/1997/11/23/nyregion/a-growing-market-in-computer-solutions.html.
[4] www.techrepublic.com/search/?q=rick+freedman.
[5] PMP: Project Management Professional, MCSE: Microsoft Certified System Engineer, CCNE: Cisco Certified Network Engineer, CISSP: Certified Information Systems Security Professional.

Many agile aspirants start by simply introducing some of the core agile ideas into their team, whatever their role. Project managers begin letting go of big, upfront plans and start inching toward a more just-in-time approach. Developers start working on what's ready versus waiting for the complete, blessed specification. Teams start meeting daily to ensure that they're on beam and uncovering issues as they arise. Unlike many agile purists, I'm not of the opinion that an official agile pilot needs to be proclaimed and the scrum guide must be followed dogmatically to start down the agile path. Agile practices are proliferating because they make sense, and because they work. Don't wait for an Emancipation Proclamation from old methods; whether you call it agile or not, start to introduce the practices that make sense in your environment and reap the benefits of the latest thinking in product development. Even if your enterprise is resistant to an official agile migration, it's hard to argue against a daily touch-base or an all-hands planning session.

The next logical step, of course, is to make it official. If you've successfully adopted some of the practices and seen benefits, start to make those benefits visible and attribute them to your team's new approach. Lobby for a pilot, or a proclamation, or whatever fits in your enterprise. Get the certifications, if they make sense for your career development (although I've known many great coaches and consultants without any letters after their names, and many weak ones with certs galore). More important, begin to work the practices, not as a bunch of isolated process improvements but as a unified framework, like scrum or kanban, and start to socialize the language, the concepts, and the mind-set. You will find, if you're successful at the team level, that agility will spread across the enterprise and give you many opportunities to expand your experience and learn the pragmatic lessons of agile evolution.

If you're a believer in the agile mind-set, and your current employer is so set against it that you can't even get a minimal pilot set up, move. There's a whole universe of agile-enlightened organizations out there that will be glad to have your enthusiasm for agile methods, and give you the opportunity to learn at the feet of coaches, consultants, scrummasters, and the agile teams whose working lives have been improved by these techniques.

You're Certifiable!

As with any new technology, especially in the IT field, there are plenty of organizations out there willing to grant you a certification in exchange for money. Most will also give you some meaningful insights and a chance to practice your craft. Some will be valued by employers as a token of your knowledge and dedication, and some will merely look nice on your wall. As technologies peak in the hype cycle, the for-profit certifiers start to come out of the woodwork.

As you can tell, I'm a skeptic, but only to a degree. There are certifications that I've seen many employers value highly, such as the Project Management Institute's Agile Certified Practitioner (PMI-ACP) and the Certified ScrumMaster (CSM) certifications. For those interested in Scaled Agile Framework (SAFe 4.0), the SAFe certification commands respect. There are a few private certification companies, like ICAgile, that have robust curricula and strong courseware (disclosure: I teach ICAgile courses through ASPE, the US-based training firm). There are also, unfortunately, lots of home-brew agile courses and trainers floating around, with courseware that may or may not be true to lean and agile principles. Some of these are lecture-based courses that fill you with slide-ware and then grant you a cert, with no chance to practice or experience the concepts.

My advice is simple; stick to the known entities. Between the agile books available, the acknowledged certifying bodies like PMI, SAFe, and Scrum Alliance, and private trainers like ICAgile, there are enough courses and certifications to fit any agile ambition.

Let's quickly differentiate some of these certifications. PMI-ACP is the Project Management Institute's exam, and that's both good and bad. Many agilists have grown up with the idea of PMI as the opposite of agility, with its rigorous, phase-gated approach, and so they are reluctant to honor any certification that comes from that source. On the other hand, there has been for years a PMI-based community of interest focused on agility. The test was developed by well-respected agilists like Mike Cottmyer and Mike Griffiths, who have built an agile body of knowledge that suits PMI yet is true to agile concepts.

I myself am a certified PMI-ACP, although I resisted the traditional PMP certification for my entire career. After studying and taking the exam myself, and witnessing its wide acceptance in the business community, I count the PMI-ACP as one of the most reputable agile certifications. Unlike the CSM, it's not scrum-focused, and it tests a wide range of agile skills, from domain knowledge to change management and consultative skills. It's not attached to a specific course like the CSM, but it's a wide-ranging test based on acknowledged classics of agile theory, and, being from PMI, gets attention from agilists and traditional Project Management Office (PMO) managers alike. I also love the fact that PMI, after years of denying agile or crying "we're agile too—we have rolling wave planning!"—has accepted the reality of agile and ratified it with this certification.

When I took the Certified Scrum Master class, there was no test associated with it at all—take the class, get the cert. Accordingly, the value received depended on the trainer, as many trainers had different material, different approaches, and, frankly, different skills and knowledge. The Scrum Alliance has since tightened up its act considerably, with a clear path through a series of standardized courseware, each culminating in an exam and leading to a logical next certification for the ambitious. We now have certified scrummasters, scrum trainers, product owners, coaches, and even agile leaders, each with a distinct curriculum. For those who aspire to get a hands-on introduction to scrum, a CSM certification is the most accessible, foundational certification. The progressive curricula that lead to Certified Scrum Developer, Certified Enterprise Coach, Certified Scrum Product Owner, or Certified Scrum Professional certifications are well-designed, pertinent, and respected in the profession and the client base.

Among the "official" scrum certifications, the Professional Scrum series is the real competitor to the Scrum Alliance's CSM. Offered by scrum.org, the organization established by Ken Schwaber, one of the originators of scrum, it also has a defined path for scrummaster, product owners, and developers, as well as a scaling course for enterprise-level professionals. This designation is not as well recognized as a CSM, with a fraction of the number of certified professionals, but it is quite rigorous and is preferred by many due to its association with Schwaber. It also has the advantage of requiring no renewals; certification is for a lifetime. Firms like Microsoft and Avenade (Accenture's digital consulting firm) prefer this cert, and have invested heavily in certifying their teams.

I'm a big fan of the progressive agile certification paths that organizations like the Scrum Alliance and ICAgile offer. From scrummaster at the team level to trainers, product owners and executives, these roadmaps can guide ambitious agilists through an entire career, as their skill and experience multiplies. While I'm not an advocate of certs for certs' sake, for those who aspire to evolve throughout their careers to higher levels of competency and agile mind-set, these escalating pathways offer lifetime learning and an opportunity to stay engaged with the development of agile theory and practice.

I started by noting that I'm a bit of a skeptic, but these certifications are certainly worthwhile and I have no reservations recommending them. My many years as an IT professional have caused me to be a bit cynical about certifications in our field, as I've seen too many come and go with the fashion, and too many unqualified job-seekers clutching at straws in an industry for which they are poorly suited. For those of you with the temperament, skill, ambition, and desire to become a professional agile practitioner, however, these certifications and their associated training and study are a great way to enhance your understanding, practice your skills, begin to build a network of like-minded agilists, and illustrate to the world that you've done your homework.

Finally, of course, the consulting skills we reviewed in the previous chapter offer an entirely different set of challenges. Those who augment their agile certifications with study in facilitation, negotiation, persuasion, active listening, and other advisory skills clearly have an advantage in their ability to add value. Some agile coaches go on to study and gain certifications in coaching as a discipline. Others migrate into organizational development or strategic planning. As agility transcends software development and migrates across the entire enterprise, these advanced advisory skills become essential.

The Agile Community

The Scrum Alliance,[6] in addition to offering certifications, is also a global community of agile practitioners who gather frequently to evolve the practices together, and share knowledge about the development and real-world results of scrum. Their Global Scrum Gatherings are considered some of the best networking and learning events in the agile world, and the relationships a scrum professional can build are invaluable. The user group and AgileCareers sections of the community web site are important resources. Whether you're a regular attendee of the conferences or an online participant in the webinars, the Scrum Alliance is a must-have membership for professionals in the scrum and agile world.

Less scrum-focused and more aligned with general agile principles, the Agile Alliance is also a global community that grants access to outstanding training materials, webinars, and global conclaves with top speakers and networking events. With active members like Steve Denning[7] and Ron Jefferies,[8] and a robust international group of user communities, distributed both geographically and by interest, membership in the Agile Alliance is another sign of commitment, participation, and passion. You'll find communities as diverse as the XP Forum of Johannesburg and the Agilni Srbija of Serbia, as well as communities across the United States.

PMI has its own agile community, which spawned the PMI-ACP exam and certification, as do the vendors of agile tools such as Rally, CollabNet, and Version One. A quick web search will uncover hundreds of local agile groups. There's even an agile Internet radio station, Agile.FM,[9] for the insomniac agilists who can't get enough.

Of course, agile communities of practice don't have to be external entities. Every enterprise large enough to have multiple cross-functional teams should also cultivate internal communities of practice, focused on both agile and on the domain knowledge of members. So, for example, MultiCorp might have an agile, scrum or XP community and might also cultivate communities of developers, testers, or architects. Agile communities in the enterprise often use activities such as reading clubs, article exchanges, and community blogs to spread and share the knowledge. As we noted in our overview of the Spotify model, it's important to keep teams connected to their domain disciplines as well as their cross-functional teammates, to keep knowledge current and

---

[6] www.scrumalliance.org.
[7] www.stevedenning.com/site/Default.asp.
[8] http://ronjeffries.com.
[9] www.incrementor.com/agilefm/.

communal. The Spotify model codifies this practice in chapters and guilds, but every enterprise can help communities form by offering technical assistance and meeting spaces, and by granting some time for participation. After all, the company benefits as much as the members do, and keeping both domain and agile knowledge fresh is an important goal and a great retention strategy.

Summary

The IT and business landscape is littered with the bones of developers, consultants, and leaders who were unable to stay current in their disciplines and management theories. Especially for the consultant, up-to-the-minute understanding of evolving trends and ideas in the agile discipline are essential. From the scores of books that make up the agile library to the study required to gain and retain certifications, the aspiring agilist and the agile professional have plenty of opportunities to expand and test their knowledge of this domain. Agilists can gain experience by bringing lean practices into their enterprise by stealth, by starting with a few ceremonies in a team or two, or by persuading the entire organization to embark on a declared agile voyage. If none of these work, the demand for agile professionals is now universal, and experience can be gained in many different settings. The agile community is robust, global, and welcoming, and agilists can join with like-minded practitioners around the world to keep growing their knowledge and network. By adding agile domain knowledge to subject matter expertise and consulting skills, we can multiply our effectiveness and our value to client enterprises.

Conclusion: Toward the Agile Enterprise

Back in 2007, James Shore[1] predicted:

> *I fully expect the big consulting companies to start offering Certified Agile Processes and Certified Agile Consultants - for astronomical fees, of course - any day now.*

He followed his prediction with this warning; "Please don't get sucked into that mess."

It's not my intent with this book to suck agile advisors into that mess, or to focus on certifications, processes, or practices. Agilists will, in any event, naturally resist any cult of experts, or any one "correct" path. My drive to write this book comes from a few simple observations from my 15 years as an agile consultant;

---

[1] James Shore and Shane Warden, *The Art of Agile Development* (Sebastopol, CA: O'Reilly Media, 2008).

© Rick Freedman 2016
R. Freedman, *The Agile Consultant*, DOI 10.1007/978-1-4302-6053-0_16

- Agility will expand beyond the software development function to influence the nature of work and of the enterprise.

- There's a significant difference in the skills required to act as a practice-focused coach and as an enterprise-focused consultant.

- As agility evolves, our skills, influence, and responsibility as advisors must mature and evolve as well.

Many of our clients are not truthful within the enterprise, denying dysfunction and relying on illusory plans and meaningless estimates to reinforce their magical belief in control and prediction. Many are not collaborative, instead competing between silos, managers, and teammates. Many don't particularly care about sustainability, and are instead focused on maximum productivity and profit no matter the human cost. Lean and agile aren't mere theoretical or methodological frameworks; they're pragmatic responses to these realities, and the failures they've engendered, with the aim of accommodating and nurturing creativity, ownership, honesty, and teamwork. Reducing waste, promoting collaboration, respecting truth and reality, and enabling sustainable, satisfying work practices are honorable pursuits, and most agile advisors engage from these motives, rather than the mere increase of profit and productivity.

For agile advisors, the purity of our intentions and the empathy we bring to our engagements are our governing success factors. Although we bring great enthusiasm to our efforts, we're not here to guarantee a specific result or drive to our particular vision of agility. Enterprises become as agile as their potential allows, and we apply our knowledge, skill, and compassion to help them achieve that level within their constraints of will, desire, and legacy. Like kanban, agile consulting is a pull, not a push. The client brings us in because its leaders know the enterprise must change, and they engage us to help the enterprise achieve its goals. If we've prepared the engagement correctly, they recognize that there will be disruption, challenge, and conflict along the way. That doesn't mean, however, that it's our job to march them to the one true vision of agility. The opposite is true; each enterprise's unique path doesn't exist until we tread it together. Agile evolution is not a death march to agile purity; it's an iterative, pragmatic, and collaborative effort to find each organization's most efficient, lean, and sustainable nature. My recent encounters with many agile coaches have illustrated to me, again, that the rule book can be our worst enemy. Clients don't care if they've achieved total compliance with the Scrum Guide. They want advisors who can accept them as they are and adapt their consulting advice to the client's reality.

We've explored many factors, historical, cultural, and procedural. We've examined the evolution of the assembly-line, command-and-control business environment and explored the factors that made it successful, and have since made it obsolete. We've looked at many different approaches to helping organizations evolve from unsuccessful and unsustainable practices to agile, responsive, and humane methods. We've outlined the skills and knowledge that agile consultants must bring to the advisory relationship to guide their clients to their utmost agility and creativity. We've emphasized that, although agilists believe these techniques go far toward the goal of a more human business culture, clients don't engage us to raise consciousness and promote happiness but to help them gain and sustain concrete business results.

Agile is cascading from information technology (IT) into sales, marketing, analysis, and leadership. It's influenced everything from the design of office space[2] to our relationships with customers and partners. A simple web search will uncover everything from agile ticketing solutions (whatever that means) to agile aerospace design, and from agile guitars (!) to agile Australia (part of Prime Minister Malcolm Turnbull's election platform[3]). Of course, there's a hefty dose of camp-following here, as folks with little understanding of the agile mind-set tag along with the movement. Be that as it may, the widespread adoption of the agile language can encourage understanding and adoption of the accompanying ideas. Or so we can hope.

If we ignore the hype and concentrate on the substance, however, we find a global IT community that has embraced agile ideas, and has become the vanguard for a revolution across the business world. In IT, agile development has led to agile deployment in the form of DevOps and continuous integration. Agile infrastructure, through the flexibility and immediacy of the cloud, has had a significant impact on IT architecture and processes. Agile leadership has begun to replace the notion of an all-knowing leader, or a supreme project manager, with servant-leadership, participative decision making, and self-organization. As agile IT pushes against the constraints and boundaries of traditional management, strategy, and budgeting, the extension of agility to these realms seems inevitable. My sincere hope, and my belief, is that, unlike some management fads of the past, the mind-set of agility, sustainability, collaboration, and value focus will transform our enterprises and interactions.

Agile consultants, and the coaches, scrummasters, teams, and leaders who embrace it, have a central role to play in this evolution. If we can apply a kaizen attitude to our own work, hone our skills, and guide clients faithfully through the challenges and opportunities of agile evolution, we will fulfill our roles as wise advisors and indelibly influence the world of work. Agilists believe that the virtues of honesty, trust, teamwork, service, and value can unleash creativity and community across the global workplace. May we be proven right.

---

[2] www.agilealliance.org/wp-content/uploads/files/session_pdfs/Agile%20Office%20Spaces%20Workshop.pdf.
[3] www.dpmc.gov.au/domestic-policy/more-innovative-and-agile-australia.

The Roots of Agile: History and Background

Take agility out of its product development context and think of it in its more familiar usage, as descriptive of a person or animal that has speed, grace, and flexibility. Agile individuals can bend and twist, turn on a dime, and switch on the speed when appropriate. Speed is one of many characteristics of agility, but certainly not the only one. The word *agile* in the physical world indicates an organism that can adapt to its environment, not over eons but by its actions right now to suit the current circumstances. Those blessed with agility are more likely to escape the perils of the moment and land in a dominant position.

Agility is defined as[1]:

1. marked by ready ability to move with quick easy grace <an agile dancer>

2. having a quick, resourceful, and adaptable character <an agile mind>

---

[1]Merriam Webster Online Dictionary, www.merriam-webster.com.

© Rick Freedman 2016
R. Freedman, *The Agile Consultant*, DOI 10.1007/978-1-4302-6053-0_17

If we move to a business context, the daily headlines illustrate over and over both the power of agility and the risks inherent in its absence. Those corporate giants, from Citicorp to Chrysler, that can't transition from historic business models and business cultures are at risk of extinction. Those, from Apple to Amazon, that reinvent themselves and respond to marketplace changes with urgency and innovation are the likely survivors.

Agility is an attribute that now ranks with stability and governance as indicators of a well-run business. For the global consumer we all serve, the pace of change in technology and business models has been positive. New capabilities at lower costs, as we see in the personal computer (PC) and cellphone markets, has now become an expected benefit of the migration to digital technologies. The life cycle of a product is now measured in months, and this speed of product refresh has fueled a global market with high expectations and a short attention span, as new, science-fiction features like voice recognition quickly become old-hat.

The Agile Manifesto: Founding Document

An understanding of the Manifesto for Agile Software Development is critical to anyone wishing to grasp the concepts of agility. The Manifesto is structured as a simple value statement, comparing one type of value with another. For example, the statement that "We value working products over comprehensive documentation" has been interpreted to mean that agile teams disdain all documentation. In fact, agile teams, and most developers, resist useless documentation that will never be referenced, the sort of ritualized document production that's become part of many development life cycles. In my experience with high-performing agile teams, they'll work hard to produce documents, like user stories or test scripts, that add value to the process. What they refuse is to spend time on non-value-producing activities like writing status reports that are never read. In this example, the key idea of the Manifesto is not that only "working products" have value and that "comprehensive documentation" has none; rather, it challenges product developers and project managers to question, project by project, which processes, tools, documents, plans, and contracts add value to this particular effort, and which ones we might be doing out of habit, or to fulfill a bureaucratic requirement.

THE MANIFESTO FOR AGILE PRODUCT[2] DEVELOPMENT

We are uncovering better ways of developing products by doing it and helping others to do it. Through this work we have come to value:

The signatories included Kent Beck, the proponent of Extreme Programming, Alistair Cockburn, the developer of Crystal Methods and author of influential works on agile development, and Jim Highsmith, who has translated agile software concepts into an Agile Project Management methodology.

In product development, as in most other human endeavors, the pendulum keeps swinging, in this case from highly structured, prescriptive, and predictive methods to more loosely defined, adaptable, and flexible approaches. In my career as an information technology project manager, I've been around long enough to see the gyration from ad hoc unstructured "cowboy coding" by "super-programmers," with no overall plan or project controls, to the tightly constrained and systematized practices of the Capability Maturity Model (CMM) and Project Management Institute (PMI)-sanctioned[3] "best practices" that require every step, action, and decision to be documented, traceable, and consistent project to project. We've now landed at a position in the continuum that fits the moment: the quest for a specific product development model that suits the project, the team, the enterprise, and the culture.

In contrast with traditional project methods, agile methods emphasize the incremental delivery of working products or prototypes for client evaluation and optimization. Traditional, "waterfall," sequential project management assumes that, at the beginning of the project, stakeholders can know, articulate, and document their entire set of requirements. It further assumes that developers can review those documented requirements and accurately predict the activities required, the resources needed, and the time and cost of that development. Both real-world experience and academic research indicate that this is a mistaken belief.

---

[2]As Highsmith has done in his book *Agile Project Management*, we've replaced "software" with "product" in the Agile Manifesto, and throughout the book, so agility can apply to all types of product development efforts.

[3]The **CMM** is a development model created for the U.S. Department of Defense by Carnegie Mellon University, which created the Software Engineering Institute (SEI). The term *maturity* relates to the degree of formality and optimization of processes, from ad hoc practices to formally defined steps to managed result metrics to active optimization of the processes.

The **PMI** is the certifying body of the project management profession and the developer and publisher of the *Project Manager's Body of Knowledge*.

The famous Standish Group CHAOS Studies,[4] familiar to project managers worldwide, studied thousands of IT projects for conformity with scope, time, and cost projections. Repeated about every four years, these studies consistently show that about 40% of IT projects are in the "challenged" category, a polite way of saying "circling the drain." At a Weapons Symposium in 1999, the results of a Department of Defense (DoD) software spending study were presented. Of $35.7 billion spent by the DoD in 1995 for software, only 2% of the software was usable as delivered. 75% of the software was either never used or was cancelled prior to delivery.[5]

Other academic research challenged project management methods in use, especially in an IT context. In a 1998 Harvard Business School study of large software projects, authors Austin and Nichols challenged many of the fundamental ideas of IT project management. As they noted[6]:

> The first flawed assumption is that it is possible to plan such a large project.

> The second flawed assumption is that it is possible to protect against late changes.

> A third flawed assumption is that it even makes sense to lock in big projects early!

At about the same time, Watts Humphrey, a respected IBM researcher, published his *Requirements Uncertainty Principle*[7] stating that,

> for a new software system, the requirements will not be completely known until after the users have used it.

Hadar Ziv of the University of California soon followed with his own *Software Uncertainty Principle*[8]:

> Uncertainty is inherent and inevitable in software development processes and products.

---

[4]www.standishgroup.com/services.php.
[5]Stanley J. Jarzombek, "The 5th Annual Joint Aerospace Weapons Systems Support, Sensors, and Simulation Symposium (JAWS S3)." Proceedings, 1999.
[6]Robert D. Austin and Richard L. Nolan, "How to Manage ERP Initiatives," Working Paper 99–024, 1998.
[7]Watts S. Humphrey, *A Discipline for Software Engineering* (SEI Series in Software Engineering) (Boston: Addison-Wesley, 1995).
[8]Hadar Ziv, Deborah J. Richardson, and René Klösch, "The Uncertainty Principle in Software Engineering" (Technical Report 96-33), University of California, Irvine, 1996.

In an influential article in 2001 that surveyed software development methods of innovative Internet companies, Alan MacCormack, assistant professor at the Harvard Business School, published a review of the history of software development methodologies.[9]

MacCormack's "Evolutionary Model of Software Development Methods" illustrates the history of IT systems development methods:

Waterfall Model – sequential process, maintains a document trail

Rapid-Prototyping Model – disposable prototype, helps establish customer preference

Spiral Model – series of prototypes, identifies major risks

Incremental or Staged Delivery Model – system is delivered to customer in chunks

Evolutionary Delivery Model – iterative approach in which customers test an actual version of the software

These academic findings and observations from real-world efforts led many developers and project managers to question the assumptions of traditional product development methodologies. Recognizing problems with existing methods does not, however, solve the predicament of revamping, replacing, or enhancing those processes. In his article on IT project management for Internet companies, MacCormack recommended a set of practices that could begin to replace the traditional methods. These simple precepts have been cited as a central foundation of the movement toward Agile approaches:

Early release of evolving design and code,

Daily build of code and fast turnaround on changes,

Deeply skilled teams.

Developments in industry, especially the lean manufacturing systems pioneered by Japanese firms like Toyota, validated many of the ideas brewing in the software and project management communities. The Standish Group finding, that around 60% of features built in to IT projects are rarely or never used, was also noteworthy. Concepts like focusing on features the customer valued and specifically requested and building in quality upfront rather than "testing it in" later resonated with these communities.

---

[9]Alan MacCormack, "Product-Development Practices That Work: How Internet Companies Build Software." MIT Sloan Management Review, 42(2): 75–84 (Winter 2001).

The development of agile methods accelerated in the 1990s, as Scrum was developed at Easel Corporation and Extreme Programming evolved at Chrysler. In the mid-1990s Dynamic Systems Development Method was introduced and quickly adopted in Europe. Finally, in 2001, the Agile Manifesto was created, and agile development methods were on their way toward mainstream acceptance.

Agile methods assume that clients can't know what they want in detail until they see a prototype. Agile assumes that, as we iterate toward a complete solution, small releases of functionality and value at a time, our stakeholders will guide us to a product that more closely fits their needs and expectations. Each iteration delivers a working product or prototype, and the response to that product serves as crucial input into the succeeding iterations.

Agile theory assumes that changes, improvements, and additional features will be incorporated throughout the product development life cycle, and that change, rather than perceived as a failing of the process, is seen as an opportunity to improve the product and make it more fit for its use and business purpose.

Let's delve into each of these statements and clarify what they mean.

Individuals and interactions over processes and tools

Process and tools don't create results, or add value for the user: only skilled people can do that. Processes and tools, when selected and applied judiciously, can offer guidelines and best practices, and can improve productivity, but agile project managers understand that it's the human interactions, within the team and with the users and customers of the desired product, that grant us the insight to deliver the right results. Many agile advocates look at the Business Process Reengineering (BPR) movement of the late 1990s as the culmination of a trend toward valuing processes over people, as if the perfect process alone could enforce success, and the skills and characteristics of the people were secondary. Agile theory asserts that even the most perfect process can do no more than guide and support skilled, motivated, and driven individuals focused on delivering value.

Working products over comprehensive documentation

This is, as stated, one of the most frequently misinterpreted principles within the Agile Manifesto. The key idea it intends to convey is that a working product or prototype can grant users insight into the actual status of development efforts far more clearly and realistically than any status report or Gantt chart can. Experienced IT consultants know that every software product under development is always proclaimed by the developer to be "90% done" until it either is delivered or fails and is discarded. This agile principle insists that the only way to know the real status of an effort, and to gauge the users' satisfaction and acceptance of the results, is to deliver something tangible that users can review and assess.

This preference of working software or product prototypes over documentation also serves to emphasize a key idea in agile development: documentation is no substitute for collaboration and interaction. Status reports are distributed through e-mail, Gantt charts are posted on a wall in the project office, and requirements documents are approved via an e-mail chain rather than face-to-face: all of these are examples of the sort of interaction-free exchanges that agile methods are expressly designed to replace with vivid, intensive collaboration.

Customer collaboration over contract negotiation

Projects based on contracts have traditionally implied that the entire scope and range of features required are documented before any development begins, and that the scope, schedule, resources, and often the price, are fixed and unchanging throughout the life of the project. Sometimes these contracts and scope documents are not even created by the teams building the product. To make matters worse, in many projects the contract becomes a substitute for collaboration with the client, and complex or innovative projects often become adversarial wrangles over terms of the contract.

Agile methods aim to move focus from the contract, and from predefined planning documents, to collaboration, with the customer and other stakeholders becoming a central element of the development effort. A key insight of this statement in the Manifesto is the idea that it's only customers who can define the value of the features development teams deliver, and that they must take ownership of the output, and must be involved throughout the effort, not just at the beginning, when scope documents are developed, and at the end, when acceptance is required.

It's important to note that this idea can create difficulties on both sides of the development effort. Project teams migrating from traditional to agile methods are often startled by the degree of client interaction required in an agile environment, and can often be troubled by the constant requirement to present their designs and prototypes to client review, and by the need to constantly incorporate changes and improvements as they work. Conversely, many clients, trained to "throw projects over the wall" to developers, often having little contact with the project team between specification and acceptance time, are often unprepared for the intensive interaction expected in an agile engagement. Preparation of teams, and expectation setting regarding this new way of engaging, is a key success factor.

Responding to change over following a plan

Developers and project teams are asked to participate in many types of projects. Some are production-style, low-uncertainty projects, like installing a new server in an existing data center, for which there may be well-known, documented rules and procedures. Others may be innovative, high-uncertainty projects, like creating a new business based on a web-based business model that is untried and untested. Agile theory contends that it's a fallacy to believe that all types of projects, from production to exploration, can be accomplished using the same, anticipatory, Plan-Do type of project approach, and that exploratory, innovative projects require a more experimental Envision-Explore approach.

Another key element of this philosophy is the changing nature of business itself. As global competition heats up, and the pace of change speeds up, driven by the Internet and our instant communication culture, the requirements of a project can change dramatically from conception to execution. Project teams are no longer simply confronting a series of minor scope changes that can be handled with change control processes; they're facing projects in which the entire set of business assumptions, technology, and infrastructure can change as the project is underway. Traditional measures of project success, such as compliance with an anticipatory plan and strict control of change requests, are a poor fit for this type of engagement.

Every project is not a candidate for an agile approach. Agile methods and approaches are uniquely suited for innovative, experimental, "never-been-done" projects, and are probably not the best fit for well-documented, low-variability projects. Projects like the 20th implementation of a bottling plant, or the 8th installation of an off-the-shelf software product, while having unique characteristics, probably don't call for the exploratory, learn-as-we-go attributes in which agile methods excel. Projects such as an innovative software application, with requirements emerging as development proceeds, or a new product development effort for a quick-moving marketplace like consumer electronics, are probably better fits for the methods we are discussing.

In biology, organisms that are dynamic, evolving over time, and adapting to the environment in which they dwell are known as "emergent" organisms. This concept of emergence is frequently discussed in agile documents, applying this biological meaning to the group interaction of a project team, and to the evolving requirements and expectations of the customer. New software, or new products in general, are subject to changing business conditions, changing technologies, changing end-customer expectations, and changing economic conditions, and so are not well-matched with static, predictive methods. These innovative products or services invite the exploration, experimentation, and creativity that are enabled by iterative, incremental, time-bound methodologies.

In addition to the innovative, emergent qualities we've discussed, agile projects also require an actively engaged, available customer. Common to most agile methods is the requirement for the customer to be a constant participant in the work sessions, daily meetings, iteration reviews, and brainstorming that exemplify the agile approach. Unlike traditional project methods, the entire requirement and work plan is not derived upfront, and so the customer is not free to participate in a requirements workshop and then disappear until acceptance time. Since agile methods assume that customers can't know what they want until they see a working example, the customer clearly needs to be there to review the deliverables and comment. The ultimate goal is to deeply integrate the customer into the process as a central member of the development team.

Projects with high regulatory compliance requirements are probably not a great fit for agile methods. Customers whose industry or culture requires that every change go through a formal committee, that every conversation be documented with detailed minutes, and that every new direction, taken in a speculative manner to improve the product, must go through a lengthy approval process, will probably lack tolerance for the lean, nimble, artifact-light approach that agile advocates.

Other important considerations when determining whether to adopt an agile approach relate to skills and culture. It's inherent in agile theory that the teams being led by these methods are composed of skilled, motivated, driven professionals. In agile environments, leadership and management are focused on serving the team, removing barriers, and fostering a creative environment, not on managing individual granular tasks.

Methods like Extreme Programming explicitly call for highly skilled team members, and explicitly state that they are not suited for large teams. This creates difficulty in many environments, where the staff is composed of a mixture of seasoned veterans and less-experienced journeymen. Most agile advocates would caution against assigning rookies to a key role in an agile team, although bringing them in to observe the process is encouraged as a training tool.

The question of dispersed and virtual teams in agile environments is hotly debated. Since many of the agile methods require attendance at a daily session, there's been some controversy about whether these can be held through video, collaboration tools, or other virtual techniques. Communication, collaboration, and customer interaction are key tenets of agility, so these concerns can't be simply discounted. Teams in which project managers and developers are working on many projects at once add to these concerns. There has been effort by members of the agile community to address both scaling and virtual teaming; Jim Highsmith has proposed both scalable agile team compositions and hub-spoke team configurations to address these concerns.

Finally, some industries, and some corporate cultures, may not be suited for agile approaches; highly regulated industries like pharmaceuticals, and safety-conscious industries like transportation, may be wary of shedding the documentation and process associated with traditional methods, for example.

The developers who gathered to develop the Agile Manifesto were more than theorists; they were dedicated practitioners who went on to develop pragmatic development systems based on the agile principles. Kent Beck, Ward Cunningham, and Ron Jefferies, all signers of the Manifesto, are also the co-developers of Extreme Programming, the agile method that attracted the most attention at the time. Alistair Cockburn, another signer, is the architect of the Crystal methods, as well as an author of influential works on use cases. Manifesto signer Jim Highsmith has been the chronicler of the agile movement, and he has done the most to migrate agile concepts from the software to the project management community. Ken Schwaber and Jeff Sutherland, also signers, were the originators of the Scrum methods. We'll explore each of these variants of agile methods, and discuss criteria for selecting one approach or another based on project specifics.

Extreme Programming

Often known simply as XP, Extreme Programming has gotten an outsize share of interest among agile methods. Extreme Programming drew attention because its audience of software developers was discovering many of its practices in real project work, and because its initial successes, including the well-known Chrysler Compensation project, coincided with the Internet movement, with its need for an approach geared to speed-to-value and exploratory, innovative projects.[10]

XP has some unique features among the agile methods surveyed here. It is focused on software development and is not touted as a project methodology. It explicitly admits that it doesn't scale to teams larger than ten or so, and that it's not well suited to virtual or dispersed teams. Like the Agile Manifesto itself, XP is presented as a series of principles. These include elements such as the following:

- **The planning game**: A recurrent workshop in which developers and customers interact in order to create and refine the "stories" that describe their project.

- **Small releases**: "Every release should be as small as possible, containing the most valuable business requirements."[11]

---

[10]http://en.wikipedia.org/wiki/Chrysler_Comprehensive_Compensation_System.
[11]Kent Beck, *Extreme Programming Explained: Embrace Change* (Boston: Addison-Wesley, 2000), p. 56.

- **Metaphor**: The overall idea of the project; the broad goal told as a narrative or story, to keep the technical jargon to a minimum and build a collaborative vision between developers and customers.

- **Simplicity**: The ideal of simplicity is central to XP. The delivered product itself should be simple, delivering the needed features in the simplest manner without trying to speculate about the bells and whistles that might be useful sometime in the future. The use of methodology and technique should be simple too; XP developers avoid documentation, other than stories and test cases, unless there's a convincing demonstration of their value to the customer. Finally, XP practitioners strive for elegance and simplicity in their actual coding practices, which leads us to refactoring.

- **Refactoring**: Refactoring is the optimization of the internal code and architecture of software, and it's a key element of XP. It's also a response to one of the hazards of iterative design, the danger that the separate iterations will be poorly integrated and internally incompatible. Refactoring is a disciplined approach to rebuilding system internals to ensure simplicity, elegance, and compatibility.

- **Pair programming**: Pair programming takes the concept of software inspections and walkthroughs to the next level. Rather than periodic reviews, the key insight of pair programming is that two skilled practitioners can review and optimize each other's code, and each other's coding practices, as they work toward the customer's goal.

- **Testing**: The vital difference between XP testing practices and traditional practices is that XP insists that test cases for all features be developed upfront, with the stories.

- **Continuous builds**: Going beyond the "daily build" that's a common practice in many commercial software companies, XP practitioners prefer the continuous build, ensuring compatibility and functionality continuously as the product is created.

- **Sustainable development**: A reaction to the 70-hour week, "death march" project that many developers have experienced, the 40-hour-week standard that XP espouses is consistent with the agile philosophy that creative developers do their best work when they're committed, energized, clear, and focused.

- **Available customer**: XP calls for the customer to be completely integrated with the development team, available to review features, builds, and tests and to review, assess, and optimize the product as it evolves.

XP's broad exposure, and the debate it has engendered, has given the project management and software development communities the chance to consider these ideas and to explore their applicability to their work.

Scrum

Ken Schwaber, who, along with Jeff Sutherland, developed the Scrum Process, states that "the core of the Scrum approach is the belief that most systems development has the wrong philosophical basis ... you can't predict or definitely plan what you'll deliver, when you'll deliver it, and what the quality and cost will be."[12] Schwaber declares that development is not a defined process, which can be repeated time after time, like the implementation of a well-known system, but is instead an empirical process, in which each project is fundamentally different, in which new discoveries must be made every time, and which unfolds differently each time based on the findings of each unique project.

It's important to distinguish the process from the content of the project in thinking about Scrum. While the Scrum process can be consistent from project to project, the content to be developed, whether a new bit of software, a new system, or a new product, will be sufficiently innovative and unique that the team will discover and integrate new ideas within each project as they work, create, and discover.

Unlike XP, which is designed to be a programming-centric approach, Scrum has more of a project management focus. With the uncertainty of predicting the outcomes quoted above, Scrum instead concentrates on creating a supportive environment for creative development, on close examination of features delivered, and on constant fine-tuning of the product as it is iteratively delivered. As in all agile methods, the supportive environment emphasizes collaboration, constant customer involvement, and the drive toward iteratively delivering real working features.

---

[12]Quoted in Jim Highsmith, *Agile Project Management: Creating Innovative Products,* Second Edition (New York: Pearson Educational, 2010).

The Scrum process has three activities:

- Pre-sprint, in which the team, in collaboration with the client (known in Scrum as the "product owner"), creates a set of three "backlogs" that catalog the features visualized for the product under development. The product backlog is the "master" list of features discovered so far, which in turn divides into a release backlog and a sprint backlog. Also defined in the pre-sprint planning is the sprint goal, a business result for the sprint to come.

- Sprint, strictly defined in Scrum as a 30-day work cycle in which team members sign up for tasks on the backlog, work with the sprint goal in mind, and participate in daily Scrum sessions. The sprint is the fixed center of the Scrum method, in which the features accepted into the sprint backlog remain constant during the sprint. Product owners can make changes or discard the entire effort once the product of the sprint is displayed for review, but during the sprint the scrummaster manages changes and suggestions to keep the team focused while "sprinting."

- Post-sprint, when the product is displayed to the product owners for review and optimization. At the end of this session, if the project is not complete, the Scrum cycle begins again with a new pre-sprint planning session.

In order to grasp Scrum, it's critical to understand the backlog concept, as illustrated in Figure 17-1. The entire product, to be delivered when the project is complete, is defined by the features and functions captured in the product backlog. Those features are then categorized by the collaborative team and product owner to determine which features will be included in the next sprint. Those selected features compose the sprint backlog. Not pictured in the diagram but also used in some Scrum projects is the release backlog, for products that envision multiple releases leading up to a final product release.

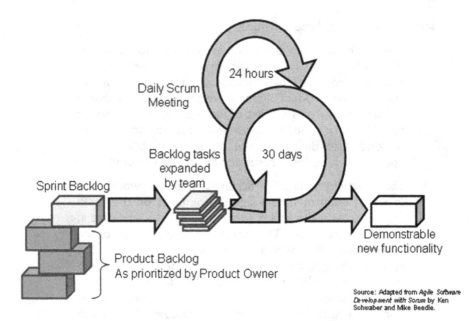

Figure 17-1. Scrum process diagram

The philosophy of Scrum centers on a few simple ideas: that predicting the outcome of innovative, creative projects is folly, that dedicated, talented teams have the initiative and creativity to build the requested features and functions if enabled to do so by a supportive environment, and that delivery of working functions and constant oversight of the content (rather than the process) makes successful development of inventive products possible.

Lean Development

In 1989, Professor James Womack and consultant Dan Jones published *Lean Thinking*,[13] a survey of the lean manufacturing techniques that helped create the "Japanese miracle" of the late 1980s and early 1990s. They chronicled the ideas of lean manufacturing, with their focus on eliminating waste, creating a smooth "flow" of work on the factory floor, and expecting workers to contribute high skill levels and an ownership mentality. These concepts helped Toyota, the exemplar of these techniques, vault over the traditional giants of the automotive industry. Lean manufacturing theories were highly influential in the creation of lean development (LD). Robert Charette, while not a signatory of the Agile Manifesto, has developed a methodology that has many

---

[13]James P. Womack and Daniel T. Jones, *Lean Thinking: Banish Waste and Create Wealth in Your Corporation*, Second Edition (New York: Free Press, 2003).

commonalities with those mentioned so far. Similar, though distinct, ideas have also been put forward by Mary Poppendieck and Tom Poppendieck in their book *Lean Software Development*[14] (we focus on Charette's version here).

LD emphasizes four key success factors that clearly illustrate LD's compatibility with other agile methods:

- Create visible customer value rapidly,

- Build change-tolerant software,

- Create only necessary functionality and no more,

- Aggressiveness, stubbornness, and belief in meeting stretch goals.[15]

Like Scrum, LD is more of a project management environment than simply a software development one; it consists of three distinct phases, startup, steady-state, and transition/renewal. Rather than the daily "scrum," it recommends a time-boxed "whirlpool" that, like all agile methods, includes the analysis, design, test, and build activities in each iteration.

Lean development is important not just for its conformance to the ideals of agile development but because the underlying philosophies of lean manufacturing have been accepted by business leaders worldwide, and so come with existing acceptance. This makes the introduction of agile methods in a lean framework more easily accepted, and presents a strategic framework that executives are likely to accept with less resistance.

There are, of course, other variants we haven't explored here, including Feature Driven Development and Jim Highsmith's Adaptive Software Development. Dynamic Systems Development Method (DSDM), for example, is a software development life cycle that embraces many of the foundation ideas of agile development, such as business value focus, iterative release, deep collaboration, and time-boxed delivery.[16] Some, like Scrum, are primarily focused on the project management element of product development, while others, like Extreme Programming, are software-centric. The agile ideas outlined here, from the early theoretical findings to the Agile Manifesto, have not just created debate and discussion but have led to the crafting of a variety of disciplined, complete methodologies that bring the theories into real-world practice.

---

[14]Lean Thinking: Banish Waste and Create Wealth in Your Corporation, Revised and Updated Hardcover – June 10, 2003.
[15]Robert Charette, *Foundations of Lean Development* (Spotsylvania, VA: ITABHI Corp., 2002).
[16]www.dsdm.org/.

Bibliography

While there are hundreds of agile titles available, these are the volumes that have an honored place in my personal library, and the ones I recommend to agilists hoping to begin their agile apprenticeship or enhance their skills. I tried to cover a wide range of topics, from software development and testing to agile scaling and leadership. Many of these titles are cited by Project Management Institute (PMI) as the basis for its PMI-ACP exam[1] and are acknowledged classics in the agile canon.

Adkins, Lyssa. *Coaching Agile Teams: A Companion for ScrumMasters, Agile Coaches, and Project Managers in Transition.* Boston: Addison-Wesley Professional, 2010.

Ambler, Scott. *Disciplined Agile Delivery: A Practitioner's Guide to Agile Software Delivery in the Enterprise.* New York: IBM Press, 2012.

Anderson, David. *Kanban: Successful Evolutionary Change for Your Technology Business.* Sequim, WA: Blue Hole Press, 2010.

Beck, Kent. *Extreme Programming Explained: Embrace Change.* Boston: Addison-Wesley, 2004.

Beck, Kent. *Test Driven Development: By Example.* Boston: Addison-Wesley Professional, 2002.

Cohn, Mike. *Agile Estimating and Planning.* Upper Saddle River, NJ: Prentice Hall, 2005.

Cohn, Mike. *Succeeding with Agile: Software Development Using Scrum;* Boston: Addison-Wesley, 2009.

---

[1] www.pmi.org/Certification/~/media/Files/PDF/Agile/PMI000-GainInsights AIGLE418.ashx.

© Rick Freedman 2016
R. Freedman, *The Agile Consultant*, DOI 10.1007/978-1-4302-6053-0_18

Cohn, Mike. *User Stories Applied: For Agile Software Development*. Boston: Addison-Wesley Professional, 2004.

Crispin, Lisa, and Janet Gregory. *Agile Testing: A Practical Guide for Testers and Agile Teams*. Boston: Addison-Wesley Professional, 2009.

Denning, Stephen. *The Leader's Guide to Radical Management: Reinventing the Workplace for the 21st Century*. San Francisco: Jossey-Bass, 2010.

Derby, Esther, and Diana Larsen. *Agile Retrospectives: Making Good Teams Great*. Location: 9650 Strickland Rd, #103-255 Pragmatic Bookshelf, 2006.

Galen, Robert. *Scrum Product Ownership: Balancing Value from the Inside Out*. Location: RGCG, LLC; 2 edition (March 2, 2013).

Griffiths, Mike. *PMI-ACP Exam Prep, Second Edition: A Course in a Book for Passing the PMI-ACP Exam*. Location Kansas City MO: RMC Publications, 2015.

Humble, Jez. *Continuous Delivery: Reliable Software Releases through Build, Test, and Deployment Automation*. Boston: Addison-Wesley Professional, 2010.

Jim Highsmith, *Agile Project Management: Creating Innovative Products, Second Edition* (New York: Pearson Educational, 2010).

Larman, Craig, and Bas Vodde. *Practices for Scaling Lean & Agile Development: Large, Multisite, and Offshore Product Development with Large-Scale Scrum*. Boston: Addison-Wesley Professional, 2010.

Larman, Craig, and Bas Vodde. *Scaling Lean & Agile Development: Thinking and Organizational Tools for Large-Scale Scrum*. Boston: Addison-Wesley Professional, 2008 Addison-Wesley Professional; 1 edition (December 18, 2008).

Leffingwell, Dean. *Scaling Software Agility: Best Practices for Large Enterprises*. Boston: Addison-Wesley Professional, 2007.

Patton, Jeff. *User Story Mapping: Discover the Whole Story, Build the Right Product*. Location: 1005 Gravenstein Highway North O'Reilly Media, 2014.

Pilcher, Roman. *Agile Product Management with Scrum: Creating Products that Customers Love*. Boston: Addison-Wesley Professional, 2010.

Poppendieck, Mary, and Tom Poppendieck. *Implementing Lean Software Development: From Concept to Cash* Boston: Addison-Wesley Professional, 2006.

Rubin, Ken. *Essential Scrum: A Practical Guide to the Most Popular Agile Process*. Boston: Addison-Wesley Professional, 2012.

Schwaber, Ken. *Agile Project Management with Scrum*. Redmond, WA: Microsoft Press, 2004.

Schwaber, Ken. *The Enterprise and Scrum*. Redmond, WA: Microsoft Press, 2007.

Shore, James, and Shane Warden. *The Art of Agile Development*. Location: 1005 Gravenstein Highway North O'Reilly Media, 2007.

Sliger, Michelle, and Stacia Broderick. *The Software Project Manager's Bridge to Agility*. Boston: Addison-Wesley Professional, 2008.

Wysocki, Robert. *Effective Project Management: Traditional, Agile, Extreme*. New York: Wiley, 2013.

I

Index

R. Freedman, *The Agile Consultant*, DOI 10.1007/978-1-4302-6053-0

Get the eBook for only $5!

Why limit yourself?

Now you can take the weightless companion with you wherever you go and access your content on your PC, phone, tablet, or reader.

Since you've purchased this print book, we're happy to offer you the eBook in all 3 formats for just $5.

Convenient and fully searchable, the PDF version enables you to easily find and copy code—or perform examples by quickly toggling between instructions and applications. The MOBI format is ideal for your Kindle, while the ePUB can be utilized on a variety of mobile devices.

To learn more, go to www.apress.com/companion or contact support@apress.com.

Printed in the United States
By Bookmasters